# THE PETROGRAD WORKERS AND THE SOVIET SEIZURE OF POWER

To what extent can the October Insurrection be seen as a workers' revolution? How did Soviet democracy fare in the first eight months following the seizure of power? What lay behind the debate between the factory committees and the trade union leadership over workers' control? These are some of the questions this book seeks to answer approaching the Russian Revolution from the vantage point of the industrial workers of Petrograd, Russia's 'red capital'.

This volume completes the study, begun in the author's earlier work, *The Petrograd Workers and the Fall of the Old Regime*. It traces the evolution of the workers' political consciousness and activity, both on the shop floor and in the broader societal arena, from their temporary defeat in the July Days through their mobilisation against General Kornilov's abortive counterrevolution, the October Insurrection, the dispersal of the Constituent Assembly, the economic collapse, the 'obscene' treaty of Brest–Litovsk and finally to the outbreak of full-scale civil war in the early summer of 1918.

Making systematic use of the wealth of source materials now available, the author strives to let the workers speak for themselves, allowing the reader to enter into the atmosphere of the period and the mind of the actors. In doing so, he questions the widely-held view of the workers as anarchistically inclined masses whose unrealistic aspirations made them the prey of demagogic leaders. The workers appear here as conscious actors, certainly no less conscious than the more educated and privileged strata of society, and as the crucial social force in the revolution's development. At the same time, the author seeks to explain why the power, so bitterly and heroically contested, won and defended, began so soon to slip from the workers' hands.

---

**David Mandel** was born in Toronto in 1947. He took his BA at the Hebrew University and PhD at Columbia University, where he was appointed Senior Research Fellow in the Russian Institute (1977–8). In the course of his research for this book he spent a year in Leningrad as a Canada – USSR Exchange Scholar (1975). He has taught at the Centre for Russian and East European Studies at the University of Birmingham, the Department of Political Science at McGill University, the Department of Sociology at l'Université de Montréal, and is presently at the Department of Political Science at l'Université du Québec à Montréal. He is the author of several articles on the Russian revolutionary period and labour movement.

STUDIES IN SOVIET HISTORY AND SOCIETY
General Editor: R. W. Davies

The series consists of works by members or associates of the interdisciplinary Centre for Russian and East European Studies of the University of Birmingham, England. Special interests of the Centre include Soviet economic and social history, contemporary Soviet economics and planning, science and technology, sociology and education.

John Barber
SOVIET HISTORIANS IN CRISIS, 1928–1932

Philip Hanson
TRADE AND TECHNOLOGY IN SOVIET-WESTERN
RELATIONS

Jonathan Haslam
SOVIET FOREIGN POLICY, 1930–33

Nicholas Lampert
THE TECHNICAL INTELLIGENTSIA AND THE SOVIET
STATE

Robert Lewis
SCIENCE AND INDUSTRIALISATION IN THE USSR

Neil Malcolm
SOVIET POLITICAL SCIENTISTS AND AMERICAN
POLITICS

David Mandel
THE PETROGRAD WORKERS AND THE FALL OF THE
OLD REGIME

THE PETROGRAD WORKERS AND THE SOVIET
SEIZURE OF POWER

Roger Skurski
SOVIET MARKETING AND ECONOMIC DEVELOPMENT

J. N. Westwood
SOVIET LOCOMOTIVE TECHNOLOGY DURING
INDUSTRIALIZATION, 1928–1952

*Further titles in preparation*

# THE PETROGRAD WORKERS AND THE SOVIET SEIZURE OF POWER

## From the July Days 1917 to July 1918

David Mandel

in association with the
Centre for Russian and East European Studies
University of Birmingham

*First published 1984 by*
THE MACMILLAN PRESS LTD
*London and Basingstoke*
*Companies and representatives*
*throughout the world*

ISBN 0 333 30937 5

Filmsetting by Vantage Photosetting Co Ltd
Eastleigh and London
*Printed in Hong Kong*

137334

For Sonia and my parents

This book was sponsored by the
Russian Institute of Columbia University
in the City of New York

# Contents

Page-numbering in this book follows on consecutively from the companion volume, *The Petrograd Workers and the Fall of the Old Regime.*

# List of Tables

# Glossary and Abbreviations

Until 14 February 1918 Russia used the Julian calendar which was thirteen days behind the Gregorian in use in the West. Events occurring before 1/14 February 1918 are dated here according to the Julian calendar; after this date – according to the Gregorian. For events occurring between 1/14 February and 15/28 February 1918 both dates are given.

census society  the propertied classes and those members of the intelligentsia who identified with them

*chernorabochii* literally, black worker: unskilled labourer

conciliator  contemptuous term applied to the moderate socialists (Menshevik and SR defencists), who argued that an alliance between the workers and peasants, on the one hand, and census society, on the other, was necessary if the revolution was to survive

defencist  after February 1917, the moderate socialists, who maintained that as a result of the revolution the war on Russia's part had ceased to be imperialist and that the people therefore had a duty to support the efforts of the Provisional Government to defend the revolution against the Central Powers.

duma  municipal government, after the February Revolution elected by universal suffrage

*intelligent* (collectively: intelligentsia) one earning (or looking forward to earning) a living in an occupation recruited chiefly from among those with a higher or at least secondary education

internationalist  after February 1917, the left socialists — Bolsheviks, Menshevik–Internationalists and

Left SRs—who maintained that the war being waged by the Provisional Government, which refused to renounce the annexationist treaties of the overthrown regime, continued to be imperialist and should be opposed

Kadet  member of the Constitutional Democrat Party, Russia's liberal party

*nizy* literally, those on the bottom; the rank and file; the lower classes

PSFMO  Petrograd Society of Factory and Mill Owners

revolutionary democracy (or simply, democracy) the workers, peasants and soldiers and those members of the intelligentsia who identified with them; for all practical purposes, synonymous with the constituency of the socialist parties

Sovnarkhoz  Council of National Economy, established by a decree of 23 December 1917, essentially replicas of the VSNKh on the regional level

Sovnarkom  Council of People's Commissars, elected by the Second Congress of Soviets in October and headed by Lenin; essentially the cabinet, formally responsible to the TsIK and ultimately the Soviet Congress

State Duma  the 'parliament' granted by the Tsar as a result of the 1905

Revolution; its franchise and powers were very narrow, particularly after the *coup d'état* of June 1907

TsIK All-Russian Central Executive of Soviets of Workers' and Soldiers' Deputies, elected by the Congress of Soviets

*verkhi* literally, those on top; the leadership stratum of an organisation; the wealthy and privileged classes of society

VSNKh Supreme Council of National Economy, set up in December 1917; its functions were vague at first but involved the state organisation of the economy

# Preface

This volume is intended to complete the study begun in *The Petrograd Workers and the Fall of the Old Regime*, taking it from the July Days through the October Revolution to the start of the intense phase of the civil war in the summer of 1918. This is a natural termination: by that time a majority of the workers of 1917, including those who had been the most ardent advocates of soviet power, were no longer in the factories. Many were far from Petrograd in remote corners of the hungry and desolate land.

The basic aims and methodology of this volume remain the same. It is an attempt to understand the revolution as viewed from below, from the factory districts of the 'red capital'. It argues that the workers' participation in the revolution can be understood in fundamentally rational terms, that their political behaviour was a response, not to internal drives and unrealistic hopes, but to a real situation, that it involved a reasoned weighing of the consequences of various possible alternative routes of action. It does not ignore the important role of non-rational factors. But it questions the often condescending and impressionistic interpretations of the workers' radicalism as elemental anarchism, chiliasm or simply political immaturity.

(In the interval between the completion of this book and its appearance in print, a number of other monographs on related aspects of the social history of the revolution have appeared that also challenge these long-standing views (in particular D. Koenker, *The Moscow Workers and the 1917 Revolution* and S. Smith, *Red Petrograd*). This long-overdue turn to the *nizy* in the West (heralded, in fact, by M. Ferro, *La Révolution de 1917* and A. Rabinowitch, *The Bolsheviks Come to Power*, which appeared several years ago) cannot help but greatly deepen our understanding of the revolution and the origins of the Soviet system. Although it is not possible to comment further on these works here, I refer the reader to R. Suny's review article 'Toward a Social History of the October Revolution', *American Journal of History*, no. 1 (1983) 31–52.)

This is not the same as arguing that the workers were 'correct' in the path they chose. The reader will have to judge that. But I do argue that the workers as a group had a realistic grasp of their situation and acted upon it in a largely conscious manner, certainly no less consciously than did the other social classes and strata in Russian society.

The previous volume traced the political attitudes and activity of the Petrograd workers during the first four and half months of the revolution, when a majority of workers, reversing their original position, turned against the liberal–moderate socialist coalition government, that represented a political alliance between the propertied classes and the workers and soldiers organised into their soviets. More and more insistently came the demand from the factories, particularly the more skilled metalworking plants, for the transfer of 'all power to the soviets', for a government of 'revolutionary democracy', i.e. for an exclusively workers' and peasants' government (the soldiers being overwhelmingly peasants). Exasperated by what they saw as the growing boldness of the counterrevolution, identified more and more with the propertied classes and aided by the Provisional Government, these workers and a part of the garrison took to the streets in demonstrations aimed at forcing the moderate socialist leaders of the soviets to assume power on their own.

Already on 4 July the reaction set in: firing on demonstrators by provocateurs and troops, indiscriminate raids, beatings, arrests and searches in workers' organisations and among the left socialists, newspaper closings, the reintroduction of the death penalty at the front. This lasted with declining intensity for several weeks. Tsereteli, the undisputed leader of the TsIK (Central Executive Committee of Soviets of Workers' and Soldiers' Deputies) and Minister of Interior, assumed personal responsibility for the arrests. Other moderates in the TsIK were less enthusiastic but nevertheless continued to support the government and the idea of a coalition.

The July Days presented the workers with a problem they had not had to face before: could they go it alone? This issue is the major theme of this book. It continued to dominate political debate among the workers in one version or another for months after the October Revolution, which had seemed at the time conclusively to have laid it to rest.

The reaction following the July Days made it clear to the workers that in a split with the propertied classes they could not count on the support of the moderate socialists and their constituency within revolutionary democracy—most of the left intelligentsia, the urban petty bourgeoisie and at least the wealthier strata of the peasantry. This isolation carried with it the threat of civil war within revolutionary democracy, infinitely more serious than any overt resistance the propertied classes themselves could muster. It also meant that the workers would have to assume the tasks of running the state and organising the economy without the aid of the socialist intelligentsia.

This new and much more threatening perspective on the revolution's development that resulted from the July Days left its mark on relations between the worker rank and file and their leadership. In this respect, the period from July to October was very different from the preceding months, when the masses held the initiative, repeatedly outflanking their socialist leaders, Bolsheviks included. This changed abruptly, if not completely, after the July Days. The leadership role of the Bolshevik Party now came to the fore, particularly in the October Revolution.

This, however, did not make October any less of a popular revolution. The identification of the workers with soviet power was to prove a major challenge to the moderate socialist opposition, a challenge that, despite the great suffering and disappointments the following months dealt the workers, it was never able to overcome.

Nearly all those whose assistance I gratefully acknowledged in the preface to the preceding volume have also aided me in one way or another in the preparation of the present one. I would nevertheless like once again especially to thank Leopold Haimson, my thesis supervisor, whose generous help in more ways than one was crucial to the realisation of this work. We differed more than once on large and small matters. But these were always honest intellectual differences. I am also again indebted to R. W. Davies of the Centre for Russian and East European Studies at the University of Birmingham and editor of this series for his helpful comments on the manuscript as well as the other practical aid he has afforded me.

To all these and others who have in some way aided and supported me in the research and writing of this volume I offer my sincere thanks.

DAVID MANDEL
*Montréal*

# 1 Rethinking the Revolution: Revolutionary Democracy or Proletarian Dictatorship?

## Census Society on the Offensive

As the workers, chastened by their defeat in the July Days at the hands of the Provisional Government and the moderate leaders of the TsIK, moved to take up defensive positions, the forces of the right hurried to cash in on this unexpected breach in the revolutionary–democratic front. Just as the Menshevik *Rabochaya gazeta* had foreseen back in May, the 'volcanic soil of the revolution' had at last cooled sufficiently for census society (the propertied classes and allied intelligentsia) to decide on a frontal attack.[1]

At the 'private' meetings of the State Duma, which despite the workers' protests continued to provide a quasi-official forum for the political representatives of census society, it was no longer considered necessary to use Aesopian language and merely hint at 'the evils of dual power'. 'The revolution succeeded thanks to the Duma', affirmed Maslennikov in mid-July in a typically brazen revision of recent history.

> But at that moment, a band of crazy fanatics, imposters and traitors calling themselves the Executive Committee of the Soviet of Workers' and Soldiers' Deputies attached themselves to the Revolution.[2]

Well-known and respected orators now spoke openly of a bourgeois dictatorship, dispersal of the soviets, a *coup d'état*, arguing emphatically that the Constituent Assembly could not possibly be convened during wartime. One of the most striking signs of the times was the reemergence from self-imposed seclusion of the notorious Tsarist reactionary and anti-semite, Purishkevich, who bluntly demanded before the Duma the abolition of the soviets and imposition of martial law.[3]

At the Second All-Russian Commercial and Industrial Congress on 3 August, the liberal banking and industrial magnate, Ryabushinskii, gave an especially vitriolic speech in which he bitterly attacked the soviets and other revolutionary–democratic organisations, stating that the government was merely a facade. 'In fact, a gang of political charlatans has been governing. (Stormy applause from the entire hall.) The soviet pseudo-leaders of the people have directed them onto the path of ruin, and the entire Russian state stands before a gaping abyss.' Decisively rejecting state intervention into the economy, Ryabushinskii declared that the revolution was 'bourgeois' and those who stood at the helm of the state had to act in a 'bourgeois manner'. Shouts of 'correct' resounded throughout the hall. Ryabushinskii concluded:

> Therefore, our task is an extremely difficult one. We must wait. We know that life's natural development will take its course and, unfortunately, it cruelly punishes those who transgress its laws. But it is bad when we must sacrifice state interests in order to convince a small group of people ... But unfortunately, it is necessary that the long bony hand of hunger and national immiseration seize by the throat those false friends of the people, the members of the various committees and soviets, in order that they come to their senses ... In this difficult moment, when a new sort of unrest is approaching, all vital cultural forces of the country must form a united harmonious family. Let the steadfast merchant's nature show itself! Men of commerce! We must save the Russian land! (Thunder of applause. All stand and hail the orator.)[4]

The non-socialist Moscow paper, *Russkoe slovo*, commented on the mood of the congress: 'A rustle of hatred, anger and scorn flew across the assembly at the mention of each socialist minister, up to and including Kerenskii.'[5]

In subsequent weeks and months, Ryabushinskii's graphic metaphor, the 'long bony hand of hunger', would be cited repeatedly at workers' meetings, in the soviets and by the socialist press, as Ryabushinskii himself came to symbolise to the workers the 'kapitalist–lokautchik'. 'Thanks for the truth', commented the Bolshevik *Proletarii*. 'The conscious workers and peasants can only be grateful to Ryabushinskii. The only question is: whose hand will do the grasping by the throat?'[6]

After the July Days, for the first time the counterrevolution began to assume the concrete shape of a military dictatorship. Speaking in July at the State Duma, Milyukov, leader of the Kadet Party (Constitutional Democrats, the main party of census society in 1917) did not mince words:

> I must say that, shaken by the events of the day, by our failures at the front and the revolt of the Bolsheviks in Petrograd, the members of the government have understood the necessity of sharply changing

course. The death penalty has been restored; maybe other measures will be adopted soon. But we feel it absolutely necessary that the Minister-Chairman (Kerenskii) either yield his place or, in any case, take as aides authoritative military men and that these authoritative military men act with the necessary independence and initiative.[7]

On 22 July, General Kornilov accepted the supreme command from Kerenskii, presenting at the same time an 'ultimatum', in which he demanded for himself full freedom in issuing operative orders and in the appointment of officers and the extension of the death penalty to the rear. He also declared that he was responsible solely to his 'own conscience and the whole people'.[8] This same Cossack general, as commander of the Petrograd garrison during the April Crisis, had ordered artillery fire against the demonstrating workers and soldiers. A massacre was averted only because the gunners insisted that the Soviet countersign the order.

As the non-socialist press touted Kornilov as the 'strong man' who would save Russia (his biography was distributed in great numbers), in soviet circles rumours of an impending military conspiracy became rife. There was talk of removing Kornilov. In response, a series of conferences of right-wing organisations (the Union of Twelve Cossack Armies, League of Cavaliers of St George, Conference of Public Figures, etc.) sternly warned the government against such a move.[9]

In the meanwhile, government repression directed at the Left continued unabated. After a brief reappearance, the Bolshevik central organ was again shut on 10 August. Arrests also continued, including those of Trotsky and Lunacharskii. But lesser figures were also swept up. On 28 July at Tsirk Modern, a popular public meeting place, a worker was arrested for denouncing Kerenskii; another was taken in for condemning the Liberty Loan.[10] On 6 August the Minister of Internal Affairs was empowered to arrest and detain without trial.

The government had by now abandoned even the pretence of a peace policy. On the third anniversary of the outbreak of the war, Kerenskii wired King George to assure him of Russia's ability and willingness to 'carry the world war to the end'. When Lloyd George refused to issue passports to the British socialist delegates to the Stockholm Conference (the cornerstone of the Russian moderate socialists' peace strategy), he cited a note from Kerenskii, in which the latter gave a negative opinion of the undertaking, calling it a 'private affair'.[11] For revealing Kerenskii's role in the failure of the conference, the Menshevik–Internationalist *Novaya zhizn'* was closed. In connection with this incident, a law was passed making it a criminal offence to 'insult in print any representative of a friendly state'.[12]

To the workers, all this attested to the capitulation of the moderate TsIK majority before census society. This view received symbolic confirmation in mid August at the Moscow State Conference. Kerenskii had called this conference in the hopes of obtaining a common expression of support for the government from all classes of society. But even though it was boycotted by the Bolsheviks, the conference was so polarised that hardly an issue came up that did not find the census delegates irreconcilably opposed to those of revolutionary democracy. 'That which gladdens one', commented *Novaya zhizn'*, 'meets with icy cold on the part of the other.'[13] The whole affair nearly ended in a brawl when a young Cossack announced that the 'toiling Cossacks do not trust their leaders'.[14] It could not, therefore, have cheered the workers, by now overwhelmingly convinced of the counterrevolutionary mood of the bourgeoisie, when they learnt of Tsereteli's demonstrative offer of his hand to Bublikov, representative of the Council of the Congress of Trade and Industry, before the entire conference.[15]

At the level of the factories themselves, the owners were now determined to withdraw the concessions they had been forced to make earlier, concentrating their fire especially on the factory committees. A circular of the Council of United Industry dated 22 August claimed the right to hire and fire exclusively for the entrepreneurs. Moreover, the latter rejected any financial obligation to the factory committees other than to supply a meeting place. The committee of the Skorokhod Shoe Factory issued the following appeal in August:

> After all the events which occurred on 3 and 4 July, you see, comrades, that the factory and mill bourgeoisie has started an offensive against your economic betterment. They act openly, comrades, and conduct a struggle against your organisations ... Comrades, the administration of our factory is already starting to intervene in the internal order [*vnutrennyi rasporyadok*] of the factory, a matter that until now was in our hands. The administration has declared that it alone will conduct hiring and firing of workers. Comrades, you know from your bitter experience how under the old régime they threw us outside the gates for any just word spoken and put in our place people whom they found to their advantage.[16]

'Everyday we hear of new attacks on the rights of the factory committees', noted the rapporteur at the second Petrograd Factory Committee Conference in August.

> In the beginning of the activity of the CS [Central Soviet] of Factory Committees, the entrepreneurs were quite open to our influence in personal negotiations with representatives of the CS. But now they are becoming less and less flexible, citing in their stubbornness the

Society of Factory and Mill Owners and refusing to recognise the CS as it is a non-governmental institution.[17]

Nor was the government itself inactive. The Menshevik Minister of Labour, Skobelev, issued a series of circulars towards the end of August upholding the owners' claims and stating further that the committees could not meet during work hours without management's permission.

But when it came to state regulation of the economy, first proposed by the Petrograd Soviet back in May, the government could not report any real progress at all. The Economic Council finally began to meet in July and continued to do so twice a week but only to hear reports upon which no action was taken.[18] 'Not one serious reform has been made', noted the resolution of the Factory Committee Conference, 'neither in the social sphere nor in that of the national economy.'[19]

On the other hand, the plan for 'unloading' Petrograd of its industrial enterprises was dusted off anew.[20] Ostensibly an economic measure, the political motives were barely concealed. The government's 8 August resolution called to evacuate medical and educational institutions and 'other establishments ... and to work out a plan for expelling ... persons who pose a threat in a counterrevolutionary sense'. (The original version of the resolution had called to 'liberate the capital from elements creating a danger of a repeat of the events of July 3–5'.[21]) It soon became clear enough what the government had in mind. Towards the end of August a list of forty-seven factories to be given priority in the evacuation had been drawn up, including all state plants, most large private metalworking factories and a number of chemical works. To add insult to injury, only a small part of the workers were slated to accompany the factories, the rest to be given two weeks' severance pay. On the other hand, the state treasury was to cover the entire moving expense of the private plants.[22]

But even without the proposed evacuation, the threat to production, employment and the integrity of the capital's working class was growing more serious each day. By early August forty-three factories had already been shut in Petrograd. These were mostly small and medium-sized plants, and relatively few workers were involved. Now, however, the Petrograd Metalworkers' Union reported that twenty-five more factories were soon to be closed and production was to be curtailed in another 137.[23] What was new was that this list included even the largest state and private factories in every branch of industry.[24] 'The storm has now broken out over everyone's head', a representative of the CS told the Factory Committee Conference.[25]

Although actual industrial unemployment was still low,[26] the trend was alarming. In the first half of 1917, the industrial work force had expanded by 10 to 12 per cent. This however, ended in July, when the employment curve began a downward swing that was not to end until several years later. Nevertheless, although the smaller establishments suffered considerably, overall industrial employment in October does not seem to have been much below the level of January 1917.[27] This, as will be seen, was the major achievement of workers' control.

After the July Days, the employers' stand on wages also hardened. In fact, the Petrograd Society of Factory and Mill Owners (PSFMO) now specifically prohibited separate wage agreements and established a fine (25 roubles per worker) for recalcitrant members.[28] On 12 July, negotiations between the Society and the Metalworkers' Union for a collective agreement broke down, with the owners rejecting the union's demand for the unskilled workers,[29] insisting instead on fixed minimum output norms. In the end, the metalworkers refused to give battle, accepting a government-sponsored compromise that included the minimum output norms. To the union it seemed clear that the owners were hankering for a fight, hoping perhaps for something along the lines of November 1905, when a city-wide lockout helped to defeat the revolution. Endless disputes and haggling accompanied the introduction of the new rates.[30]

At the same time, the Textile Workers' Union was being deluged with complaints about the improper calculation of wages. Despite an agreement with the PSFMO on a 25 per cent raise, several owners were pleading ignorance. Others said wages were already too high, while still others paid the raise selectively. Negotiations on a new contract, begun 27 June, dragged on for over two months, the owners fighting tooth and nail over each demand. It took two days of hard bargaining for them to agree to supply boiling water, and even then 'only due to exceptional circumstances'.[31]

All this time the workers were being treated to exposés in the socialist press of war profiteering by the industrialists. One of the more notorious scandals involved the revelation that Rodzyanko, Chairman of the State Duma, had been supplying the army with defective rifle butts all during the war at highly inflated prices.[32]

August also saw the beginning of a long period of decline in the workers' real wages relative to the spring. According to one estimate, the cost of living in Petrograd rose by approximately 70 per cent in January–June 1917 but by 75 per cent in July and August alone.[33] Data on a limited but fairly representative sample of Petrograd factories published by Stepanov indicate that the movement of real wages after the February Revolution reached its highest point in May and June. In the following months nominal wages continued to rise, though at a slower pace, but inflation drastically eroded their buying power. Thus, at Obukhovskii, Parviainen, Baltiiskii (metalworking), Kersten, Novaya bumagopryadil'nya (textile) and Shaposhnikova (tobacco), real wages rose on the average by 110 per cent in the first six months of 1917, well beyond the rise in the cost of living. (Although if Moscow is any guide, real wages still failed to catch up to their pre-war level. Government figures for Moscow show a rise of 515 per cent in wages between July 1914 and July 1917, while prices of food staples in the same period rose by 566 per cent and of other basic necessities by 1109 per cent.[34]) In July and August, however, the average wage in these factories rose by only 12 per cent, indicating a drastic decline in real wages, in most cases below the February level. The collective agreements signed in the metal and textile industries in mid August and early September helped the workers temporarily to recoup some of the lost buying power, but in face of the galloping inflation the general downward trend in real wages relative to the spring was not arrested.[35]

It was also in the summer that the food shortage (not to mention the scarcity of manufactured goods) really began to be felt for the first time since the winter of 1916–17.[36] At one point, the capital was down to only two days' supply of grain. The irregular arrival of food shipments caused serious distribution difficulties, such that, according to the Vyborg District Food Authority, the queues in front of bakeries 'have in fact turned the eight-hour day into a twelve and thirteen-hour day, since proletarians go from their factories directly to the queues where they spend four to five hours and sometimes right up to the next work day'.[37]

At the August Factory Committee Conference, the Bolshevik Milyutin offered a summary of the post-July situation that was later incorporated into a resolution approved by an overwhelming majority:

In the economic and political spheres one is forced to note of late a changed situation. In the economic sphere Russia has already entered a period of real catastrophe because the economic break-down and the food crisis have reached extreme limits. One already feels an acute scarcity of grain, and the picture of real hunger looms before us in all its immensity ...

It is in this atmosphere of approaching economic disaster that the political life of the country has recently been evolving ... Here the distinctive note is the open organisation of the counterrevolution. The disgraceful legacy of the past—capital punishment, administrative exile and arrests, attacks on the workers' organisations and press—these are the striking manifestations of the counterrevolution that occur in plain view of all. Parallel to this are the fanning of the war and the influence of international capital on the entire life of the country ...

All power has in fact passed into the hands of the counterrevolution despite the fact that half of the cabinet consists of 'socialists'.[38]

**The Workers' Response**

*The Death Throes of 'Conciliationism'*

July and August witnessed the near total collapse of the remaining working-class support for the governmental coalition of census and soviet representatives and also for the moderate socialists who advocated it. Until July, the radicalisation had affected mainly the urbanised, skilled elements, especially in metalworking, and machine construction in particular. Accordingly, most of the shift had occurred within social democracy from its moderate (defencist) wing to the Bolsheviks. The SRs (Socialist Revolutionaries), however, had managed to retain considerable worker support. After the July Days their decline was all the more dramatic with the massive radicalisation of the unskilled workers, who had been attracted originally by the party's peasant–populist accent, which accorded better with their still strong economic and cultural ties to the village than social democracy's class and urban emphasis. The Left SRs (internationalists on the war issue), who, like the Menshevik–Internationalists, opposed the coalition but did not advocate soviet power as the alternative, picked up some of this support. But most workers turned to the Bolsheviks, whose position on state power seemed clearer and more consistent. In addition, the Bolsheviks, unlike the internationalist wings of Menshevism and populism, were not tainted by organisational ties with the defencists.

The 20 August election to the city duma (municipal council), the second of three city-wide elections in 1917, showed a remarkable increase in Bolshevik support over the spring (see Table 1.1). Not only did their share of the vote jump from approximately one-fifth in May to one-third, but the Bolsheviks were the only party to register an absolute increase in votes, despite a 30 per cent decline in turnout. (Actually, the relative turnout was even lower since new districts had been incorporated into the city boundaries since May.)

The Bolsheviks drew strongly on the working-class vote,[39] winning absolute majorities in the heavily proletarian Vyborg and Petergof Districts and pluralities in the more heterogeneous but still quite industrial Vasilevskii ostrov and Petrograd Districts, and in Lesnoi and Novaya derevnya, adjacent to Vyborg[40] (see Table 1.2).

The strong Bolshevik vote in some of the central districts seems to have come largely from the garrison. In the Admiralty District, for example, which had no factories, 86 per cent of the Bolshevik votes were cast by soldiers.[41]

The moderate socialists, and by August this meant mainly the SRs, were on the decline everywhere but still quite strong among the workers in the three semi-rural outlying districts with industry, Nevskii, Moscow and Polyustrovo-Porokhovskii, as well as among the white-collar and petty bourgeois population and the soldiers.

TABLE 1.1: *Returns in Petrograd Elections to District Dumas (27 May – 5 June), Central Duma (20 August), and Constituent Assembly (12–14 November 1917) (number of votes cast, in 1000s)*

| Election date | Bolshevik | | SR | | Menshevik | | Kadet | | All parties | |
|---|---|---|---|---|---|---|---|---|---|---|
| | Number | % | Number | % | Number | % | Number | % | Number | % |
| May | 160 | 20.4 | 431[a] | 55.0[a] | | | 172 | 21.9 | 785 | 100 |
| August | 184 | 33.4 | 206 | 37.4 | 24 | 4.3[b] | 114 | 20.8 | 549 | 100 |
| November | 424 | 45.0 | 152 | 16.1 | 29 | 3.0[c] | 247 | 26.2 | 942 | 100 |

[a] These figures included both the SR and Menshevik votes, as the two parties ran a joint list.

[b] The Menshevik list in the August election was exclusively Internationalist.

[c] Includes Defencist as well as Internationalist vote, 1.8 per cent and 1.2 per cent respectively.

Sources: May – W. Rosenberg, *Liberals in the Russian Revolution*, p. 162; August – *Delo naroda* (23–4 Aug 1917); November – *Nasha rech'* (17 Nov 1918).

TABLE 1.2:   District Breakdown of Petrograd Duma Election Returns, 20 August 1917 (percent of total district vote)

| District | Bolshevik % | SR % | Menshevik % | Kadet % | Total number votes cast[a] |
|---|---|---|---|---|---|
| Admiralty | 35.7 | 35.8 | 2.2 | 21.3 | 11865 |
| Aleksandr–Nevskii | 28.0 | 52.4 | 3.4 | 13.8 | 43552 |
| Kazan' | 17.1 | 29.9 | 3.5 | 41.0 | 13375 |
| Kolomna | 29.7 | 38.3 | 2.3 | 26.2 | 23609 |
| Lesnoi | 36.5 | 29.3 | 5.3 | 24.6 | 15830 |
| Liteinyi | 16.9 | 35.2 | 4.0 | 38.5 | 31236 |
| Moscow | 21.3 | 34.8 | 4.5 | 33.0 | 39967 |
| Narva | 33.3 | 50.2 | 3.2 | 11.3 | 69621 |
| Nevskii | 20.1 | 66.8 | 2.8 | 8.5 | 30812 |
| Novaya derevnya | 37.5 | 28.1 | 4.3 | 28.5 | 9825 |
| Petergof | 61.7 | 31.5 | 1.6 | 3.4 | 27949 |
| Petrograd | 38.0 | 25.9 | 5.4 | 26.3 | 70515 |
| Polyustrovo-Porokhovskii | 34.5 | 55.0 | 2.3 | 6.8 | 19690 |
| Rozhdestvenskii | 15.5 | 39.3 | 4.9 | 33.9 | 34287 |
| Spasskii | 16.8 | 39.7 | 3.6 | 33.0 | 17970 |
| Vasilevskii ostrov | 38.1 | 32.9 | 8.2 | 17.7 | 64726 |
| Vyborg | 63.0 | 23.9 | 3.5 | 7.6 | 35711 |

[a] Includes votes for several minor socialist and non-socialist parties that together received 4.0 per cent of the vote in Petrograd.

Sources:   Rosenberg, Liberals in the Russian Revolution, p. 220; Delo naroda (23–4 Aug 1917).

Judging from the overall voting trend in 1917, the Kadets suffered most from the low turnout. The party's slight decline in August was no doubt largely due to the absence of the wealthier elements of the capital, who failed to heed the Kadets' pleas to return from their dachas to vote. The Kadet vote also suffered from the recent incorporation of six outlying districts with few wealthy inhabitants. The liberals won pluralities in only two districts, both central and overwhelmingly well-to-do—Liteinyi and Admiralty. But they did manage to increase their share of the vote relative to the results of the spring election by 3 to 4 per cent in four other districts (Moscow, Spasskii, Petrograd and Rozhdestvenskii),[42] indicating that a part of the middle strata that had supported the socialists in the earlier, halcyon days of the revolution was having second thoughts under the impact of the deepening social and political polarisation.

Among the district soviets, elected exclusively by wage and salaried elements and the garrison, only three that had any significant working-class constituency—Narva, Nevskii and Porokhovskii—retained their moderate socialist majorities to the end of August.[43] But these soviets had, in fact, already ceased to represent the dominant political sentiment among the local workers.[44]

In the factory committees, the Bolsheviks consolidated their already very strong positions. At the 7–12 August Second Conference of Factory Committees, the Bolshevik resolution was passed by 82 per cent of the vote with 10 per cent opposing and 8 per cent abstaining.[45] (At the first conference in late May, the resolution for soviet power received 63 per cent.)

With the exceptions of the Printers' and the Paper Workers' Unions, the Bolsheviks now held majorities in the executives of all of Petrograd's industrial unions. Seventeen of the twenty-three members of the Petrograd Trade Union Council were Bolsheviks.[46]

The reaction against the Bolsheviks provoked by the bloodshed of the July Days, in any case limited mainly to workers who had not participated in the demonstrations, had thus proved remarkably short-lived. Less than a month had passed since the workers of the Thornton Textile Mill had recalled all their Bolshevik delegates when they restored them all to their former posts in new elections.[47] By August, even the hitherto staunchest bastions of defencism were crumbling.

This shift was especially striking in the largely unskilled and overwhelmingly female textile industry,[48] where before July the demand for soviet power had the support of majorities in only two or three mills. On 13 August the delegates' assembly of the Petrograd Union of Textile Workers (80 delegates from 24 mills) for the first time passed a resolution demanding the transfer of state power to the soviets.[49]

In elections to the Petrograd Soviet held in June at the Petrograd Pipe (Trubochnyi) Factory (20,000 workers, 30 per cent female and less than 10 per cent skilled[50]) the Bolsheviks took only a third of the seats. But on 17 August, a factory-wide delegates' meeting resolved to condemn Kerenskii's 'government of salvation and its counter-revolutionary essence'.[51] At the Skorokhod Shoe Factory (4900 workers, two-thirds female[52]), according to one of its workers, 'now [after July], even the most backward workers turned away from the SRs'.[53]

This was also the period when anti-coalition sentiment began to make headway in the large state factories (for the most part, heavily involved in ordnance production), among the most conservative in the capital. The Patronnyi and Arsenal Factories, defencist exceptions in the Vyborg District, elected their first Bolshevik Soviet delegates in August (though the defencists retained majorities for several more weeks).[54]

Especially dramatic was the change in political mood at the Obukhovskii Steel Mill in the Nevskii District, where the Bolsheviks had been terrorised after the July Days. The workers here had the distinction of forming the only volunteer workers' unit put at the government's disposal in its preparations for the June offensive.[55] Following elections to the district duma on 10–11 August, the Bolshevik paper, *Proletarii*, published this report:

> Was it not recently that the defencists ruled undividedly at the huge [12 000 workers] Obukhovskii Factory, which sets the tone for the entire proletariat and semi-proletariat of the Nevskii District? Not long ago Deich and Aleksinskii [prominent right-wing Menshevik and SR] were welcome guests, and a Bolshevik could not show his face. At the elections, the defencists received only one mandate. And the SRs, to hold onto their following, had to hastily repaint themselves in a protective internationalist hue. Of the 38 mandates they received [out of 52], 26 consider themselves as belonging to the left wing of the SR Party.[56]

It is true that the SRs held onto their attraction for the inhabitants of this semi-rural district (the factory in question was 15 km from the centre of town[57]): of the total popular vote of 43 000, the SRs won 74.4 per cent, the Bolsheviks—11.2, Mensheviks—5.6 and the Kadets 5.1.[58] But support for the coalition government was fading quickly. According to the same article, at a recent factory meeting it was the Bolshevik speakers who enjoyed the greatest success and were repeatedly interrupted by applause.

In fact, as the city-wide duma elections showed, both wings of the SR Party were in serious trouble. Apart from the precipitous drop in electoral support, the party was plagued by mass rank-and-file defections from within its own ranks. Reports from the districts on the situation during July–August at the 23 August meeting of the SR PC

(Petrograd Committee) noted the party's declining influence among the workers, with rank-and-file members complaining of the party's right-wing policies and leaving in droves to join the Bolsheviks. The only exceptions to this general picture were the Nevskii, Porokhovskii and Moscow Districts, where the SRs still retained considerable, if declining, working-class support.[59] By contrast, the Bolshevik Petrograd organisation (not including soldiers) grew by a fifth, from 30 620 members to 36 015, in the month of July alone.[60]

As for the by now very weak Menshevik Petrograd organisation, it had shifted decisively to an internationalist and anti-coalition stand (though the minority defencist wing enjoyed slightly larger electoral support). At the city conference in early August, the left wing had a majority of fifteen among a little over one hundred delegates.[61] And the rank and file was constantly pressing the leadership leftward. It succeeded, for example, in thwarting the PC's intention of entering into an electoral alliance with the defencists in the duma elections.[62] Even on the national level the defencists were on the run. At the All-Russian Menshevik Congress on 19 August, Tsereteli prevailed over Martov (the Internationalist leader) by the unprecedentedly narrow margin of 115 to 79.[63]

The post-July political evolution of the Rozhdestvenskii District Soviet offers a somewhat more specific glimpse into the processes at work among the elements that had still supported the coalition at the start of July and condemned the demonstrations. This was a small district in the 'bourgeois' centre of the city with only about 10 000 factory workers, a little less than half of whom were employed in two textile mills. The rest were scattered among several small metalworking and electrical factories, printing plants and a tram depot. Several military units were barracked here.[64] Accordingly, Bolshevik influence in the soviet before the July Days was small, and on 6 July, the plenum (general assembly of workers' and soldiers' sections) of the soviet condemned the Bolsheviks as an 'irresponsible minority leading benighted masses in an unconscious manner toward civil war within democracy and threatening to turn the revolution onto the path of reaction and counterrevolution'.[65]

However, under the impact of the ensuing reaction, the soviet's attitude towards the Bolsheviks and the 'danger on the left' began to soften. A week after the above meeting, the soviet once again condemned the 'irresponsible agitation of anarcho-Bolshevik elements', but now hastened to add that 'as a result of the defeat of the unconscious counterrevolution from the left, the counterrevolution from the right has raised its head and is trying to open active operations'. Summoning the workers to rally behind the TsIK, the soviet demanded that the latter 'take measures against the increasingly militant counterrevolution on the right'. It also protested against the bias of the commission investigating the July Days in which the workers and soldiers were inadequately represented: it was concentrating exclusively on the 'anarcho-Bolshevik' organisations without attempting to get to the root of the counterrevolution, which lay on the right.[66] The balance of opinion was clearly beginning to shift from concern with the Bolsheviks and their supporters, now defeated, to growing alarm at the onslaught of reaction as well as at the TsIK's virtual capitulation before it.

Four days later, the soviet decisively rejected the proposed disarming of the district's workers by a special military unit, saying that it would itself investigate whether there were any illegal arms. To the soldiers it pointed out the necessity rather of disarming 'the supporters of the counterrevolution among the bourgeoisie of all ranks and stations'.[67]

About this time, the government reintroduced the death penalty at the front, long a demand of the Right (particularly the military and the Kadet Party). The TsIK approved this measure. It was on this issue that the Rozhdestvenskii District Soviet finally broke with the moderate TsIK majority, voting thirteen against five (with five abstentions) to condemn the new measure. This resolution merits being quoted at length because of the symbolism for the workers of the death penalty, which perhaps more than anything else smacked of a return to the repressive ways of the old régime. Many workers could still recall the mass executions following the defeat of the revolution of 1905, and many more had participated in strikes and demonstrations in the following years to save their comrades and leaders from the Tsarist hangman. The sentiments expressed in this resolution were echoed at numerous working-class gatherings of this period.[68]

One of the most valuable achievements of the Great Russian Revolution—the abolition of capital punishment—has been destroyed with a single stroke of the Provisional Government's pen.

Already under [Tsar] Nikolai, in the fiercest and darkest times of reaction, the death penalty provoked the unanimous indignation of the toilers, on the one hand, and a feigned squeamish attitude from the bourgeoisie, on the other; and a rumble of anger rolled across Russia from one end to the other.

The victorious people, having overthrown the autocracy, first of all abolished the death penalty as a barbarism unworthy of a free country.

Now the Provisional Government, on the demand of the generals and of people incapable of appreciating this great achievement, and also on the request of the Minister of War [Kerenskii], who has acceded to these demands, has again restored this legalised murder ... Soldiers, appointed to the role of executioner, will hastily drag away their comrades, exhausted and driven senseless by the savage three-year slaughter and sentenced to death ... They will shoot them like dogs only because they did not self-sacrificingly give up their lives in the interests of their class enemies, the imperialist bourgeoisie, which has thrown the toilers of one side against those of the other.

A great absurdity occurs: a free country abolishes the death penalty for highly placed criminals, all those Nikolais, Sukhomlinovs, Stürmers and Protopopovs [Tsarist ministers], etc. and retains it for soldiers worn out by a senseless three-year slaughter, whom the base and cowardly bourgeoisie is now slandering with the undeserved title of cowards and traitors ...

It is a crime to pass over in silence this attack by the Provisional Government against the achievements of the Revolution. In no place and at no time have the toilers reconciled themselves to this disgrace nor have they ever looked coldly upon that form of murder called the death penalty ... Down with the death penalty! ... Down with the war as the cause of this horrible result that disgraces humanity! Long live the Revolutionary International![69]

(A month later, the plenum of the Petrograd Soviet met (after a four week recess, itself testimony to the atrophy of the defencist-led soviets) and in a dramatic break with the TsIK voted 900 to four for the abolition of the death penalty. The four opposing were Tsereteli, Dan, Liber and Chkheidze, Menshevik leaders of the TsIK.[70])

This same meeting of the Rozhdestvenskii Soviet demanded a serious struggle against the 'counterrevolution grown bold, which is now coming out into the open, having found its leadership in the June-Third Duma, the clergy, the landowners and the capitalists'. The soviet called on the TsIK to 'put an end to the comedy' and finally disperse the State Duma,

> this insignificant band of counterrevolutionaries and recent toadies of autocracy, who have pretensions to speak for the Russian people who have never empowered them for anything, who permit themselves intolerable insults and call for the dissolution of the legitimate organs of revolutionary democracy ... The TsIK must turn the most serious attention of the government and especially of its socialist ministers to the necessity of applying the full force of repression against the counterrevolution from the right that is growing more insolent each day.

Not one word about the 'anarcho-Bolsheviks' and the 'counterrevolution from the left'.

The same transformation was occurring in the other districts that had experienced an anti-Bolshevik reaction after the July Days, particularly the Nevskii and Porokhovskii Districts, SR strongholds. Already on 16 July the delegate from the Nevskii District to the Bolshevik City Conference was able to report that the 'pogrom mood' had passed. 'A calm now appears to have set in, if events don't develop further. Protest signatures [against the repressions] are being collected. Many SRs and Mensheviks are signing.'[71]

It is significant that this was also the period when the workers of Moscow abandoned the moderate socialists en masse. The industrial working class of Moscow was significantly different from that of Petrograd: there the overwhelmingly unskilled textile sector predominated over metalworking, the former employing about 37 per cent of the industrial labour force, as opposed to 11 per cent in Petrograd. On the other hand, the more skilled metalworking industry employed only 26 per cent of the factory workers as opposed to 60 per cent in Petrograd. Moscow's workers also retained stronger ties to their peasant origins than those of Petrograd. According to the 1918 industrial census, 39.8 per cent of Moscow's workers in August 1918 had owned land before the October Revolution; in Petrograd—only 16.5 per cent. Finally, Moscow's workers were much less concentrated in large factories than Petrograd's. Average factory size in Moscow was 159 workers as opposed to 389 in Petrograd.[72]

In many respects then, the Moscow working class resembled that segment of the Petrograd proletariat, mainly unskilled workers, that still followed the moderate socialists and the coalition in the July Days (as had the bulk of the workers in Moscow, where the July Days passed almost unnoticed). At the start of July even Moscow's factory committees were still dominated by defencists.[73] Muscovites often commented on the relative quiescence of the city's workers compared to the activism and militancy of Petrograd. 'I'm very struck that the Moscow organisation is so weak', noted the Bolshevik Efimov at a July meeting of the Bolshevik Moscow Committee. 'In Piter they're holding the masses back all the time. Here we have to conduct intensified agitation to get any demonstration.'[74] 'Many are those who have sung the meekness and patriarchal spirit of Moscow', commented Sukhanov.[75]

All the more startling, therefore, was the virtually unanimous general political strike that greeted the 11 August opening of the State Conference. Moscow had been selected over the capital to host the conference precisely because the government wanted to avoid the latter's embattled atmosphere and class polarisation. Yet not only had Moscow's workers brought the city to a virtual standstill, but in doing this they were openly defying the will of the Moscow Soviet, which had voted 354 to 304 against the strike.[76] (The Central Council of Trade Unions, however, supported the strike, with only the representatives of the Printers' and the White-collar Employees' (*sluzhashchie*) Unions dissenting.[77])

This belated radicalisation of the main mass of less skilled workers (and the provinces tended to resemble Moscow in this respect) can be explained by the much more tangible character assumed by the counterrevolution and the economic crisis (in the workers' minds the two were closely connected) after the July Days. These were issues that even the most apolitical and cautious workers[78] could no longer ignore or dismiss. All the arguments in favour of soviet power that they had heard earlier and rejected, were now being proven correct 'on their own hides' (*na sobstvennoi shkure*), as the workers would say.

Referring to the peasants, soldiers and also 'that significant part of the proletariat' still closely tied to the peasantry, the Left SR Kamkov told the All-Russian Factory Committee Conference in October:

Only the sad experience of the past seven months of the revolution could create the conditions for the final elimination . . . of the politics of conciliationism and the transfer of power to the hands of re-volutionary democracy . . . In the beginning, during the first govern-mental crisis [April], the broad masses were not able to understand the slogan 'All power to the soviets', hurled at them by the left wing of revolutionary democracy. The masses were too backward, *their development had not reached the point where they could accept this slogan without experience.* Through artificial, technical (if one can use such a term) means, through individual actions, the minority could not graft this slogan upon the masses. Now the sad experience of all the coalitions is there for all to see. It has *concretely* proven the unsoundness of the principle of coalitions . . .

The question of peace evolved in the same way. Posed *abstractly* at the start of the war, the question of peace could not be sufficiently mastered by the peasantry, the army and a significant part of the proletariat. Now all feel *concretely* that the government not only has done nothing to bring closer a democratic peace but that it has even created all sorts of obstacles to this . . . [italics added][79]

Kamkov's incisive analysis underlines the limited (though, for all that, no less crucial) role played by leadership in shaping the political attitudes of the unskilled workers. The capacity for abstract, theoreti-cal thought, the facility in passing from personal, direct experience to general political issues lacking immediate, concrete referents were much less developed in the unskilled workers than in their skilled counterparts.[80] For this reason, party agitation alone was unable to persuade them that 'conciliationism' was harmful to their interests. However, it is equally true that without the credible alternative to 'conciliationism' offered by the Bolshevik organisation and its political programme, the unskilled workers would in all probability have turned to unorganised spontaneous economic actions on the factory level or else would have sunk back into political apathy. Both reactions did, in fact, occur to a limited extent in the weeks following the Kornilov Affair, when the Bolshevik Party failed to put forth concrete political goals towards which the workers could orient themselves.[81] The leadership, therefore, played a crucial role in providing a political alternative, but only first-hand, tangible experience could drive these workers to embrace it.

Thus, in the case of the Russian working class, at least, economic insecurity and poverty did not correlate positively with political radicalism. They tended rather to foster caution and political inertness. Yet another possible factor in the unskilled workers' slower radicalisation was the fact that soviet power, which in 1917 was understood by all as the direct assumption of state power by the masses, went against the grain of traditional peasant mentality, which was still a potent element in the consciousness of the unskilled newcomers and women workers. To the Russian peasant mind, the state had always appeared as alien, something to petition for redress against local powers but with which one could never actually identify.[82] Dual power fitted this conception very well, with the soviets acting as intercessors for the masses before the state. It was all the more difficult, therefore, to abandon it in favour of soviet power, which represented a conception of the state that belonged to a new world which the unskilled workers had for the most part only just begun to experience.

### Attitudes Towards Census Society

The radicalisation of the bulk of unskilled workers in the summer restored the political unity that had characterised the Petrograd working class in the early period of the revolution. This unity was based on the shared perception of the counterrevolutionary nature of census Russia, and this in turn called for an end to the politics of 'conciliationism' and for the direct assumption of power by the popular classes.

Never before, it seems, had Petrograd society been so polarised, as the anger and hatred of May and June turned into rage and loathing in July and August. 'When you meet up with the street [the masses], what do you observe?' asked the Kadet leader Shingarev at a meeting of his party's CC (Central Committee) on 20 August.

Yesterday in Novaya derevnya [a small district next to the heavily industrial Vyborg District], they simply would not let Milyukov speak. [I myself] only with great difficulty was able to finish a meeting at Goryachee pole in the Labour Exchange building, which was attended only by Kadets and Bolsheviks [!] and by some curious onlookers. Seeking common concepts, common terms, I mentioned the fatherland, and a worker with a savage expression on his face shouted spitefully: 'A worker has no fatherland—he has a fist!' When I reminded them that such mutual bitterness in France ended in people chopping of each other's heads, a sailor shouted: 'And your head should be chopped off too!' ... Benighted and embittered people, having thrown aside their recent leader, Tsereteli, are taking to rebellion [*buntarstvo*]. It is reaching the point of shooting, as words are no longer of any avail.[83]

Although Shingarev seems to have caught the popular mood, his reference to *buntarstvo*, which implies an unconscious, elemental spirit of revolt, must surely be taken with a grain of salt. In Petrograd of August 1917, there was very little sign among the workers of a resolve for such drastic action. On the other hand, the protocols of the Kadet CC meeting are rife with allusions to an imminent 'surgical intervention' (one week before the Kornilov Uprising), and not all by any means were of a disapproving nature. Shingarev himself admitted that 'one can already see a dictator on the horizon'. Should, then, the party leave the coalition, he asked. No, because even if the dictator were later to turn power over to the Kadets, the origins of such a régime would be tantamount to political suicide for the party. All the same, he admitted that the dilemma tormented him.

Buzinov, a worker at the Nevskii Factory, offered the following illustration of how much the political temper had changed. When in April 1917 a former Black Hundred (a monarchist, arch-reactionary, anti-semitic organisation founded in 1905) worker reappeared in the Nevskii District and began agitating openly, the workers left him alone, 'because in those days of general ecstacy amidst the young freedom, the workers showed a striking tolerance toward alien convictions'. But in the summer of 1917, 'when the political atmosphere had already grown incandescent, an SR worker at the Nevskii Factory gunned him down in broad daylight'.[84]

There had always been more involved in the workers' hostility towards census society than the perception of opposing economic and political interests. The workers' offended sense of class honour had already played an important role in their forceful reaction to the Milyukov note and the street clashes in April. But after July this became a major theme. The resolution of the Rozhdestvenskii District Soviet cited earlier refers to the 'pretensions ... of this insignificant band of counterrevolutionaries ... who permit themselves intolerable insults ... [and who are] growing more insolent each day'. Over and over during this period workers' meetings emphasise the intolerable 'insolence' (*nakhal'stvo*) with which census society was conducting itself and its 'mocking' (*izdevatel'stvo*, *glumlenie*) of the working class and its organisations.

Facing mass dismissals, in early August the workers of Pulemet met to protest against

> the hidden lockouts by the factory owners, who cite and find support in our ministry while firing workers and shutting our factories ... With such hidden lockouts the capitalists put the army at the front and the peasants in the rear without agricultural tools in a helpless situation, while all the time they shout about the salvation of the fatherland. Is this not a mockery of the working people?![85]

'The current moment places the revolution in extreme danger', declared the workers of the Anchar Factory on 25 July in a resolution passed by 310 against 14.

> Yet all the conciliations of the Mensheviks and SRs with the bourgeoisie cannot lead the country out of its dead-end but only bring it to further disorganisation ... We workers declare that the fear of the majority of the Soviet to take power into their hands proves the bankruptcy of their policies and allows the right-wing counterrevolution to mock the working class ... We see salvation in the transfer of power to the hands of the peasants, soldiers and workers, to the hands of the soviets which will be supported by the people. For only the entire people, united around a revolutionary soviet, can save the country and the revolution, which they are now trying to reverse.[86]

Skorinko, then a sixteen-year-old worker at the Putilov Works, has left a striking account of the 'incandescent atmosphere' of the late summer and the intense emotion surrounding this sense of class honour. On one of the long summer evenings, Skorinko and some other young Putilov workers were sitting around at the Bolshevik district headquarters, as was their custom, talking politics, trying to imagine what a communist society would be like, singing, and simply enjoying each other's company, when a battered comrade suddenly appeared. He had just come from the centre, where he had been beaten up for defending Lenin. The Putilov youths at once hopped on a tram for Nevskii Prospekt 'to defend Lenin's honour'. It did not take long before the author himself was twice beaten up, ultimately landing in jail, where he was again treated to a sound thrashing. On returning home early next morning, he had to recount his adventures to his parents, lest they suspect 'immoral' behaviour.

> In the course of my story, I noticed the frame of mind of my father, a revolutionary worker. (As my father, on previous occasions when I

had landed in trouble, he would add a little of his own.) This time he grew furious and broke into uncontrolled abuse directed at the bourgeoisie, Kerenskii and the police. Then he suddenly became bellicose and swore that the Putilov Factory alone would scatter the bourgeoisie and grind Nevskii to dust for insulting comrade Lenin. When I told of the two prostitutes [the only people to offer the semi-conscious Skorinko help], tears welled up in his eyes. And, after all, he tended to look at them from the 'social' point of view.

But when I mentioned that at the Spasskii police station I was punched in the mouth, he leaped up, knocking over his chair, and shouted to my mother's horror: 'And you let him get away with it, you *parshivets* [mangy one]? You should have given him one in the mug, with an inkwell, a revolver, a chair. A worker should not tolerate a blow from a bourgeois. He hit you? Well, then return it. Akh, you *zasranets* [shithead]!'

'Look at the old fool,' my mother jumped on him. 'He's gone crazy himself and now he wants to drive his son mad. Bolsheviks? You'll see. Your son will soon come home without a head, thanks to his father. The officers will take it off.'

I strongly doubted I would show up in such a form, as it was 'technically' impossible. But my father, paying no attention to her, stamped his foot and let loose a barrage of abuse addressed at my head, saying that I was good even without it. 'To the devil with her!' (Actually, this was expressed in a somewhat different manner.) 'For Lenin, for the Bolsheviks, let them tear it off. But we'll tear off a hundred for that one.'

After that, he dashed about the apartment swearing and mumbling something, when our lodger, a baker at a large plant, an SR, entered the room. He ran up to him and shouted at the top of his voice: 'Out of this apartment, the devil take you, damned SR! Go to Kerenskii [a Trudovik—Right SR] for whose sake they beat children! Get out!'

That same day the lodger left, and my father, jubilant, declared that from now on he was a Red Guard, despite his forty-eight years.[87]

(One can readily see here the moderating influence women generally exerted on their husbands. On the other hand, in the elder Skorinko, a worker in the Putilov forging shop and a veteran of 1905, there is none of the proverbial peasant meekness.)

The atmosphere in the capital was thick with class hatred. Nevertheless, it soon became clear that it was one thing to demand an end to the coalition and to census influence on state policy, but quite another, after the sobering experience of the July Days, to decide what sort of government should take its place.

*Attitudes Towards Revolutionary Democracy*

The TsIK's repeated capitulations before census society and its condonation, if not outright approval, of the repressions against the workers and left socialists, cast doubt in the workers' minds on the validity of the very concept of 'revolutionary democracy' and of soviet power as its proposed political expression. After all, the moderate socialists, who controlled the TsIK, still enjoyed very significant support in the country, particularly among the peasantry and the left-leaning intelligentsia, who along with the workers and soldiers made up revolutionary democracy. Yet, as the workers saw it, the moderate socialists were aiding the counterrevolutionary forces (though few workers were yet prepared to say that they were consciously counterrevolutionary). It was necessary, therefore, to find an answer to the questions: Who should take power if not 'revolutionary democracy'? Was there anything that could replace it without condemning the revolution to defeat? And even if there was, how would this affect the nature and course of the revolution?

In this connection, it is worth examining the debate on tactics at the Bolshevik Petrograd Conference in mid July, as it offers the clearest formulation of the issues facing the workers. While one cannot claim any *a priori* correspondence between the views expressed here and attitudes current among the worker rank and file, in this instance, at least, data emanating directly from the workers indicate that there was a rough coincidence. Also, one should bear in mind that a good part of the conference delegates were workers. According to Golovanova's data, about three-fourths of the Bolshevik district committees between February and July 1917 were workers,[88] and it was from among these people that conference delegates were most likely to be chosen.

Moreover, the Petrograd party organisation as a whole was strongly working class. On the basis of national figures, Stepanov estimates that in October 1917 workers made up 66 per cent of the Bolshevik Party membership in Petrograd (including the Petrograd Military Organisation).[89] But this may be an underestimate. The registration book of the Second City District, which was a central district with relatively little industry, shows that of the 913 new members joining in the four months March–June, 789 or 86.4 per cent were workers. The next largest group were the sailors and soldiers, 49 and 25 people respectively, together 8.1 per cent. Professions that even by stretching the term one could call intellectual—bookkeeper, instructor, pianist and student—amounted to no more than eight people. The others were all low wage or salary earners.[90] This, of course, is not to deny that the balance of opinion within the party was probably to the left of that in the working class as a whole and that formulations at the conference were no doubt more articulate than what one might hear from the average worker.

The debate revolved around the following question: should the workers break with the moderate-socialist-dominated soviets, abandon the slogan of soviet power, and thus sever relations with the 'petty bourgeois' elements of revolutionary democracy that continued to support the 'conciliators'? An affirmative reply meant replacing revolutionary democracy with a purely working-class alliance of the urban and rural proletariat, in effect, a dictatorship of the proletariat.

There were basically two positions: one wanted to retain 'all power to the soviets'; the other wanted to replace it with a new slogan being urged by Lenin: 'a government of the workers and poorest peasants'. 'This is the crucial point of our disagreements', noted Volodarskii.

> The question is: are the petty bourgeoisie and the TsIK an appendage of the counterrevolution or are they wavering between revolution and counterrevolution? It is a matter of what conclusions to draw. If we recognise that the petty bourgeoisie is counterrevolutionary, *then in the future we are alone*. [italics added][91]

'There is no basis to change slogans', seconded Kharitonov.

> Elections to the organs of self-government show that all strata of the peasantry follow the Mensheviks and SRs. We cannot declare a dictatorship of the proletariat when we are an overwhelmed minority. By saying 'All power to the soviets', we do not mean to give it to Dan and Liber. The key questions have not been resolved and so the revolution is not over, and the wavering petty bourgeoisie, under the influence of events, will inevitably move to the left. To write off the petty bourgeoisie is to ruin the revolution.[92]

According to this position, without a revolution in the West an isolated Russian working class could not hold power on its own. In any case, it was argued, a proletarian dictatorship could not 'rest upon bayonets'. The petty bourgeoisie should not be written off into the camp of the counterrevolution. Rather, it was unenlightened and vacillating, and its own interests, particularly land reform and peace, would drive it to the side of the working class and against census society.

The opposing current of opinion maintained that the peasants represented by the Executive Committee of the Peasant Congress belonged to the wealthier rural stratum, which together with the right-wing SRs were thirsting for workers' blood. These elements would not follow the workers. The working class could ally itself only with those rural elements that shared its interests—the poorest peasantry. The July Days represented a fundamental shift in the correlation of political forces, not merely a temporary wavering of the soviets. The counterrevolution had emerged victorious, and this effectively ruled out peaceful, parliamentary means of struggle for power. As proof of this, the warrant for Lenin's arrest, preventing him from addressing the conference, was cited. This, therefore, was no longer the pre-July situation. Now, even if the soviets wanted to take power, they could not, since they had lost the real power they once had.[93]

The supporters of the old strategy answered this by arguing that 'poorest peasantry' was not a political entity nor a Marxist category. It smacked rather of a lumpen element. Besides, it was wrong to say the counterrevolution was victorious so long as it could not shut the mouths of the workers and soldiers. And this clearly was not the case. The peasants voluntarily supported the soviet majority and would learn better through concrete experience. An insurrection against the soviet leadership and the peasantry was unnecessary. In the meanwhile 'our presence in the soviet prevents it from making a deal with the bourgeoisie. Our duty is to stay in it and conduct our former decisive line.'[94]

In the end, the conference voted 28 to 3 (with 28 abstentions) for the compromise position which had been adopted earlier by the CC, where Lenin had found himself in a minority.[95] This resolution called both for a government based upon the 'proletariat and poorest peasantry' and for the transfer of power 'to the revolutionary soviets of workers' and peasants' deputies'.[96] The concession to the advocates of a new strategy lay in the word 'revolutionary' as well as in the summons to prepare for a 'decisive battle', a euphemism for insurrection. The resolution was, therefore, ambiguous, speaking simultaneously of workers and peasants and of workers and poorest peasants, of soviet power and of insurrection. It thus left unanswered the crucial question of the attitude towards the peasantry. However, given the retention of the soviet slogan, it is clear that the supporters of Lenin's position got the short end of the compromise.

This group, although defeated, was nevertheless a very sizeable minority at the conference. Its resolution was rather narrowly defeated by 22 to 15. Moreover, most of the 28 who abstained in the vote for the victorious resolution belonged to the opposition, including the entire delegation (eleven people) from the Vyborg District, who complained that the resolution was ambiguous and that Lenin's theses had not been read before the conference.[97]

The basic question was, thus, left open, the majority opting to continue to try to win over the rest of revolutionary democracy, while paying lip service to the need to prepare for insurrection. Even after the Sixth All-Russian Party Congress two weeks later called for a government of workers and poor peasants (with no mention of the soviets), various factories and working-class organisations continued to call for soviet power or a government of revolutionary democracy, including the Textile Workers' Union and the Factory Committee Conference[98] (though many others did adopt the new slogan). This indicates that the congress had not resolved the issue for a very large part of Petrograd's workers nor even for the Bolsheviks themselves.

This is certainly the conclusion that emerges from the proceedings of the Second Petrograd Conference of Factory Committees of 12–14 August. While the debate at the Bolshevik City Conference centred explicitly around the peasantry, there was another part of revolutionary democracy towards which the workers were now forced to define their relationship—the democratic or socialist intelligentsia. ('Intelligentsia' refers to those earning (or students looking forward to earning) their living in an occupation requiring a higher or at least secondary diploma. The socialist intelligentsia were those who identified with one or another of the socialist parties.) This problem was understandably given much attention at the Factory Committee Conference, where the scarcity of technical and administrative skills among the workers was a source of grave concern.

In demanding soviet power before July, the workers knew they were writing off the active support of the part of the intelligentsia that would choose to side with the propertied classes. But it was only after the July Days that they realised the full extent of their isolation from educated society, since the great majority of even the socialist intelligentsia were 'conciliators', supporters of the TsIK, which had turned against the workers and their goals in the July Days.

The Factory Committee Conference showed a new awareness among the committee activists of the eventual necessity for the workers to assume full control of production in face of the impending collapse of industry that was being prepared by the capitalists' opposition to state regulation and by their direct sabotage on the plant level. In this work, the intelligentsia could not be counted upon. As one delegate put it:

We must exert all our energy in this struggle [to have ready their own workers' economic apparatus for the moment of capitalist collapse]. Especially as class contradictions emerge more and more clearly and the intelligentsia leaves us, we have to rely on ourselves and take all our organisations into our own workers' hands.[99]

These workers were acutely aware of the immense difficulty of the task they saw before them. 'Throughout all the reports', remarked one delegate, 'the cry of a lack of [qualified] people runs like a red thread.'[100] 'Tsarism did everything to leave us unprepared', lamented another, 'and naturally, everywhere, in both political and economic bodies we lack [qualified] people.'[101]

This was, in fact, the main argument of the Mensheviks against an attempt by the workers to seize state power and to organise industry on their own. They constantly stressed the numerical and cultural weakness of the working class, its poor organisation, its ignorance and isolation. 'We are alone', emphasised Sedov, one of the few Menshevik workers at the conference to take the floor.

We have few workers capable of understanding state affairs and of controlling. It is necessary to organise courses in government affairs and in control of production. If we take power, the masses will crucify us. The bourgeoisie is organised and has at its disposal a mass of experienced people. But we do not and, therefore, we will not be in a position to hold onto power.[102]

But as before, these warnings had little effect. This was so in large part because even the Menshevik workers were forced to agree with the Bolsheviks' general assessment of the economic and political situation. Something had to be done and done quickly, but the Mensheviks had only warnings, no positive proposals. It is not surprising, then, that the vast majority of the delegates rejected Sedov's position in favour of the one put forth by Maksimov, the delegate from the Wireless Telephone and Telegraph Factory:

The bourgeoisie knows its interests better than the petty bourgeois parties [Mensheviks and SRs]. The bourgeoisie fully understands the situation and has expressed itself very clearly in Ryabushinskii's words, who said that they will wait until hunger grabs us by the throat and destroys all that we have won. But while they are reaching for our throats, we will fight and we will not back away from the struggle.[103]

'The working class has always been isolated', argued Derbyshev, a Bolshevik member of the CS of Factory Committees and a highly skilled printer formerly at Soikin.

It always has to conduct its policy alone. But in a revolution the working class is the vanguard. It must lead the other classes, including the peasantry. Everything depends upon the activity of workers in various organisations, commissions, etc., where we must be a majority of workers. Against the advancing hunger we must pit the activity of the masses. We have to disown the Slavic spirit of laziness and together cut a path through the forest that will lead the working class to socialism.[104]

Again and again the speakers called for a spirit of self-reliance. When it was suggested that the number of working sections at the conference be limited because of the complexity of the issues and the limited number of 'active forces', Voskov, a carpenter and chairman of the Sestroretsk Arms Factory Committee, retorted indignantly:

The absence of *intelligenty* in no way impedes the work of the sections. It is high time the workers abandoned the bad habit of constantly looking over their shoulder at the *intelligenty*. It is necessary that all participants at the conference enter some section and work there independently.[105]

Chubar', a member of the CS and a skilled metalworker employed at Orudiinyi until the revolution, similarly admonished the assembly: 'The hopeless situation in industry forces us to take upon ourselves the entire burden of the economic ruin ... but we have become so used to tutelage that it is hard to free ourselves from the habit.'[106]

Fighting back their fears, the workers at this conference were struggling to throw off the cultural legacy of their traditionally subordinate position in society. Those who all their lives had been on the receiving end of orders were trying to envisage themselves as a governing class.

The growing rift between the workers and the intelligentsia alluded to by various speakers at this conference was not limited to the sphere of economic management. At a conference on extra-scholastic education, Lunacharskii, a Bolshevik intellectual and cultural activist, caused considerable controversy when he spoke of a great thirst for knowledge among the workers that was going unsatisfied 'because at present one observes that the proletariat is itself isolated from the intelligentsia ... Even the ranks of the worker-intelligentsia have thinned significantly thanks to the fact that the proletariat in its great majority has crossed over to the banner of the extreme left of democracy while the intelligentsia found itself to the right.'[107] Others protested against this characterisation, but Lunacharskii replied that 'not the proletariat is to blame, but the intelligentsia, which has a sharply negative attitude to the political tasks that the proletariat has put forward'.[108]

Nowhere, however, was this rift more pronounced than in the political sphere. Both of the socialist movements in Russia, populism and social democracy, were split between right (defencist) and left (internationalist) wings, the vast majority of the socialist intelligentsia siding with the right wings, while the left attracted almost exclusively workers, peasants and soldiers. As Radkey points out in his study of the SRs, with the split in the party, it is clear ... that nearly all the sailors and a large majority of the workers and the army went with the L[eft] SR, most of the intellectuals and white collar workers stayed where they were, and the peasantry divided into two camps, the larger loyal to the PSR, but the lesser one already sizeable and steadily growing ... From every quarter came complaints of a dearth of intellectuals which seriously impeded the activity of the new party. Sukhanov termed it the party of the rural plebs and ranked it even lower on the cultural scale than the Bolsheviks, the party of the urban plebs.[109]

A similar process occurred within social democracy. Although the Bolsheviks are often mistakenly depicted as a sect of fanatical intellectuals, the fact is that this party, with notable exceptions to be sure, was very much shunned by the radical intelligentsia. At the Bolshevik City Conference in July one speaker went so far as to complain of the 'wholesale desertion of the intelligentsia'. Volodarskii, who headed the PC's agitation department, added:

The intelligentsia, in accord with its social make-up, has crossed over to the defencists and does not want to carry the revolution farther. It does not come to us and everywhere it is in a position of resisting the revolutionary steps of the workers.[110]

He reaffirmed this a few weeks later at the Party's All-Russian Congress in his report on the Petrograd organisation:

Work is being conducted by local forces from among the worker masses. There are very few intellectual forces. All organisational work, and a significant part of the agitational work, is carried out by the workers themselves. The members of the CC [intellectual in its majority] took little part in our organisational work. Lenin and Zinoviev very rarely, as they were preoccupied with other work. Our organisation has grown from below.[111]

In the provincial organisations, where there were even fewer intellectuals available and where the workers were generally of a lower cultural level than in the capital, this rift was felt especially acutely. In fact, the Bolshevik CC was being constantly bombarded with urgent requests to send 'literary forces', 'at least one intellectual'. But Sverdlov, the CC secretary, almost invariably replied that the situation was little better in Petrograd and no one could be spared.[112]

As a result, there was a growing identification by the workers of the Mensheviks (and partly SRs) with intellectuals and the Bolsheviks with workers. Walking about the working-class districts during the July Days, Andreev, a Menshevik journalist, came upon a worker making a speech in support of the Bolsheviks. Andreev remarked that the Bolsheviks were in fact working for the counterrevolution. At this, 'A worker standing behind me shouted furiously at me: "You stroll about in a pince-nez [sure sign of an intellectual to the people] and you can still talk about counterrevolution!?" '[113]

Another Petrograd Menshevik recounted his visit in June to a Moscow tea-packing plant where all the factory committee members but one were Mensheviks. When he inquired about this, the non-Menshevik replied that although he belonged to no party, he did vote for the Bolsheviks because 'on their [electoral] list there are workers. The Mensheviks are all gentlemen [*gospoda*]—doctors, lawyers, etc.' Furthermore, he added, the Bolsheviks stood for workers' control and soviet power.[114] Speaking in the autumn before the Orekhovo-Zuevo Soviet (in the Central Industrial Region), a certain Baryshnikov declared:

> Due to the fact that the ideology and politics of the working class assume an immediate radical transformation of the current system, the relationship between the so-called intelligentsia, the SRs and Mensheviks, and the workers has become very strained. And therefore, there already exist no ties between us, and in the eyes of the working class they have finally defined themselves as servants of bourgeois society.[115]

It would, however, be wrong to see this rift as solely the product of the 1917 revolution and the workers' radicalisation during its course. The roots of this mutual alienation go back at least to 1905. The memoirs of worker activists on the interrevolutionary period are replete with complaints of the 'flight' and 'betrayal' of the intelligentsia. The background to this was the growing class polarisation within Russian society during and particularly following 1905. The radical intelligentsia had been frightened away by a labour movement that was less and less willing to limit itself to the struggle against Tsarism, as it increasingly directed its fire equally against the capitalist class and (though only implicitly until 1917) against the socio-economic order it represented.[116]

February, which bore the appearance of an all-national democratic movement, temporarily papered over this class polarisation and created the ground for a *rapprochement* between the workers and radical intelligentsia on the basis of their shared 'revolutionary defencism', and support for dual power. However, this turned out to be only a brief interlude. By the late summer, defencist and 'conciliationist' sentiment had all but disappeared among Petrograd's workers and with it the basis for the worker–intelligentsia *rapprochement*.

It was thus with some justification that the Bolsheviks, in the autumn of 1917, could speak of themselves as the party of the proletariat. For not only did they enjoy the support of the vast majority of workers, but their party consisted of and to a large extent was run by workers (and certainly to a much greater extent than any other socialist party). One should not be misled by the prominence of intellectuals in the CC. The party in 1917 was run on a democratic basis, and throughout that year it was the more radical working-class base that predominated over the quite moderate majority of the central body.

In sum, at issue in this debate over strategy was the prospect of the total isolation of the working class from its one time allies—the peasants and the left-leaning intelligentsia. The question was: could the revolution be saved without running this risk?

The Factory Committee Conference seemed prepared to answer this negatively and to take up the challenge. In the discussion on workers' control a resolution calling for the transfer of power to the 'proletariat and those strata of the peasantry adhering to it' was passed by 198 votes against 13 (with 18 abstentions).[117] In fact, an attempt to amend this formulation with 'the transfer of power to revolutionary democracy' collected only 23 votes (22 abstentions).[118]

But then came a surprise. Just when it seemed that the matter was settled, the debate flared up anew when Larin, a recent convert to Bolshevism from left Menshevism, in his report on unemployment proposed a resolution calling for the transfer of power to 'revolutionary democracy'. Naturally, it was at once proposed to change this to 'proletariat and poorest peasantry' or 'proletariat supported by the poorest strata of the peasantry'.

Larin, however, replied that these formulations were unacceptable, particularly the second, which seemed to give preference to the workers and would only play into the hands of those trying to bait the peasantry against the workers. Evdokimov's reply was blunt. This was not a matter of choice of words. His formulation had a specific intent: 'The proletariat is the vanguard. It must have hegemony and it will take along with it certain strata of the peasantry.' Larin remained adamant, calling this a formula for the ruin of the revolution.

Supporting Larin, Lunacharskii emphasised that the peasants had to participate in the movement and should not be pushed to the side or given the impression that their role was subordinate to that of the workers. Besides, no clear line separated the poor from the non-poor peasantry, and one could not tell beforehand which elements would join the workers. It was better, therefore, to leave the issue open.

At this point, Skrypnik interjected that the conference had already taken its position and could not reverse itself in just three minutes. And when the conference did, in fact, uphold Larin, Evdokimov claimed it did not know what it was voting for, that it had 'whipped itself'.

In view of the fact that the debate on both resolutions had dotted all the i's and that this conference was drawn from among the politically most sophisticated workers in Petrograd, it does not seem likely that Evdokimov was correct. On the other hand, one cannot help but be struck by the close parallel between the two contradictory votes at this conference and the internally contradictory resolution passed three weeks earlier by the Bolshevik City Conference.

This indecision reflected a basic unwillingness on the part of the workers to accept in practice the consequences that followed from their own analysis of the post-July situation. The prospect of total isolation and a civil war within democracy was a bitter pill, indeed, to swallow. While the Factory Committee Conference's first resolution made this isolation appear a certainty, Larin's left open the possibility of a reunification of the ranks of revolutionary democracy. Though defiant and unyielding, the workers were still licking their wounds from the July Days and were afraid of repeating the same experience on an even more bloody and disastrous scale.

This was the mood of the conference: an impressive display of independence and defiance along with intense inner struggle against self-doubt and fear. And the conference's atmosphere, though very determined, was also much less ebullient, more modest and business-like than that of the previous conference in May. Judging by the talk of the need for legislation to entrench the rights of factory committees and the debate over whether or not to participate in state economic organs, it was clear that the goal of a non-census government, what-ever its specific class composition, was not seen as an immediate prospect.

To be sure, many factory meetings did demand a government of 'the workers and poorest part of the peasantry', but in light of the above, these resolutions cannot of themselves be taken as evidence of a practical readiness to take power against the will of the TsIK and its supporters in revolutionary democracy. Just the opposite would seem to be the case. Even in the 'red Vyborg District', according to the local commander of the Red Guards, one could observe at this time 'a political lull and even a certain indifference to red guard training'.[119] It was relatively easy to vote for a resolution; acting on it was a different matter. This problem had not arisen with the old slogan of 'soviet power' because it was a slogan of peaceful transition and entailed no split or threat of civil war within revolutionary democracy.

Some workers, no doubt, were even then prepared to accept the practical conclusions of the new slogan. Some resolutions were accom-panied by extremely harsh denunciations of the moderate socialists.

For example, Voenno-podkovnyi, a consistently militant metalworking factory that had been among the first to demand soviet power, resolved in early August:

> Only the poorest classes of the population with the proletariat at the head can suppress the greedy appetites of the predators of world imperialism and lead this long-suffering country onto the wide road, giving peace, bread and freedom, and liberate humanity from the bondage of capitalist slavery.
>
> We declare that, having thrown aside all the turncoats from socialism to the bourgeoisie, who hide their betrayal behind defencist slogans, we will support only those who hold high and honestly the banner of revolutionary internationalism.[120]

Similarly, the decisiveness of the resolution of the young Putilov workers has a very convincing ring:

> We, the youths, having learnt from the experience of our fathers how dangerous it is to fraternise with the bourgeoisie, declare that it will be a fearful hour when we, the youth, for the salvation of the revolution take to the streets to destroy with our young hands those parasites who live off the blood and sweat of the toilers . . .
>
> [We express] our profound scorn for the SRs and Mensheviks who continue to cohabitate with the bourgeoisie and allow themselves to be led on a leash by Kerenskii and Tsereteli.[121]

These were Skorinko's friends, young militant workers prepared at a moment's notice to do battle in defence of the workers' honour against the 'burzhui' and 'philistines'.

On 18 August, when the Petrograd Soviet voted for the repeal of the death penalty, Tsereteli asked:

> Why, your resolution shows a lack of confidence in the Provisional Government. And what if the abolition of the death penalty does not follow? Will you keep on trying . . . and overthrow the government?

At this question, all hell broke loose. Sukhanov writes:

> Shouts rang out: yes! yes! We'll take to the streets again! Others shouted about Bublikov and the handshake. Still others whistled and stamped their feet, while others applauded madly . . . But Tsereteli waved his hand—he did not believe they would take to the streets again to overthrow the coalition.[122]

Undoubtedly some readiness to act existed, but this was far from the dominant mood. Kerenskii's diplomatic notes (which made Milyukov's note, that had set off the April crisis, seem pale by comparison) did not produce so much as a strike or small demonstration. True, all socialist parties, Bolsheviks included, were constantly appealing for calm and restraint. But this had not stopped the workers in April or July.

This decline in activism should not be interpreted as a weakening of oppositional sentiment. Reporting on the Rozhdestvenskii District (to be sure, never a hotbed of militancy), the Left SR *Znamya truda* noted: 'Everywhere confusion and apathy among the workers and soldiers and dissatisfaction with domestic and foreign policy.'[123] The confusion was over how to proceed to change this government whose policies were so harmful. The Moscow workers, who had only recently abandoned the Provisional Government, had not experienced the defeat of the July Days and could still resort to general strikes and similar actions. But in Petrograd, the time for such tactics had passed. After the July Days, a general strike, a mass demonstration, or any 'coming out' (*vystuplenie*) could make sense only as the prelude to insurrection. And for this, most of Petrograd's workers were obviously still not prepared.

This is why, paradoxically, the workers first heard the news of Kornilov's march on Petrograd with a certain sigh of relief.

# 2 From the Kornilov Rising to the Eve of October

## The Kornilov Rising

At the Moscow State Conference Kornilov had warned lest it require the fall of Riga to restore 'order' to the rear.[1] A week later, on 21 August, news of a broad breach of the front near Riga reached Petrograd. Soon after, Riga fell, threatening the capital. Immediately, the non-socialist press and the census politicians joined in a chorus of condemnation of the army ranks and placed the blame for their demoralisation on the Bolsheviks, the soviets and revolutionary democracy generally. Yet Stankevich and Voitinskii, defencist commissars at the front, observed in independent reports that the soldiers were retreating in orderly fashion, giving battle. The decisive factor was the overwhelming numerical superiority of the enemy's artillery. Both particularly commended the Lettish Riflemen for their discipline and valour.[2] The soldiers of this regiment, staunchly Bolshevik almost to the man, later served as shock troops in the Red Army. By 25 August the offensive had been halted, and Petrograd was out of danger. After Kornilov's abortive rising, it was widely believed among the workers and in socialist circles that Riga's fall had been planned or, at least, not prevented in order to discredit the soldiers and the soviets as a prelude to the *coup*.

In the meanwhile, on 24 August, while such Bolshevik-led organisations as the CS of Factory Committees, the Petrograd Trade Union Council, the Workers' Section of the Petrograd Soviet were busy planning for the capital's defence, Kerenskii once again shut down the Bolshevik press. From here events moved swiftly. Cossack units were called to the capital, allegedly for its defence. Insistent provocational rumours of an impending Bolshevik 'action' timed for the half-year anniversary of the revolution were circulated. On 26 August, the Commander of the Petrograd Military Region, under Kornilov's direct command, put the capital on a military footing, positioning troops in the working-class districts. The next morning, all the Kadet ministers resigned, State Controller Kokoshkin declaring that a coalition government was no longer feasible.[3]

(On 30 August, when Kornilov's failure had already become evident, the front page of the Kadet central organ *Rech'* appeared with blank space. The deleted editorial was revealed two weeks later: 'Kornilov's aims are the same as those we feel necessary for the salvation of the country. We adhere to his formulation—we advocated it long before Kornilov. True, it is a conspiracy; but it is not counterrevolutionary.'[4] Stock prices soared on 28 August, the high point of Kornilov's fortunes.[5] As for Prime Minister Kerenskii, he admitted to knowing of the conspiracy long before it occurred—he had even been offered the role of dictator. The Left SR *Znamya truda* summed up a broad current of thought on the left: 'It was not a conspiracy against the Provisional Government but an agreement with it against the democratic organisations, and a chance dispute prevented its execution.'[6])

The news of Kornilov's march on Petrograd broke on the working-class districts on the night of 27–8 August in an atmosphere of pent-up rage and frustration that was unable to find a meaningful outlet in action. And partly because of this, the workers' response was far from panic. In fact, the howl of the factory horns announcing the emergency seemed to dispel in one swoop the sluggish, depressed mood of the preceding two months. There followed a show of enthusiasm and activism, the like of which had not been seen since February. For Kornilov was offering the workers a way out of their impasse, the opportunity to deal the counterrevolution a decisive blow, not against the will of the rest of revolutionary democracy but in unison with it. Moreover, it was widely believed that now that census society had literally taken up arms against the revolution, the moderate socialists would have no choice but to abandon their 'conciliationism'. Here then, at long last, was a way to move forward without risking civil war within democracy.

Reports from the factories to the CS of Factory Committees on 29 August all noted high spirits and feverish activity: meetings, searches for arms, organisation of Red Guards, fortification construction. 'Everywhere the same picture', summarised *Rabochii*, 'energy, restraint, organising.'[7] Reports received by the SR committees of the Petrograd and Kolpino Districts were similar: 'The mood is cheerful, unanimous, decisive.'[8] The Soviet historian Startsev estimates that 13 000 to 15 000 workers signed up at this time for the Red Guards.[9] *Izvestiya* put the figure closer to 25 000.[10] But in any case, the number was severely restricted by the shortage of arms. The TsIK was deluged with demands from the factories for arms. One district reported that it had only 420 rifles for 4000 workers that had registered.[11]

The TsIK's role in mobilising the workers was minimal. In fact, it advised the district soviets to 'calm the workers and take no measures until directed by the centre'. It agreed to distribute only 300 rifles per district, while Petergof alone had requested 2000.[12] The main organising centres were the Military-Revolutionary Committee (set up by the Petrograd Soviet EC (Executive Committee) and including representatives of the three main soviet parties, the Trade Union Council and the Petrograd Soviet) and especially the factory committees, their CS and the district soviets. Trotsky noted that 'the task of the Defence Committee [Military-Revolutionary Committee] was not so much to keep watch over and to call the workers to action, as to merely direct them. Its plans were always anticipated.'[13]

The Putilov Works, which had shown signs of fatigue after July, set the tone. 'It was as if the Putilov Factory was reliving the Revolution', observed *Izvestiya*. Working round the clock, the cannon shop put out over 100 artillery pieces in three days, three weeks' normal output. In all, about 8000 workers were sent out by the factory, including eight Red Guard units, fortification construction detachments and agitators to work among Kornilov's troops.[14] Even the sleepy Nevskii District sprang to life, its district soviet of factory committees demanding 10 000 rifles and urging all factory committees to 'more firmly take the initiative into their hands and, united, to resist with all their forces the counterrevolutionary designs of the bourgeoisie'.[15]

As this resolution indicates, the workers needed little convincing of the bourgeoisie's complicity. 'In view of the counterrevolutionary bourgeois movement', declared the workers of Trubochnyi, 'and also the infringements by former Tsarist *oprichniki* [political police under Ivan the Terrible] on the freedom and the democratic achievements of the Russian [*Rossiiskii*] proletariat . . . all power must be transferred to the soviets.'[16] 8000 workers at Metallicheskii unanimously 'express our distrust of the socialist ministers and demand the creation of a united, decisive revolutionary government for the struggle against the counterrevolutionary clique organised around Kornilov and the general staff and inspired by the traitors to the revolution, the Kadets, who call themselves the Party of Popular Freedom'.[17]

The resolutions also reflected some of the emotional intensity of the workers' response. Demanding arms, a trial of the conspirators and the release of the political prisoners of July, No. 6 Shop of the Trubochnyi Factory unanimously declared:

> On our part, we swear to die in the name of the liberation of the toiling class. And let the entire bourgeois clique not think that we have forgotten our tasks, that we are preoccupied by our party disputes. No. When self-sacrifice is needed, then let that vile clique know that we are ready to die or achieve victory.[18]

A meeting of 3000 workers at the Old Baranovskii Machine-construction Factory addressed the following to the TsIK:

Recognising that the workers in the factories have always marched at the head of the movement of revolutionary democracy against the age-old oppression of the toiling people and that the bourgeoisie has always tried to direct the point of the sword against the workers, and, not disdaining any method, has attacked and baited the working class in an attempt to cut off the head of the revolutionary movement—to crush the workers, as the most united and organised proletariat . . . , [we have] decided:

In this grave moment, when . . . the clouds of counterrevolution hang over us, ready at any moment to choke us with their poisonous gases, we, the revolutionary proletariat, cannot stand by passively as that pack of scoundrels and traitors moves against revolutionary Petrograd. . . We demand that the TsIK give arms to the workers, who, not sparing their lives, will stand as one in defence of the just rights of revolutionary democracy and, together with our brethren soldiers, will erect an impassable barrier to the counterrevolution and will tear out the poisonous fangs from the snake that has dared to poison the Great Russian Revolution with its lethal venom.

Demanding the release of the prisoners of July and the abolition of the death penalty, with Kornilov, 'who preached its introduction', as the last exception, the resolution concluded:

Believing in our bright future, we raise high the banner of Freedom—long live the Great Russian Revolution: To the defence, comrade workers and soldiers, of Freedom so dear to us, against the executioners who would lead it to slaughter, who are determined to drink of our fraternal blood. To the defence, comrades! All as one![19]

This resolution illustrates some key traits of the mentality of the skilled metalworkers'. Despite the fear of isolation from the rest of revolutionary democracy, there was never any doubt in their minds that the workers, as the most active, organised and enlightened segment of democracy, stood at the 'head of the revolutionary movement'. This was yet another aspect of working-class honour. The historical perspective of the resolution is also characteristic of the skilled workers and largely absent among the recent arrivals from the village. Finally, despite the obvious deepening of the social and political content of the revolution since February, it was nevertheless still seen in essentially democratic terms. It was the 'Banner of Freedom' that was raised. Socialism is not mentioned. What had changed since February, however, were the 'objective' circumstances: the bourgeoisie had actively turned against the revolution, and the economy faced collapse, forcing new radical measures. But these were conceived first of all as means of protecting the democratic revolution. Socialism—and all these workers were socialists—was not yet an immediate goal.

As it turned out, the workers did not have to join battle with Kornilov (though their efforts were not in vain: they were made use of later in preparing the October Insurrection). Since Kornilov had nothing to offer his troops, whose interests were totally inimical to all he stood for, they simply melted away en route, as had the Tsar's troops in February. But much of the credit for this belonged to the working-class agitators who infiltrated Kornilov's echelons and to the railroad workers who dispersed the troop trains and sabotaged the lines before Kornilov could get close to the capital.

In many ways, the workers' reaction to the uprising paralleled their response to the July reaction: on the one hand they rallied even more decisively behind the Bolsheviks and the demand for a government without census representation; on the other, the threat of counter-revolution once again aroused the strong desire to restore unity within revolutionary democracy. Thus, the Trubochnyi workers, cited above, warned the bourgeoisie not to be misled by 'our party disputes'. 'We feel', declared the Nevskii District Soviet of Factory Committees, 'that the most important thing is for all workers to act together.'[20] 'At Langezipen', observed *Znamya truda*, 'the moment has brought all party groups together. The squabbling has died down. At Lorents, a *rapprochement* between the Bolsheviks and SRs has occurred. And so on, although it was noted that this is a temporary phenomenon in face of the common misfortune.'[21]

M. Zhdanov, a worker, wrote to the paper:

> Only in complete unity is there strength, and only in an organised rebuff is there defence of the revolution. Until Kornilov it seemed that the most needed slogan of all, the slogan of unification, was buried by the vain leaders. It floated to the surface only in the moment of grave danger to which the Russian Revolution has been subjected. It floated up and was seized by the masses, those benighted masses, as the 'political leaders' have grown accustomed to calling them.[22]

But as in July, unification had to be based upon the platform of the left. Zhdanov concluded: 'There can be no talk of a coalition. Only democracy; no bourgeoisie.' In referring to the 'vain leaders', Zhdanov expressed a still widespread belief among the workers that the split in the socialist camp, or rather, the reason why the defencists so stubbornly clung to their 'conciliationism', was somehow due to personal vanity that prevented them from coming to terms with the left.

The Kornilov affair raised hopes that the TsIK would at long last abandon its alliance with the bourgeoisie. This seemed only logical to the majority of workers, who saw the TsIK majority and its supporters as misguided, but not consciously counterrevolutionary. Speaking somewhat later before the Kolomna District Soviet, the Bolshevik Kharitonov noted: 'After the Kornilov conspiracy, a temporary united front of democracy was established which could have been consolidated by immediately calling a Congress of Soviets [to take power].'[23] On 28 August, M. Lebedev, a Bolshevik joiner in the port, told the Kronstadt Soviet:

> The TsIK must know, if it is to represent democracy, that until now it has been mistaken in its understanding of the political situation and must say that now it must correct its errors. Kronstadt has always been on the right path, and, in view of the events, from this moment our differences and disagreements will not be so deep.[24]

'The abyss between the proletariat and petty bourgeois democracy was filled in by the Kornilovshchina', noted Sukhanov.[25] Even Lenin, who after July placed the defencists firmly in the camp of the counter-revolution, for a brief period at the end of August and early September offered the TsIK a compromise, whereby it would take power and the Bolsheviks, enjoying full freedom of agitation, would act as a loyal opposition to the soviet government.[26]

The workers, however, could not throw aside their misgivings. 'We express full confidence in the Soviet of WS and PD [Workers', Soldiers' and Peasants' Deputies, i.e. the TsIK]', declared the factory committees of the Nevskii District, 'insofar as it will express the political will of the worker and peasant masses.'[27] Here was February's formula of conditional support, applied originally by the workers to the census government, now addressed to the TsIK itself! Others, particularly in the machine-construction factories, were even less sanguine. The workers of Langezipen resolved:

> 1. Freedom is in danger, and we are ready to defend ourselves to the last drop of blood, regardless of who is in power . . .
> 5. We demand that the Soviet of W and SD as well as the Provisional Government end their criminal bargaining with the bourgeoisie. If, however, the Soviet cannot change the direction of its policies, we demand that its members resign at once and yield their places to more worthy representatives.
> 6. We declare that the Kornilovist experiments carried out on our backs thanks to the criminal accommodation [to the bourgeoisie], have cost us dearly and we suppose that the Kornilov rebellion has washed your sleepy eyes clear and enabled you to see the situation in its true light.

7. We declare that you have long spoken for us, but not our views, and we demand that you begin to speak the language of the proletariat or else we reserve for ourselves freedom of action. [28]

Here the conditional support takes the form of an ultimatum.

In the aftermath of the rebellion, the TsIK did in fact veer to the left (it finally got around, for example, to demanding the release of July's prisoners), clashing sharply with Kerenskii over the composition of a new government. The affair actually seemed to be turning the moderate socialists away from 'conciliationism'. On 31 August, the Menshevik CC declared that participation of Kadets in a new government would be unacceptable.[29] The SR CC followed suit the next day.[30] It was clear to all that to reject the Kadets as coalition partners meant to exclude direct representation of census interests in the government, since the Kadets had become the hegemonic party in census society.

Accordingly, after the Kadets resigned on the eve of the uprising, the TsIK decided to keep the vacant portfolios for itself until a 'pre-parliament', a body consisting exclusively of representatives of revolutionary democracy, could be convened to form a revolutionary government responsible to it until the Constituent Assembly could meet. Kerenskii, however, insisted on his right unilaterally to appoint a 'directorate' and at once began to negotiate with the Kadets. Another dispute arose over Kerenskii's appointment of Savinkov, his military commissar, as Governor of Petrograd. Savinkov had been so totally compromised by his role in the Kornilov affair that even the very tolerant SR Party was forced to expel him. He lasted as Governor only three days. But to add insult to injury, Kerenskii replaced him with Pal'chinskii, notorious to the workers for his pro-capital policies while Acting Minister of Trade and Industry. And true to form, no sooner had he assumed office, than he shut down the Bolshevik and Menshevik–Internationalist press, this in the very midst of the alarm over Kornilov! According to Sukhanov, the mood in the TsIK was angry and strongly opposed to a coalition.[31]

But, apparently, not angry enough. For in the end, the TsIK gave its sanction to Kerenskii's 'directorate of five', in return, to be sure, for certain concessions: dissolution of the State Duma, proclamation of a democratic republic (a demand the government had previously rejected under the pretext that only the Constituent Assembly could decide) and the pledge that the directorate would resign once the pre-parliament was convened. On 2 September, the TsIK resolved:

The tragic situation created by the events at the front and the civil war begun by the counterrevolution makes necessary the formation of a strong government capable of executing the programme of revolutionary democracy and of conducting an active struggle against the counterrevolution and the external enemy. Such a government, created by democracy and resting upon its organisations, must be free of any compromise with counterrevolutionary elements.

It went on to call for a conference of revolutionary democracy to decide on the organisation of a new government.[32]

This undoubtedly marked a shift leftward. But the sanction, even if provisional, of Kerenskii's government and the vagueness of the resolution (who was the 'democracy' and who were the 'counter-revolutionary elements'?) could not but give rise to doubts. Indeed, why a democratic conference at all, when the Congress of Soviets was due for mid September (three months after the last) and was quite capable of taking power in the name of revolutionary democracy—if, indeed, that was intended?

These questions would soon find answers. But in the meanwhile the workers seemed remarkably unimpressed. On the contrary, the worker and soldier delegates to the Petrograd Soviet proceeded directly to show their lack of confidence in the moderate leadership by passing at the 31 August plenum for the first time a Bolshevik-sponsored resolution demanding a government of 'the revolutionary proletariat and peasantry'. Tsereteli's resolution supporting the Provisional Government garnered only fifteen votes. Even in March 1917 the Bolsheviks had been able to boast more support! Even after the defencists demanded a roll-call vote that forced many Mensheviks and SRs to leave rather than openly oppose their leaders, the vote was still 279 against 135.[33]

Since many delegates had been absent, involved in the efforts against Kornilov, the real test came on 9 September, when all fractions appeared in force. The EC challenged the 31 August vote and presented a motion of support for the defencist praesidium. During the debate Trotsky asked the moderate leaders if they still considered Kerenskii a member of this praesidium. Their affirmative reply sealed its fate. Despite the numerical preponderance of soldier delegates, much more moderate and loyal to the defencists on the whole than the workers, the vote was 519 to 414 (67 abstentions) in favour of dismissing the praesidium.[34]

On 5 September, the Moscow Soviet adhered to the 31 August resolution of the Petrograd Soviet. By the end of September almost all urban soviets in towns with any large-scale industry or garrison had decisively abandoned the coalition in favour of some version of the Bolshevik position on power.

In Petrograd itself, the SR organisation, the only party still competing—though less and less successfully—with the Bolsheviks for working-class support, had become overwhelmingly internationalist. Nearly all the delegates to the party's City Conference on 10 September adhered to its left wing, which had its own newspaper and had all but formally broken with the CC.[35]

What separated the Bolsheviks from the Left SRs and Menshevik–Internationalists was not the issue of ending the coalition, on which all were agreed, but rather the nature of the government to replace it. The latter argued that a government of workers and poor peasants or a soviet government (the Bolsheviks put this demand forward again after the Kornilov affair) did not provide a sufficiently broad social base to be viable. However, what they specifically had in mind was not very clear to the workers (nor, it would appear, to themselves). As a result, even the Left SR rank and file tended to support the Bolshevik position. *Znamya truda*, which spared no effort in its criticism of the Bolsheviks' 'dictatorship of the proletariat and poor peasants', arguing that the latter category was politically and economically meaningless, had to recognise that 'workers pass these resolutions, SRs vote for them'.[36] 'Several comrade workers and soldiers', wrote a prominent Left SR, 'came to me to ask why the SR fraction voted against the Bolshevik resolution on August 31.'[37]

As for the defencists, the Kornilov affair dealt them the *coup de grâce*. In the Moscow District, for so long an SR stronghold, new elections to the district soviet gave the Bolsheviks fourteen seats to the SRs' six. None of the latter were defencists.[38] A worker from Patronnyi, a state factory, and one of the most moderate in the capital, reported in the Bolshevik *Rabochii put'*:

Our factory (8000 workers) has been the nucleus of the petty bourgeois bloc (of Mensheviks and SRs) in the red Vyborg District. Only the brass shop invariably supported the Bolsheviks but it was drowned in the mass of the factory.

As representatives to the Soviet, the factory sent Mensheviks and SRs and two, then one, Bolshevik ... Only a month and a half ago, the Bolsheviks were unable to speak at meetings. Now the circumstances have dramatically changed. A trifling matter occurred. On September 4 at the general assembly of our factory, first the SR and then the Menshevik delegates to the Petrograd Soviet spoke openly of that which until now had passed over in silence. They told what they had voted for and what against in the Petrograd Soviet. Thus, on land [the prominence of this issue was characteristic here], they voted against its immediate transfer into the hands of the people, and on the secret treaties—against breaking them. And they advised the workers to wait on these matters until the Constituent Assembly. And that was enough. It has become clear to the workers that to wait on these matters until the Constituent Assembly and to postpone the convocation of the Constituent Assembly means to leave the decision to the landowners and capitalists; it means to leave the peasants without land and to endlessly drag out the war.[39]

'At elections to the soviet at the Obukhovskii Factory', went another report,

> the defencists were dealt a total defeat. Not one SR, not one Menshevik got through. Of thirteen delegates, eleven Bolsheviks and two syndicalists were elected. Who could have conceived of this a month ago? Thus fall the last bastions of defencism.[40]

Meetings here during the Kornilov rebellion witnessed some dramatic scenes. At one of them, a former defencist worker mounted the rostrum and with tears in his eyes begged forgiveness from his comrades, promising personally to wring Kornilov's neck. Another appeared with a huge portrait of Kerenskii, which he proceeded to tear to shreds before the assembly.[41]

But the real significance of the Kornilov affair for the revolution lay elsewhere, in the conclusive swing of the garrison to the side of the workers and especially in the massive radicalisation at the front and in the provinces, where the worker and soldier masses finally pulled abreast of Petrograd's workers, ending the latter's isolation. (At the same time the impact of the Kornilov affair should not be exaggerated, as one can already observe the beginnings of this shift in the provinces in early August.[42]) In fact, the provinces were now often ahead of the capital—many local soviets refused to relinquish the power they had assumed as an emergency measure during the crisis.

Thanks to the elimination of the defencist influence from the majority of soviets, the workers' opposition to the coalition could once again take the form of the demand for soviet power. Of course, this by no means eliminated fears of isolation and civil war within democracy. The fact that the soviets were to be the organs of state power in no way guaranteed that the mass of peasants and the socialist intelligentsia would support the new régime. Nevertheless, the fact that the new revolution was carried out through and in the name of the soviets made it easier for the workers to face these dangers. The soviets, despite their atrophy during the months of 'conciliationist' rule, had struck deep roots in the workers' consciousness. These were *their* organs. If the defencists refused to support them, then, from the workers' point of view, they were writing themselves out of revolutionary democracy and the split had to be accepted.

**The Democratic Conference**

Immediately after Kornilov's defeat, however, the issue was not the Soviet Congress but the Democratic Conference. On 3 September, the TsIK made public the conference's mode of representation which was heavily weighted towards the defencist wing of democracy, strongly suggesting that the conference was not, after all, designed to give power to revolutionary democracy. The final version of the list gave the soviets 300 representatives (with a major chunk going to the TsIK and the Peasant EC, both elected back in June), the soldiers' committee (also elected in the spring)—150, trade unions—100; railroad and post-telegraph unions—35, dumas and zemstvos (organs of urban and rural self-government, elected by universal suffrage and, therefore, not exclusively 'revolutionary democratic' organisations)—500, cooperators (of whom Lenin wryly remarked that they represent the political will of their members in much the same way as the postmen represent letter writers)—150; national organisations—100; and a host of small groups including doctors, journalists and Orthodox clergy. (*Rech'* was incensed that the midwives had been forgotten.) In all, 1425 votes, with much overlapping representation, so that certain delegates had up to four or more votes.[43]

The list was testimony to the tenacity of the defencists' view that the revolution was doomed without the support of the liberal elements of census society. Since Kornilov's adventure had shown rather conclusively that the political representatives of the landowners and the bourgeoisie supported the counterrevolution, the defencists were forced to smuggle census society back in through the dumas, the peasant cooperators (mostly well-to-do elements), and the intellectuals, who were deathly afraid of a government resting solely upon the popular masses and would not willingly support the break with the propertied classes and the world they represented.

The clearest expression of working-class attitudes on the Democratic Conference are the protocols of the 10 September (Third) Conference of Petrograd Factory Committees. These give a definite sense of how the Kornilov affair had cleared the air. It was as if a great weight had been lifted from the workers. There was a new sense of movement, of passing to the offensive. The conference had been called to discuss the circulars issued in late August by the Menshevik Minister of Labour, Skobelev, seeking to restrict the *de facto* rights of the committees, and the mood was very hostile and aggressive. 'Comrade Kolokol'nikov [a Menshevik representative of the Ministry of Labour] believes that only minor reforms are needed, a certain cleansing', stated Rovinskii, a Langezipen worker. 'But you are cleaning up by laying new obstacles, and the workers will themselves have to clear away such organs as the Ministry of Labour.'[44] Levin, a left SR member of the CS, warned:

Let the Minister of Labour know that for us the two recognised forms of the movement [unions and parties] are insufficient. The workers will seek out their own forms and, having found them, will

not cede their positions without a fight and will sweep away the
Ministry of Labour if it stands in their way.[45]

Nevertheless, a resolution calling for a boycott of the Democratic
Conference unless the factory committees were allotted 100 delegates
was overwhelmingly rejected. Evdokimov expressed the prevailing
ambivalence that the Kornilov affair had not been able to dispel:

> Our enemies are strong, they are organised, they will put forward
> new Kornilovs and will find aid in the person of Kerenskii. But even
> this would not frighten us if the conciliators were able to understand
> the situation. If the Democratic Conference really reflected the
> mood of the broad masses, it would play a great role. But, unfortu-
> nately, the odds are great that the Democratic Conference will
> become a revised edition of the Moscow Conference.[46]

Then why go at all? Because the wavering masses who still support the
'conciliators' could yet be won over to the revolutionary path. A
boycott could mean only one thing: a write-off of the 'conciliators' and
a course set directly for insurrection. Despite all that had occurred
since July, the delegates were apparently still not ready for this.

There is also no evidence of boycottist views in the factories, and one
is forced to conclude that despite the general scepticism, the workers
were still willing to give the Democratic Conference a chance. For it
held out the enticing, if doubtful, prospect of the assumption of power
by a united revolutionary democracy. At a meeting of the Admiralty
Shipyard, Belov, a local worker, reported that the Factory Committee
Conference had 'found the [Democratic] conference to be bourgeois'.
But Levitskii, who followed him, qualified this: 'Going into more
detail, [he] found, all the same, that at the conference the left wing will
have enough to dominate the representatives of the bourgeoisie.' The
meeting decided to send a delegation to the conference to read out a
statement of the workers' demands.[47] Many other factories did the
same. 'The conference has aroused much interest among the Petrograd
working class', noted *Proletarii*, adding, however, that the mode of
representation was a source of profound dissatisfaction.[48]

At the same time, the workers' attitudes on the Democratic Conference must be viewed against the background of the failure of their
Bolshevik leaders to put forth any practical alternative. If, as noted
earlier, the workers ceded the political initiative to their leaders after
the July defeat, the latter showed little sign of taking it up. This, in fact,
was a cause of much discontent in party ranks. To many activists, the
party's policy after the Kornilov affair seemed hopelessly muddled.
The Soviet's 31 August resolution, to which so many factories had
adhered, called for a 'government of the revolutionary proletariat and

peasantry'. This position, adopted by the party in August, was supposed to have meant a practical orientation towards insurrection. But now, after Kornilov's defeat, the Bolshevik leadership once again began to entertain the prospect of a peaceful transition through the assumption of power by the TsIK.

At the 7 September session of the Bolshevik PC, Slutskii, reporting for the EC, noted a leftward shift in the correlation of forces after the uprising. He argued that the soviets had regained their former power, that events would lead to a major clash between the government and the TsIK, opening the way for a peaceful transition of power, though the Mensheviks and SRs should not be expected to lead this. He specifically warned against a 'coming out', as it could only play into the hands of the bourgeoisie, which wanted nothing better than to see the petty bourgeoisie and the defencist parties frightened away from the proletariat.

This report immediately drew fire for offering 'nothing with which we could guide ourselves in our internal organisational work.' 'I demand', declared one speaker, 'that the PC unfold all the material on what is taking place and in what direction we must act.' 'Comrade Slutskii', seconded another, 'in his resolution gave us neither old nor new slogans. The central organ [*Pravda*] does not sufficiently clarify our position, and for this reason our entire party finds itself in a state of uncertainty, and our comrades in the localities are confused.'

Slutskii's defenders countered that the situation itself did not permit a more definite formulation on power:

> I consider correct the exposition offered by the CC and EC, although one could see in it a lack of clarity. We are offering a programme for the realisation of which we will fight. But to say which organs will form the government, to show a concrete path—this we cannot do.

The debate over the need for or possibility of clarity really involved much deeper political differences. Those who insisted on clarity wanted to retain the orientation towards armed insurrection, forgetting about the soviets. They saw the leftward shift of the TsIK as ephemeral.

> The shift does not yet make it possible to believe the Soviet will take a revolutionary path ... It is funny to think of compromises now. No compromises! When we were weak, then it was permissible. We are frightened, we are running blindly. The counterrevolution has taken the first step, but one should not forget that it is preparing a second. Our revolution is not like that of the West [the French Revolution]. Our revolution is proletarian. Our task is to consolidate our posi-

tions and unconditionally prepare for armed struggle. I propose that the CC more clearly, more definitely, elucidate the political moment in its organ.

On the other hand, those defending the vagueness argued: 'We have entered a stage of peaceful development of the revolution. We have no cause to talk of insurrection now.'

Though no vote was taken, judging from the trend of the debate, the supporters of the CC and EC seemed to be in the majority. The Bolshevik position, then, was 'wait and see' or, as one speaker put it, 'amassing forces'. In place of a definite, practical orientation on the question of power, the party merely repeated its call for restraint, vigilance and not to yield to provocation.[49]

The same confusion plagued the Left SRs. On 14 September, the SR organisation of the Moscow District resolved: 'We find that the articles in our papers do not at all satisfy the workers and we ask for a clearer and more definite position on the evaluation of the current moment in the articles.'[50]

One consequence of this state of affairs was the dissipation of the enthusiasm and energy mobilised during the Kornilov affair, as the workers began to sink back into what many observers again took to be political indifference. 'As soon as the news of the uprising of General Kornilov ... reached working-class Petrograd', wrote *Znamya truda* on 16 September,

> the working class amazed many people with its energetic activity, restraint and will to repulse the usurper. The working class armed itself, sent several thousands from its midst for trench work and took upon itself the creation of a militia to which it entrusted the guarding of the factories.
>
> But the immediate danger has passed ... and in the worker milieu a certain apathy has already appeared. They are refusing to do night guard duty, refusing to come to military training, even though they demand universal arming, and again factory meetings are attended by small numbers, and you have to lock the gates to keep them from leaving, and even that does not help since they craftily leave before the whistle.

Although the article went on to observe that 'such indifference is especially strong in the small, so-called craft industries, where workers are scattered in small workshops' (these had always been the least active working-class elements), there is little doubt that the same phenomenon, perhaps in less extreme form, also characterised large-scale industry. 'We have 4000 people', went a Bolshevik report of 24 September on the Red Guards. 'That many are registered. But as far as those who want arms, one can find 400. So it was during the Kornilov

Days. Now one can observe a cooling off, in the first place because the mood has already passed, and secondly, and mainly, because there are no arms.'[51]

This 'indifference' stemmed largely from the fact that the workers, hard pressed on the economic front where the situation bordered on the desperate (see Chapter 4), had grown tired of meetings and speeches that offered no concrete solutions. 'Everywhere one observes a desire for practical results', Skrypnik, a member of the CS of Factory Committees, told the Bolshevik CC. 'Resolutions no longer satisfy.'[52] 'It is necessary to take the most decisive measures and to carry them out in practice', resolved the Moscow Dinamo Factory. 'For playing with words destroys all that is left and only irritates the hungry proletarian working class.'[53]

The only real alternative to the Democratic Conference and simply waiting was insurrection. Yet there is no evidence that the worker masses were pressing for this. Can one, therefore, conclude that the Bolshevik leadership was in tune with the rank and file? Possibly. But given the constant counselling of restraint by all the workers' organisations, the sad experience of July and the deepening economic crisis, it is also clear that this time the initiative would have to come from above. In any case, the policy of marking time was only demoralising the workers, and in this lay the gravest threat to the revolution.

As it turned out, even the lopsided representation of the Democratic Conference yielded a surprisingly close vote, testimony to the growing polarisation throughout all of Russia. On 19 September, the conference voted by 766 against 688 (38 abstentions) for a new coalition government. Only the urban soviets and the national organisations gave opposing majorities. But in most other contingents the pro-coalition majorities were quite small. As it turned out, it was the vote of the cooperators (who along with Kerenskii refused from the start to recognise the binding character of conference's decisions) and the zemstvos that was decisive (140 against 23 (1 abstention) and 84 against 30 (1) respectively).[54] Were it not for these, the conference may well have decided to take power!

But the biggest surprise was yet to come. An amendment to exclude the Kadets from any coalition government was proposed and passed by 595 against 493 (72 abstentions). Yet it was obvious to all that there were no significant elements in census society that did not completely sympathise with the Kadets' positions. The original resolution for a coalition was, thus, rendered meaningless.

Accordingly, the amended resolution was voted down by 183 against 813 (80).[55] The conference was a living expression of the dilemma facing the TsIK's moderate leaders: they insisted on the absolute necessity of a coalition with the 'vital forces' of census society for the success of the revolution, but Russian society had become so polarised that any meaningful coalition between the workers and peasants, on the one hand, and the propertied classes, on the other, had become quite impossible.

Undaunted by this setback, the TsIK's leaders proposed the formation of an enlarged praesidium to seek an acceptable solution to present to the conference. But when this body met on 20 September it actually voted by 60 against 50 to oppose any coalition with census representatives, much to Tsereteli's chagrin and consternation.

What followed is much too involved and lengthy to be recounted here. Suffice it to say that it served as an object lesson to the workers in the moderate socialists' professed attachment to democratic principle. It all ended in Kerenskii once again unilaterally forming a cabinet which included not only the members of the 'Directorate of Five' but such well-known census figures as: Konovalov, a big industrialist, former Minister of Trade and Industry in the first coalition who had resigned in protest against plans for state regulation of the economy; textile magnate Smirnov, whose recent lockout of 3000 workers had been found lacking economic justification by several government commissions, prompting the Ministry of Internal Affairs to request sequestration;[56] Kishkin, a prominent Kadet who had been forced to resign as Government Commissar in Moscow because of his less than ambiguous role in the Kornilov affair; and Tret'yakov, Chairman of the Moscow Stock Exchange. Not a cabinet designed to inspire confidence among the workers. Yet the TsIK agreed to this in return for Kerenskii's agreement to the formation of a 'pre-parliament'. This body was to consist of 15 per cent of the delegates to the Democratic Conference supplemented by an additional 156 census delegates. Even so, Kerenskii would only permit it consultative powers.[57]

Thus, by the time the Democratic Conference closed on 23 September, the workers' worst fears had been confirmed: nothing remained of the TsIK's declaration of 2 September. After this show of contempt for the expressed will of the Democratic Conference (itself a biased expression of the will of revolutionary democracy), the workers would have little patience with the defencists' justification for walking out of the Soviet Congress on 25 October – that in starting the insurrection a few hours before the congress could pronounce itself, the Bolsheviks had forced its will.

**Setting Course for Soviet Power**

On the day of the Democratic Conference's closure, the TsIK, under strong Bolshevik pressure, reluctantly agreed to summon the Congress of Soviets of Workers' and Soldiers' Deputies for 20 October (later moved back to 25 October). This single act carried more significance for the workers than the entire week of behind-the-scenes machinations at the Democratic Conference, or, indeed, than anything that had occurred since the Kornilov rising. From that moment on, the Congress of Soviets became a magnet for all the political concerns of the workers, a repository for all their hopes and fears. The pre-parliament, set to open 7 October, was seen as no more than the illegitimate offspring of a totally compromised Democratic Conference, this in spite of the Bolsheviks' decision to participate in it (to Lenin's great displeasure).

*Iskra*, a Menshevik–Internationalist paper that was urging the workers to make use of the pre-parliament to achieve a united revolutionary-democratic government, sadly noted that 'the workers are profoundly indignant at the outcome of the Democratic Conference', and that this indignation was driving them towards the Bolshevik slogan 'All power to the soviets'.

> To the broad masses it seems self-evident and as clear as day. They say: the Democratic Conference disappointed because it was rigged. The soviets are the true representatives. Let the Congress meet and take power.[58]

Henceforth, virtually every workers' meeting, after declaring its irreconcilable hostility to the new coalition, demanded that the congress, or simply 'the soviets', form a new government. The general assembly of Voenno-podkovnyi warmly applauded the Petrograd Soviet's

> definitive shift to a revolutionary line of conduct ... We look with scorn upon the pitiful conciliators, trying by means of detours and machinations to avert the new approaching wave of the revolution, trying to slip by the firmly demonstrated will of the masses, trying to hide the failure of their entire policy of conciliations.
>
> We declare that you cannot fool us with any democratic conferences, with any pre-parliaments. We believe only our soviets. For their power we will fight for life or death.
>
> Long live the immediate All-Russian Congress of Soviet WS and PD!
>
> Long live revolutionary Social Democracy!
>
> Long live an early peace among the peoples and the Third International!
>
> Long live the last decisive battle and our victory![59]

'The Democratic Conference', decided the workers of the Admiralty Shipyard, [was called] by the leaders of the TsIK in such a composition as to totally distort the will and face of genuine and revolutionary democracy of Russia. This distortion, this fraud, was required by the leaders of the petty bourgeoisie for a new attempt to save the government of open and concealed Kornilovists, protecting it from the workers and peasants of Russia by the screen of a pseudo-popular Democratic Soviet or Pre-parliament.

Recognising that this fraud failed and that the defencists tricked no one but themselves ..., the workers once more decisively declare their total irreconcilability toward the coalition government that can only bring catastrophe and civil war to the country and [we] demand the establishment of a truly revolutionary government, a government of the Soviet of WS and PD ... To such a government the workers will give our deepest trust and full support ... Only such a government ... will be able to offer its hand with an open face to the oppressed of all lands in the full certainty that they will reply with a shout: Long live the Russian Revolution! Long live the International Revolution![60]

When the Bolshevik leadership, itself under strong rank-and-file pressure and a continuous barrage of indignant letters from Lenin in Finland, decided to walk out of the pre-parliament's opening session, no tears were shed in the factory districts. On the contrary, this was taken with a sigh of relief as marking the transition from word to deed. It gave a sharp boost to flagging political interest and activism. On 9 October, the plenum of the Petrograd Soviet met to discuss the boycott of the pre-parliament 'amidst great excitement', according to newspaper accounts.[61] Almost all delegates, the full 1000, showed up, a striking change from the absenteeism that had plagued sessions in September. According to *Novaya zhizn'* (which opposed the boycott), the spirit here 'remained one of the first days of the Revolution'. Trotsky's speech in particular was repeatedly interrupted 'by stormy applause from the entire hall'. 'We left', he concluded, 'in order to say that only soviet power can raise up the slogan of peace and toss it over the heads of the international bourgeoisie to the proletariat of the entire world. Long live the direct and open struggle for revolutionary power in the country!'[62]

Trotsky was followed by the defencist Liber, who observed that even the Bolsheviks were not unanimous about leaving the pre-parliament. In fact, the decision had been taken by a narrow majority. When he stated: 'Let Trotsky, Kamenev, Zinoviev and Lenin find themselves in power—they will not be able to solve the problems ...', he was cut short by a burst of applause. But he went on to accuse the Bolsheviks of breaking the united front of revolutionary democracy (a charge that in a few weeks would return to haunt the defencists when they left the Soviet Congress). But it was Martov who with real or feigned naïveté hit the nail squarely on the head. He could not understand why the Bolsheviks had left the pre-parliament. The only conceivable reason would be to form a government by force of arms. 'But this is unthinkable now.'

Only 146 delegates opposed the Bolsheviks' position, while Liber's resolution of support for the pre-parliament garnered no more than 100 votes. Since the Bolshevik fraction was not nearly so large, it is clear that most rank-and-file Mensheviks and SRs voted with the Bolsheviks and against their own leaders. (The same session elected delegates to the Congress of Soviets of the Northern Region on a proportional basis: 15 Bolsheviks, 10 SRs and 5 Mensheviks.) [63]

The factories were in complete accord with the boycott. Old Parviainen, a machine-construction factory, called on all 'genuine representatives of the revolutionary soldiers, peasants and workers to leave' and declared:

> We fully and with all our means support materially and morally the soviets of WS and PD and on their first call we are ready to rise to the defence of the achievements of the Revolution. [64]

The general assembly of the Armour-piercing Shell Factory unanimously (700) resolved to

> hail the Bolshevik fraction that has left that auction hall, the 'Soviet of the Russian Republic' [pre-parliament], where, together with the enemies of the revolution, the inspirers of Kornilov, behind the back of the people, fraternisation is being conducted by representatives of the Menshevik and SR Parties. Those who entered the Soviet of the Republic have left the soviets of WS and PD, and, we assume, for good ... Only the Congress of WS and P, can, having taken power in its hands, give the Constituent Assembly, land and a democratic peace to the exhausted peoples. [65]

There was scarcely a factory in which a good majority of the workers were not eagerly awaiting soviet power and looking to the congress to establish it. This does not mean that there were still no serious doubts or that the mood was overly optimistic. This was not the case (see Chapter 4). Nevertheless, the time was late, the situation was growing more desperate by the day, and the immediate seizure of power by the soviets appeared as the only viable alternative to economic collapse and certain defeat at the hands of the counterrevolution.

With the Bolsheviks' departure from the pre-parliament, the stage was set for the final act. There were no more distractions along the way, no other straws to cling to and paralyse the will. The same session of the soviet that overwhelmingly approved the Bolsheviks' boycott decided, again by a huge majority, to set up a revolutionary defence committee, ostensibly to 'collect the necessary data' to defend the approaches of Petrograd from the Germans (who had just captured the Moon-sund Archipelago in the mouth of the Gulf of Finland), to arm the workers and secure the capital against any new counterrevolutionary attempts. In these defensive terms the soviet had set up the organ that would lead to the overthrow of the Provisional Government in little over two weeks.

# 3 Class Struggle in the Factories

The months from July to October were a period of contrasts in the labour movement: on the broader political scene (with the exception of the Kornilov affair)—a certain sluggishness, marking time and abdication of initiative to the leaders; in the factories—a continually intensifying struggle for power, with the factory committees under constant pressure from the rank and file. It was here that the workers concentrated their main energies in a desperate effort to avert economic collapse and mass unemployment and to maintain the working class physically and morally intact.

## The Factory Committees Under Attack

If the workers' defeat in the July Days gave rise to a more aggressive policy towards labour on the part of the industrialists, Kornilov's defeat did not deter them. It seemed rather to strengthen their determination. In the Kornilov affair the political card had been played and beaten. Command of the economy was the bourgeoisie's last and best trump, although a very risky one since it involved the very core of the class's existence, beyond which there could be no further retreat.

In early September, the industrialists launched a full-scale offensive against the factory committees. Buoyed by Skobelev's circulars restricting committee meetings to extra-work hours and abolishing their *de facto* right of control over hiring and firing (not to speak of control over production), the Committee of United Industry decided that payment of wages to the various elected worker delegates would be discontinued as of 15 September, in contravention of the March agreement between the Petrograd Soviet and the PSFMO.[1] The owners even tried to have the military deferments of the factory committee members lifted on the grounds that they were not really engaged in production, threatening to remove even the most prominent members of the CS of Factory Committees.

At about this time, the Committee of United Industry outlined its 'Conditions for the Restoration of Industry' in a note to the Minister of Labour. It urged the government to adopt the following measures to regulate worker–management relations: hiring and firing was to be made the exclusive prerogative of management; management was to be given the power unilaterally to impose punishments up to and including dismissal; factory committees, soviets or any other organisations were to be forbidden from interfering with management, and the latter was to be freed of all responsibility to these organisations; and finally, any worker who failed to attain the previous year's level of productivity was to be fired. The note concluded ominously: 'Without these measures to influence the worker masses, industry is threatened with complete shutdown.'[2]

To the workers it was more than clear that this assault on the factory committees had but one real aim—to remove the last obstacle preventing the industrialists from a massive shutdown. The almost simultaneous resurfacing of the plan to 'unload' Petrograd's industry, seen as merely another route towards the same goal, only reinforced this view.

In fact, as the socialist press pointed out, the note was based upon the self-serving premise, adopted soon after the February Revolution, that the chief cause of the declining productivity was the workers' abuse of their newly-won freedom. All the blame that the census politicians had heaped upon the autocracy for the economic dislocation in the months preceding the revolution was quickly forgotten. It did little good to remind the industrialists that productivity had been declining since 1915 due to shortages of fuel and raw materials, the failure to replace worn-out machinery, the physical exhaustion of the workers and the influx of a mass of inexperienced new workers to meet the needs of expanded war production.[3]

· The industrialists' formula for curing the economy thus boiled down to putting a leash on the workers. They still showed no readiness to suffer state regulation. When the reformed Factory Conference (*Zavodskoe soveshchanie*), a public body charged with overseeing the economy, finally got on its feet in August, the CS of Factory Committees began to turn to it with considerable success to prevent unjustified closures. As a last resort, the conference could and did sequester factories. However, the industrialists, in disregard of the law, simply boycotted the conference, appealing instead to Pal'chinskii, who now headed the Special Conference of Defence.[4]

For the workers, then, rather than a formula for the restoration of industry, the employers' recommendations were a *carte blanche* for its destruction. And this they were fiercely determined to prevent.

### The Struggle for Production—Workers' Control Checked

The mood among the workers was one of growing desperation over the deteriorating situation in the factories, where life had become a continuous series of crises. The gnawing sense of impending disaster became all-pervasive, as workers engaged owners and management in a dogged holding action to save their factories, their livelihood and ultimately, their revolution.

The prospects for success did not appear very bright. Experts told the August Factory Committee Conference that in the coming year Petrograd's industry could at best hope for two-thirds of the quantity of fuel received in the current year, itself one of acute shortage. As for the railroads, the Ministry of Communications was in the same mess as before February. Unless immediate emergency measures were taken, one could expect the system to collapse by the end of September.[5] All speakers warned against optimism: 'In deciding how to get out of the catastrophe that threatens us, we can talk only of how to make it less painful.'[6] 'We see hunger approaching', stated a worker from the Orudiinyi Factory, 'unemployment is growing, and all measures to regulate economic life are repulsed. The execution of control also meets resistance on the part of management . . . The country is heading towards ruin, the people are exhausted, labour productivity is falling. We must take measures.'[7] Two months later, at the Fourth Conference, Skrypnik could already report: 'We are no longer standing in the antechamber of the economic collapse; we have entered the zone of collapse itself.'[8]

The atmosphere in the factories became so strained that violence threatened to erupt over every minor conflict. The Putilov Factory Committee wrote to the CS of Factory Committees complaining of management's 'provocative' attitude and offered the following incident as an illustration. In early September, the workers learnt that certain lathes stored in the factory were being prepared for shipment and that the administration was taking inventory of the artillery shops as part of a plan for evacuation.

All this coincided with the appearance in the press of facts and entire treatises on the evacuation of Petrograd's industrial enterprises. Keenly attentive to anything relating to the situation of the industrial enterprises, the workers of the factory immediately grew alarmed, seeing in the shipment of the aforementioned lathes and machines (which were being loaded onto barges) the start of the evacuation of the Putilov Factory, and they turned to their organisation, the factory committee, to clarify the matter.

To clear up the issue that was 'agitating the workers and threatening to disrupt the normal flow of work', the committee asked the administration who the owner of the machines was and where they were destined. Both the director and the Main Artillery Authority refused to give out any information.

Considering the further 'quest for truth' about the shipment to be useless, the committee, to calm the excited workers and avoid excesses during the loading, informed the administration that shipment would be halted unless documentary materials were furnished by 25 September.

As there was no reply, the workers refused to release the barges. On 6 October, the administration sent the factory committee a copy of a letter from the Artillery Authority warning that the delay threatened 'state defence with irreparable harm'.

Knowing full well in what consists this 'state defence' and from what quarter it is threatened with irreparable harm, the workers' committee, precisely to avoid real damage to state defence (the workers agitation could erupt in the form of a work stoppage), continued to insist on documentary materials.

At last, after lengthy negotiations, papers were produced, showing that the machines did not belong to the factory. The loading was allowed to proceed. 'Thus', concluded the committee's letter,

> an affair which could have been put to rest in the course of an hour dragged on for a whole month because the 'bosses' wanted to follow their authoritarian inclinations to the very end and refused to enter into the necessary contact with the controlling organisations of the workers on these issues.[9]

It is difficult to convey in words the full extent of the workers' outrage at the policies of the industrialists and the Provisional Government. The following resolution of the workers of the Lebedev Aircraft Factory offers some idea. On 8 July, in the presence of a government commissar, the administration informed the factory committee that unless output reached a specified level by 15 August, the plant would have to be shut. The target was reached and surpassed. Then, in September, the administration announced that it was evacuating the factory to Yaroslavl' in central Russia but could take only half the work force. In their resolution, the workers admitted that 'the country is in a critical situation'. They outlined the various aspects of the economic crisis and placed the ultimate blame on the war.

> Meanwhile, lately the factory owners and together with them our boss, V. A. Lebedev, with the help of the Provisional Government, have taken to curing the country after their own fashion. A radical measure has been invented: to evacuate the factories to the materials and the workers to the food. To do this the government is giving away millions from its devastated coffers.

But we know that messieurs the industrialists are not capable of curing the country by these methods ... These 'doctors' are capable only of stuffing their already bulging purses with millions in subsidies given by the government ... We know that it is better to ship food to the population, it is easier to ship the materials to the factories than the factories to the materials. We are sure that the time of miracles has passed, that the mountain should not go to Mohamed, but Mohamed himself to the mountain. We are certain that these methods are not intended to cure the country but only to aggravate the industrial crisis, since under the guise of an evacuation they are organising mass dismissals of workers and swelling the army of unemployed.

The owner Lebedev tries to scare us by saying that there might be Zeppelin raids on the airport and that, anyway, we are not capable of continuing work here in Petrograd.

But we ask: who allowed the Germans to advance so close to Petrograd? Will Lebedev guarantee us that the Germans will not be allowed to advance to Yaroslavl', to Penza and Taganrog, and will we not be forced, like a cat with her kittens, to be carried away from there too? Can Lebedev assure us that there is in general a threat of 'German' attacks and not attacks of Lebedevs, Ryabushinskiis and the whole capitalist class on the working class? The facts of the last few days have shown that the external German is not more dangerous than the 'Germans' in the person of Kornilov and his class.

All the above leads us to the conclusion that ... the war and all the other aforementioned delights will continue as long as the conciliationist policy of our government continues, as long as our government follows on a leash behind the Lebedevs, Ryabushinskiis, and the Lebedevs and Ryabushinskiis— the English and French governments.[10]

The resolution concluded with the demand to transfer power to the workers and poor peasantry, and for the immediate proposal of democratic peace terms, the publication of secret treaties and full workers' control of the country's industry.

The Lebedev workers also protested against the position of the CS of Factory Committees on the evacuation. The latter had decided to allow evacuation in individual cases where justified and under the supervision of the workers.[11] To the Lebedev workers this appeared as recognition, in principle at least, that there was a legitimate basis to a measure that served only the interests of capital and the counter-revolution.

Of course, it did not help that the workers were being offered the Yarosalvl' jail as temporary quarters.[12] 'One comes across reports that provincial jails are being adapted for the evacuated workers', noted a delegate to the Conference of Factories of the Artillery Authority.

But you, comrade workers, have sat out too much time in prison under Tsarism to again enter the jails. Or, for example, there is one report that two houses of prostitution have been requisitioned as dwellings. This is a mockery that should be rejected with indignation.[13]

Actually, most factories agreed with the position of the CS and sent out delegations to inspect the proposed sites. But in very many instances they found that the conditions were totally unsuitable for a rapid resumption of production, and this, after all, was the rationale for the entire operation. At the September Factory Committee Conference Nikitin, a worker from the Parviainen Machine-construction Factory, slated for evacuation to the south, reported:

A delegation returning from Yuzovka found that fourteen totally unfinished structures had been prepared for the factories and even the floors had not been laid. Little houses were being built for the workers that you could puncture with an iron rod. Some have already collapsed. Wages are low. The day—ten hours. The food situation is about the same as in Piter; clothing—more expensive. The construction is not well organised: cement is brought on horses. They requested presses from here, but the foundation has not been prepared for them. The administration displays total negligence, as it does with the whole of production, when mountains of shells exist without copper rings, and copper can't be found anywhere.[14]

The management of the Treugol'nik Rubber Factory even refused to give the workers assurances that the machines and materials to be evacuated would in fact reach their stated destination. As a result, the evacuation was stopped.[15] And this is what happened in most factories as the workers remained unconvinced of the economic and defence motives being offered by the managements and the government.

Many factories resembled besieged fortresses, the defenders rushing frantically from breech to breech. The situation at the Vulkan Machine-construction Factory and Foundry, which is particularly well documented, though otherwise by no means unique, illustrates this graphically. One of the owners of this plant, Lianozov, a Kadet sympathiser, appears in John Reed's Russian notebooks as well as in his *Ten Days that Shook the World*. According to Reed, 'Mr. Lianozov is emphatic in his opinion that whatever happens, it would be impossible for the merchants and manufacturers to permit the existence of the workers' factory committees or to allow the workers a share in the management of industry.' Lianozov told Reed that international intervention would probably be necessary to stop the spread of such ideas as 'proletarian dictatorship' and 'world social revolution', ideas which threatened the West as well. There was a chance, however, that this could be avoided. 'Transport is demoralised, the factories are closing down and the Germans are advancing. Starvation and defeat may bring the Russian people to their senses . . .'[16]

Lianozov's factory employed about 2900 workers, almost 80 per cent men. In June the administration announced it was forced to curtail production and possibly close due to a drastic fall in productivity. The factory committee responded by establishing a commission to investigate the causes of the decline. On 4 July its recommendations were presented to the workers' general assembly, which decided to set up a commission of workers and white-collar employees to ensure the introduction of needed technical improvements as well as measures to reduce the proportion of defective goods and to enforce labour discipline, including strict observance of the eight-hour day, an end to lateness, etc. Overtime was to be allowed when the interests of production required it.[17]

As a result of these measures, a significant rise in productivity occurred. However, the administration resisted the technical measures on the grounds that they fell outside the factory committee's sphere of competence. Meanwhile, it announced its intention of dismissing 640 workers, with more to follow shortly. It cited financial and supply difficulties caused by declining productivity, high wages and the rising cost of raw materials. But the factory committee argued that the administration's policy of farming out a part of the production of shrapnel shells to subcontractors who were late in delivering was responsible in large part for holding back production. If the appropriate lathes were installed at Vulkan, the output of an eight-hour day would surpass what was currently being produced in ten hours. As for the administration's claim of supply difficulties, the factory was fully stocked for up to a year of continuous production.[18]

On 9 August, after a long debate on the scheduled dismissals, the factory committee addressed the following resolution to the director:

Having exhausted all peaceful means available to the working class and having achieved no results on the matter of the dismissal of our comrade workers and clerical employees, the factory committee of the Vulkan Factory, after all the clashes both with the ministries and the capitalists, has concluded that the reduction of the work force is intimately connected to the 'unloading' of Petrograd. Therefore, standing on guard for the Revolution, it is necessary to demand through the united forces of all the factories where production is being cut back that all such factories be transferred to the charge of the state and to put forth the following conditions as an ultimatum: in case the government rejects the demand of the entire proletariat, we will declare ourselves to be standing on guard for the interests of the revolution and in no way will we allow the dispersal of the revolutionary forces through the unloading of the revolutionary centre or through dismissals until the Conference of Factory Committees has taken a decision.[19]

On 16 August, after the intervention of the Ministry of Labour and long bargaining over the conditions of dismissal, 633 workers were fired.[20]

This crisis resolved, the next one was not far off. After the publication of the Skobelev circulars, Vulkan's management decided to reduce by a half the wages paid to the workers' delegates to the factory committee, the soviet and various other organisations.[21] The workers saw this as an attempt to weaken their resistance by making it impossible for the members of the factory committee to devote themselves fully to its work, thus preparing the ground for the final blow. Indeed, only a few days elapsed before management announced that the plant was closing because of financial difficulties. The factory committee, however, found that the problem stemmed from the administration's failure to press the Naval and Artillery Authorities for a review of prices to bring them into accord with rising costs due to inflation.

The general assembly met on 6 September to discuss the situation. All speakers took note of director Minkevich's 'offensive' against the factory committee: besides his refusal to pay full wages, he had forbidden clerical employees from giving out any information to the committee and was stubbornly resisting the introduction of necessary technical improvements, simply ignoring recommendations for the more rational deployment of technical personnel. It seemed obvious to the workers that Minkevich and the owners could not have cared less what the actual state of the factory really was. They had already decided to close, and no commission findings would make any difference. But what raised the workers' anger to fever pitch was Minkevich's 'insolence': at business meetings with their representatives he used such expressions as 'keep your tongue behind your teeth'.

The meeting was extremely turbulent. The workers were seething over the director's recent actions, viewed on the background of the general situation in the factory and the city. At this point a worker proposed from the floor that Minkevich be removed within forty-eight hours in the interests of the factory. If this did not happen, the 'general assembly should absolve the factory committee of responsibility for any actions the workers might take in relation to the administration'. Although the secretary of the factory committee pleaded that such an ultimatum could lead to serious consequences and that it was better first to contact the competent labour organisations, the resolution passed. The members of the factory committee either voted against the motion or abstained.

When the owners replied that Minkevich was staying, the factory committee resigned. But it had already been in touch with the factory's representatives to the Soviet as well as other organisations, who set to work at once. In the meanwhile, the factory's party organisations, Bolshevik (by far the dominant one), Menshevik and SR, issued a joint appeal for restraint. Workers were chosen to go around to the most volatile shops to try to keep the lid on. And, in fact, the veiled threat of violence was never carried out.

After meeting with the defunct factory committee, a commissar of the Ministry of Labour accompanied by representatives of the Factory Conference (*Zavodskoe soveshchanie*) put the following proposals to the workers: (1) the immediate establishment of state control through a commission consisting of government and management representatives; (2) the establishment of a 'workers' bureau' consisting of representatives of the workers and management on a 50–50 basis; and (3) an investigation into Minkevich's activity by an interministerial commission including representatives of the Metalworkers' Union. If he was found to be obstructing production, he would be removed. On their part, the workers insisted that any control commission must include representatives of the workers' organisations. As for the 'workers' bureau', they preferred a 'control-conflict commission'. The solution was accepted in this form.[22]

In an article in *Rabochii put'*, the factory committee secretary admitted that the workers did not put much store in this 'state control' by a government that was not truly democratic and when no consistent workers' control existed on the national level. Still, it was a definite 'victory for life', and the factory committee had by now developed an excellent technical-control apparatus and had established strong ties with the central institutions.[23]

But the workers' troubles were very far from over. The administration next announced that it was completely stopping payment of wages to all factory committee members. The committee wrote to its CS:

As you know, the factory committee has already defended the existence of the factory in relation to finances and raising productivity. But the administration's sabotage continues. It expresses itself both in the extreme technical defectiveness of the basic shops as well as in the extreme difficulty in which the factory committee is forced to administer the general wage agreement at the factory. But now the administration is taking new measures of sabotage. It has decided to completely withhold the money necessary to pay the factory committee, in all eleven people, including the technical control commission, the wage commission, the investigation commission and the arbitration chamber. This measure is not only a general offensive against the factory organisations (the administration cites Skobelev) but it strikes at the very existence of the factory itself. For it is anyway only with great difficulty that the factory committee now exists in the midst of extremely tense workers, who stand at defective lathes, who are poorly paid, and with the factory administration constantly threatening to shut the factory and cut the work force.[24]

This was not the last conflict, but Vulkan, largely thanks to the efforts of its factory committee, survived well past the October Revolution, which its workers wholeheartedly supported.

Vulkan was characteristic of the situation in the factories of Petrograd in several respects. First, in the continuously escalating power struggle between labour and management, the factory committee was being drawn away from its original controlling functions (in the sense of monitoring and overseeing) towards more and more direct intervention into the management of production, particularly in efforts to bolster productivity.

Secondly, in contrast to the situation on the more directly political level, the 'masses', the rank and file, were clearly holding onto the initiative, prodding their somewhat reluctant leaders into increasingly militant stands.

Finally, as before, the struggle for production led directly to the question of state power. Vulkan called for state takeover of all factories where production was declining. Its factory committee secretary expressed the general view that real control required a 'truly democratic' government and workers' control on the national level. The following discussion will take up these three aspects of the movement.

*From Workers' Control towards Workers' Management*

The workers first began to intervene directly in management functions in the spring, when some factory committees took it upon themselves to seek out new orders and supplies of fuel and raw materials. But as the Vulkan case shows, this was often not enough to ensure that production continued.

The committee of the Parviainen Machine-construction Factory achieved considerable notoriety for its activity in August that saved the jobs of 1630 workers. These workers were to be fired because, according to the administration, only three-fifths of the required fuel had arrived. In response, the factory committee aided by the CS set up an investigative commission that found that fuel was being consumed in an extremely irrational manner, that a 30 per cent saving could be effected without loss of normal output. After putting up some resistance, the administration was finally forced to confirm these findings.

The factory committee also worked out new rules for stokers, machine operators and other workers to eliminate fuel wastage. *Rabochii put'* commented:

> Here the factory committee has already entered onto the path of technical improvement of production. It would be of interest to know what the former Minister of Labour and former social democrat Skobelev would say. Can a factory committee work out these rules ... during work hours? ... The workers are creating a new life. The past and present ministers, toadying to the capitalists, only hinder this activity.[25]

In August, the fuel supply at the Sestroretsk Factory outside of Petrograd ran out. The water supply, another source of energy at the plant, was also drawing low. The factory committee took upon itself to dig a canal to a source of water supply on a nearby estate (the landowner protested vigorously, but in vain), which was able to keep the factory going for some time. *Znamya truda* wrote this up in an article entitled 'What Would the Factories be Without the Factory Committees?'[26]

These encroachments on management's traditional prerogatives were not the expression of a lust for power on the part of the factory committees or the worker rank and file. Practice was indeed changing, but the basic motive behind the activity of the factory committees remained the same: to keep the factories running. Workers' control in its original monitoring capacity, like dual power in the state, was born of the workers' mistrust of the capitalists. But at the same time it implied a belief that the workers and the owners could cooperate, even if the latter required some rather forceful prodding from time to time. In essence, workers' control meant that the workers entrusted the administration with running the factory, while they reserved for themselves the right to monitor management's activities and to intervene if there was any abuse of this trust. But there was the rub. Workers' control came up against the same obstacle as dual power: the other party refused to cooperate because it felt its interests were opposed to those of the 'controlling' workers. In fact, the 'controlled' party seemed prepared for the entire enterprise come to a halt rather than suffer the workers' newly-won power to assert their interests.

The plain fact was that there was no way to 'control' an executive that refused at almost any price to be 'controlled'. The workers reached the conclusion that management was not doing its job in good faith, that it was, in fact, fast losing any interest in maintaining production. In their view, they had no alternative but to move in to fill the void left by management's inactivity or conscious sabotage. 'We are told that we must control', complained a Dinamo worker at the

August Factory Committee Conference. 'But what will we control if we have nothing left but walls, bare walls?'[27] Levin warned the same assembly:

It is very likely that we stand before a general strike of capitalists and industrialists. We have to be prepared to take the enterprises into our hands to render harmless the hunger that the bourgeoisie so heavily counts upon as a counterrevolutionary force.[28]

Levin himself was far from being an anarchist. After the October Revolution he consistently opposed takeovers that were not absolutely justified by the sabotage or flight of the management.

Not surprisingly, the demand totally to remove the owners from command of the factories began to be raised in this period for the first time on a significant scale. Vulkan, as noted, demanded that the state take charge of all enterprises where productivity was declining. A report on the Soikin Press in *Rabochii put'* also recommended that the state requisition and confiscate all plants being sabotaged or closed. The owner of Soikin had refused to make repairs or to replace worn parts and was found selling his machines piece by piece to speculators.[29] The Kolpino and Obukhovskii District branches of the Metalworkers' Union both recommended that the unions themselves take over the enterprises 'as the only radical measure of struggle'.[30] The question of confiscation or nationalisation was also being raised in the textile union.[31]

At the time, these were still minority voices in the labour movement, and little came of these demands. The workers' attention was still focused on control, though control in an expanded sense. But it is not difficult to see that full takeover of management was but a few steps away in the logical progression of events that had led from control in the strict sense to control as direct intervention into the management of production.

*Factory Committees under Pressure from Below*

Reporting on the factory committees, Skrypnik told the Bolshevik CC in October, 'It is felt that the leaders do not entirely express the mood of the masses. The former are more conservative.'[32] Both the Vulkan and Putilov cases cited earlier show the worker rank and file as a constant spur to the factory committees. The Lebedev workers' opposition to the CS stand on the evacuation is yet another instance of the often greater militancy of the worker masses when it came to defending the factories.

The shift in the factory committees' activity towards increasingly direct intervention into the management of production occurred largely under pressure from the rank and file exerted against not always enthusiastic factory committee activists. 'One notes under the pressure of the workers', wrote the director of the Admiralty Shipyards, 'a deviation of the committees from their proper [*pryamoi*] and fruitful activity directed at preliminary [*predvaritel'nyi*] control of the administration, in other words, in the direction of management of the factory.'[33]

The background for this was the widespread disappointment with the limited success of workers' control in forestalling the industrial crisis. In retrospect it is clear that this movement played a crucial role in the victory of the October Revolution by postponing the economic collapse for several months. October would not have been possible with a massively unemployed, demoralised and dispersed working class. The fact remains, however, that despite the great popularity of the slogan and the energetic activity of the committees firmly backed by the workers, genuine control, in the sense of full access to documents and systematic monitoring of management, largely eluded the workers before October. One can sense the frustration in the report of the Putilov Factory Committee cited earlier: an affair that could have been put to rest in an hour dragged on for a month, agitating the workers and wasting their energy, simply because management refused to cooperate with the factory committee.

The limited success of the movement was readily admitted. On 26 September at a meeting on the forthcoming dismissal of 5000 Putilov workers, Glebov told his colleagues in the factory committee:

The administration has given up and it is hardly likely to take the dismissals upon itself, and in all probability we will have to supervise this dirty work ourselves. [The dismissals were due to a fuel shortage.] To blame in this, of course, are the representatives of the higher ups [*verkhy*] who refused to allow us close to control.[34]

Another committee member, Voitsekhovskii, urged:'We must succeed in getting the right to control, and it is about time we put an end to our traipsing about the shops of the factory.'[35]

Even in the best of cases the workers only managed to mount a strong holding action, to patch up the leaks temporarily. But everyone could sense the waters rising, and it was obvious that more than patchwork was needed. 'At the First Conference [of Factory Committees] we expected to greet the Second amidst brilliant success', lamented Surkov, a delegate to the Second Conference.

But the revolutionary wave has stopped, and those for whom it is profitable have been able to exploit this, and as a result our activity has been paralysed to a significant degree. The factory committees have lost their authority [with management].[36]

Two months later at the Fourth Conference, Zhuk, the delegate from the Schlusselburg Powder Factory, was still trying to fight this disillusionment:

> Many take a sceptical attitude toward the coming [All-Russian Factory Committee] conference. The conference will give us not vague resolutions but concrete answers to all the cardinal questions that arise in connection with the unprecedented anarchy that has seized all of industry. The conference must solve the question of the factories that are closing and of those where clear acts of sabotage have been exposed ... We must carry this out in deeds and not only in words.[37]

Under these circumstances it is not difficult to understand why the workers were pressing for a more active and direct role of the factory committees in management and for more militant tactics generally. What does require some explaining, however, is the reluctance often shown by the committees in taking on these new functions and supporting more aggressive tactics.

Most factory committees and their organisations firmly refused formal participation in management, rejecting any responsibility for the state of the factories. In October a conference of representatives of the factory committees and of other labour organisations in Petrograd specifically rejected the idea of sending workers' representatives to participate in the administration of the factories.[38] The same position was taken by the All-Russian Conference of Factories of the Artillery Authority and the Conference of Factories of the Naval Authority:

> Having discussed the question of control by the factory committees over the economic, technical and administrative aspects of production, and considering that responsibility for production lies exclusively with the administration of the factory, [the Conference of Factories of the Naval Authority] recognises for the factory committees through their control commissions the right to be present at all meetings of the administration and to demand exhaustive explanations to questions and to receive them.[39]

This was still control in its original sense. At about the same time the Putilov Factory Committee, backed by the workers, turned down a proposal by Pal'chinskii for a standing conference of representatives of the workers and the administration to 'regulate all the work of the factory'.[40] It was decided that the factory committee should enter solely for purposes of control but should reject any responsibility for the management of the factory.[41]

There were several interrelated reasons for this position. In part, it was reluctance to take responsibility for a task that the factory committees were not at all sure they could handle, particularly in the current harsh economic conditions. They felt that unless there was absolutely no other alternative, responsibility for the direct day-to-day running of the factory should be left with the administration. The Putilov resolution of 28 September explained:

> Having discussed the question of participation in the institution regulating the entire life of the factory, and taking into account the current state of the factory, which as a result of various causes must be recognised as catastrophic, and that the reorganisation of the administration of the factory and the regulation of production are an extremely complex affair requiring time, [we resolve:]
> 1. The workers cannot take upon themselves responsibility for the course of work at the factory in the near future.
> 2. Representatives of the workers should enter the council being created in order to actively participate in the control and regulation of the entire productive life of the factory and to oppose any attempts to hold up the proper course of factory life mainly on the part of external forces.[42]

Consciousness of the difficulties involved in management was, thus, a restraining factor. On the other hand, the rank-and-file workers, more distant from these problems, tended often to react more spontaneously to events. A situation similar to the one at Vulkan arose at the Petrov Textile Mill in late September, when the owners, again citing Skobelev, refused to pay wages to worker delegates for time spent outside of production. The workers called a meeting to which they invited representatives of management. But the latter stood their ground and, according to a report by one of the workers present, replied in an 'insolent manner'. They continued to refuse to budge even when a crowd of angry workers threatened to ride the administration out in wheelbarrows. After this, one of the management representatives resigned, asking not to be touched. At this the meeting simply broke up, the workers evidently balking at the prospect of losing the entire administration.[43]

This threat was a very real one, and in a few cases the workers actually did take up the challenge. On 19 October, the workers of Aivaz decided to fire an engineer, Abratanskii. The available documents do not specify the reasons except to say that he was responsible for 'all forms of oppression of the workers'. Abratanskii, however, refused to leave and at one point struck a worker. In the reigning atmosphere such an affront could only lead to an explosion. (Such incidents were very prominent in sparking off violence.) A group of indignant workers rode Abratanskii out in a wheelbarrow, touching off a strike of the entire engineering staff. (The foremen and clerica employees remained solidary with the workers.) The next day, the general assembly condemned the violence against the administration, but nevertheless, decided to continue under a worker-appointed management, calling for strict labour discipline, conscientiousness and a 'decisive struggle against all phenomena that disorganise our midst and disgrace the name of conscious workers'.[44]

But concern for the factory committees' lack of expertise in dealing with the technical and economic difficulties facing the factories was not the major consideration in the refusal of responsibility for production. Prepared or not, it was generally agreed that capital's 'Italian strike' would sooner or later leave the workers with no alternative. More important was the fear on the part of the committees that under the coalition government, and in the absence of workers' control on the national level, they would simply lack the power effectively to tackle the problems faced by industry and end up being exploited by the administration and compromised in the eyes of the worker masses.

This was made clear in the Putilov Factory Committee's discussion of Pal'chinskii's proposal. It was noted that Pal'chinskii was offering the committee only five places in the proposed council and that no other workers' organisations (e.g. the CS) would be permitted to participate. With this 'sawed-off' (*kutsyi*) control there was every likelihood the administration would merely use the committee as a screen for actions directed against the workers' interests. Grigor'ev summed up this view:

> The entrepreneurs at present are seeking all means that the workers might whip themselves ... Without genuine control, we should not enter this organ. When it turned out that the Government [the factory had been sequestered in 1915] could not do without us and that things were in a bad way, then it came to us for help. But we will give it help only when it gives us a guarantee that we are real controllers. Otherwise, why should we take the bait being tossed to us? We must not get caught.[45]

The same attitudes were expressed at the All-Russian Conference of Factory Committees in mid October in response to a suggestion that the factory committees delegate one member to each department of the administration. According to this proposal, the delegates would have a consultative voice and would make sure that the administration was following a general plan to be drawn up by a proposed central economic organ staffed by a majority of workers' representatives. Chubar' of the Petrograd CS objected that 'such a formulation is unfortunate, since it puts the workers in the role of some sort of aides to generals'. He referred to the decision of the Conference of Factories of the Artillery Authority against entering the administration.

The members of the factory committee would turn into pushers [*tolkachi*], whom the administration will use as extra help, itself remaining outside of active work. Such phenomena have already been observed in the practice of the state factories. Besides, if the workers enter the factory administration even with only a consultative voice, in a critical moment (and at present, this can be any moment) the workers will direct all their discontent at the factory committee, blaming it for not having taken measures to prevent the hitches in production. It will, therefore, sow discontent among the workers themselves.[46]

Chubar' recommended control through a commission entirely separate from management.

Antipov, a worker from the Vyborg District, seconded Chubar', adding that one could indeed observe of late a desire among management to offer the factory committees a place in order to foist upon them responsibility for its own failures.

Such a pitting of undeveloped masses against their factory committees can be successful, and in some cases one can already observe a certain straining of relations between the worker masses and their elected organs. A recent meeting in Petrograd of all the representatives of the workers' organisations discussed the issue of entering the factory administration and decided against it.

The conference vote was 83 to 4 for control through a commission separate from management.[47]

There was, in addition, a related 'ideological' issue: by becoming involved in production while the factories were still in effective control of the capitalists, were not the factory committees thereby participating in the exploitation of the workers, even if their motive was to save them from mass unemployment? Although circumstances were forcing the committee activists to go beyond control in the narrow sense, they were nevertheless sensitive to such criticism, which hit at a core value of the 'conscious workers'—class separateness from the bourgeoisie.[48]

Lenin himself had reproached the factory committees back in May for acting as the 'errand boys' of capital in seeking out fuel and new orders in the absence of soviet power and workers' control on the national level that alone could ensure that their efforts would be in the workers' interests.[49] This was a reproach that union leaders were particularly wont to express. Ryazanov, an old-time trade unionist and one of the moderate Bolsheviks hostile to the activity of the factory committees, told the All-Russian Factory Committee Conference:

The union movement does not bear the stain of the entrepreneur, and it is the bad luck of the committees that they seem to be component parts of the administration. The union opposes itself to capital, while the factory committee involuntarily turns into an agent of the entrepreneur.[50]

Similarly, Gastev, a leader of the Petrograd Metalworkers' Union, noted a 'touching solidarity [on the part of the factory committees] with the administration'. Provincial committees were sending representatives to the government in Petrograd to praise their factories and support the owners' requests for orders and subsidies. 'Such a coming together of the factory committees with the administration forced the Petrograd Metalworkers' Union to pass a whole series of resolutions aimed at curtailing this independent activity of the committees or at diverting it into a more defined channel.'[51]

*The Struggle for Production and the Issue of State Power*

The search for a solution to the problems facing the factory committees on both the practical and 'ideological' levels thus led them directly to the issue of state power. At the Fourth Factory Committee Conference in October, Skrypnik had some harsh words for those delegates who expressed disappointment with the meagre results of the activity of the factory committees:

They apparently flattered themselves with illusions. But our conference said from the very start that under a bourgeois government we will not be able to carry out consistent control. The future centre [of factory committees to be set up by the All-Russian Conference next week] will find itself in the same conditions, and to speak of a control board under a bourgeois government is impossible. Therefore, the working class cannot bypass state power, as comrade Renev [an anarchist] proposes.[52]

Egorov, a Putilov worker, fully agreed with this assessment:

We are only too well acquainted with factory life to deny the need for the [all-Russian] conference. We know how often the factory committees turn out to be helpless, knowing how to avert a stoppage of production in the factories but lacking the possibility of intervening. The conference can give valuable directives. But we should not fool ourselves that the conference can get us out of the dead-end. Both private and state administrations sabotage production, referring us to the Society of Factory and Mill Owners. They are still strong. The conference must first of all point out those obstacles which prevent the people of action from saving the country. These obstacles are placed before us by the bourgeois government. Only the reorganisation of state power will give us the possibility of developing our activity.[53]

If, as has often been argued, Bolshevik success in the factory committees was due to their allegedly opportunistic support for workers' control, then the anarchists, fervent advocates of factory committee power, for whom the committees played a central role in their vision of the new order, should have shared in this success. But they remained weak in the committees. At the August Factory Committee Conference, Volin, an anarchist from the Shtein Factory, proposed an amendment to the resolution on workers' control: the reference to the 'transfer of power to the proletariat' should be deleted. To this Milyutin, speaking for the Bolsheviks, replied: 'I decisively disagree with the amendment because it crosses out the essence of the resolution. We are not anarchists and we recognise that a state apparatus is necessary and it must be further developed.' Volin's amendment was rejected by an overwhelming majority.[54]

Later Voskov commented on Volin's anarcho-syndicalist model for organising the economy:

Volin has accused us of lacking a broad plan and he pointed to the syndicalist movement in the North American United States. Indeed, the American syndicalists, who, by the way, can all sit around the same table [Voskov had been in emigration in the US], have the broadest of plans, which, however, the workers will not follow. We need a practical plan of work.[55]

But if the anarchists were not making gains among the factory committee activists, their influence among the rank and file in certain districts was finally beginning to grow in this period. Skrypnik reported to the Bolshevik CC in October on the 'growth of anarchist influence in the Narva and Moscow Districts'.[56] At about this time Gessen told the Bolshevik PC that in the Narva District 'among the backward masses, there is an indifference to politics', while the other Narva representative added that 'at the Putilov Factory the anarchists are working energetically, so that it is hard to hold the masses back in an organised structure'. In the Rozhdestvenskii District, 'the mood has declined in connection with the dismissals due to the evacuations. The influence of the anarchists has increased noticeably.'[57]

The picture that presents itself, although the direct evidence is admittedly limited, is one of the growing appeal of the anarchists' direct-action tactics, particularly among the unskilled workers, disillusioned with the political struggle that seemed to be dragging on endlessly somewhere in the centre without any tangible results while the economy continued to deteriorate. The industrial labour force of the Narva, Moscow and Rozhdestvenskii Districts contained a high proportion of unskilled workers, mainly women and wartime workers, who initially had been attracted to the SRs.[58] 'Where our influence is weak', went the report from the Petrograd District, 'there is political apathy. There a struggle is taking place with the factory committee.'

But the contemporary references to the 'growth of anarchism' refer to the popularity of the anarchists' tactics rather than their principled rejection of the state and of political struggle. This explains the anarchists' continued weakness in the factory committees, as well as the Bolsheviks' continued success in getting elected to all workers' organisations and the virtually unanimous worker support for soviet power. This is apparently what Gessen meant when he added: 'But there is no decline in the authority of our party.'

Despite the increasing frequency of 'excesses' in worker–management relations, there were still very few takeovers. When they occurred, it was because the administration had shut down or left. At Respirator the workers held several administrators 'under arrest' for a few hours. The circumstances are obscure except that the workers were demanding the rescindment of an order issued on 31 August (possibly relating to the Skobelev circulars). In response to the 'arrest', the entire administration resigned. The workers decided to continue on their own, asking the government to appoint a commissar 'from the juridical point of view' to be responsible for obtaining raw materials from Respirator's idle client factories. The workers also demanded a 'democratic trial' of the administration charged with 'desertion from the rear'.[59] Very typical of such takeovers was an accompanying call for state sequestration, hardly an anarchist-inspired demand.

Workers' control remained first and foremost a practical response to the concrete problems the workers faced and not, as the dominant view in Western historiography has maintained, an anarchistic or anti-authority movement.[60] Even in the state factories, where the right to control was asserted at the very start of the revolution and where the practice of control was most developed, the authority of the state managements was recognised and supported by the factory committees.[61] On 3 October, the factory and shop committees of the Izhorskii Factory met to discuss their relations with the administration. The resolution passed stressed that the committees should cooperate with the director and that:

Any order of the foremen, subforemen and senior workers must be unwaveringly executed. In all cases of doubt as to the propriety of an order, one should immediately notify the shop committee without making any independent objections or putting obstacles before the execution of the given order.[62]

The regulations governing worker–management relations at Orudiinyi asserted the 'right of control over all acts of the administration in the area of the mutual relations among workers and in the general course of production'. But they left the appointment of higher administrative personnel to management. Moreover

Each worker is obliged to execute the legitimate demands of the administrative personnel who are their direct supervisors, maintaining polite address throughout. In case of a disagreement between a worker and a representative of management, the matter is taken up to the shop committee. In extreme cases, it is taken to the factory committee or to the conciliation chamber.[63]

These rules speak directly against an anarchist interpretation of workers' control. The need for authority was clearly recognised although subject to broad control. The conception, as noted earlier, closely resembled that of the 'dual power' established in February on the political level.

### The Quiet on the Wage Front

The workers' realisation that there was no salvation from industrial collapse without the seizure of power, along with their preoccupation with keeping the factories open, explains in large part the surprising calm that reigned in the capital in the traditional area of the struggle over wages, when the rest of Russia was experiencing an economic strike wave of unprecedented proportions.[64]

The September Conference of Factory Committees warned the workers against

scattered and premature actions that can only be utilised by the counterrevolution. On the contrary, it is necessary to concentrate all the workers' energy on organisational work for the forthcoming solution of the question of constructing state power and a swift end to the three-year-old slaughter.[65]

The workers seem to have heeded these warnings. Petrograd witnessed only two major industrial strikes in August–October, the 24–7 September strike of 7000 workers in the railroad workshops (part of the national railroad strike) and the 16–28 October strike of 25 000 woodworkers. In addition, there were a few small strikes, the most notable being that of 21 printing plants (12–22 August) and a strike of 2500 paper workers (21 September–4 October). No more than 10 per cent of Petrograd's 417 000 industrial workers participated in strikes in the three-month period preceding the insurrection.[66]

By way of contrast, in the Central Industrial Region around Moscow, even if one includes only the industry-wide strikes of this period, well over 40 per cent (closer to 50 per cent counting the smaller strikes) of the region's 1 030 000 workers took part in economic strikes. These included 110 000 leatherworkers, 300 000 textile workers and 15 000 rubber workers (as well as workers in the railroad workshops and individual metalworking factories).[67]

Not that the grounds or the desire to strike were lacking in Petrograd. Between the opening of negotiations on a collective agreement in the metalworking industry at the end of June and the signing of the agreement six weeks later, the union prevented conflicts in some 180 factories from developing into strikes.[68] At a meeting of the central and district union executives on 1 July, the Bolsheviks successfully spoke against a strike and for a compromise on wages, arguing that all the workers' demands were subsumed in the demand for soviet power and that the workers should conserve their energy towards achieving that goal.[69]

About three weeks later the PSFMO broke off talks, rejecting, as noted earlier, the union's demands for the unskilled categories and insisting, in turn, on fixed output norms. In response to this the union's Delegates' Assembly gave the executive a strike mandate to be used as a last resort.[70] However, a few days later the Delegates' Council accepted a government-sponsored compromise on wages and agreed to the output norms 'in view of the serious economic situation of the country'. The council noted that in the existing conditions of inflation and economic ruin, only ending the war, real control over production and the transfer of power to the working class and its allies could save the workers' from 'unbearable conditions of existence'.[71]

This, however, did not end the matter. The introduction of the new rates met with considerable resistance from some of the owners and particularly the managements of the state factories, not members of the PSFMO. Moreover, it had become clear during the negotiations that inflation had already eaten up most of the rise.[72] Many disputes also broke out over the classification of jobs. While scattered strikes did occur, the mass of workers, though not unsympathetic, did not support them. In response to a strike by a group of workers at the Putilov Works in late September protesting their classification, 5000 workers in the Cannon Department resolved

to call the above-mentioned comrades back to work immediately, as their strike suits only the entrepreneurs and disorganises the close ranks of the Putilov workers ... While summoning the striking workers back to work, the factory and shop committees will strive to satisfy their just demands.[73]

The general assembly of the Parviainen Factory of 12 October also refused to support a strike of 200 mechanics and turners, declaring:

> We workers feel the grasping hand of hunger. We see perfectly well that the capitalist factory owners, having grown insolent, are trying to tear from the workers whatever they can at every opportunity, that they artificially create cadres of unemployed, provoking strikes by their refusal to meet the most essential demands. But we firmly declare that we will go out into the streets only when we find it necessary. We are not frightened by the coming battle that is drawing near and we firmly believe that we will emerge from it victorious.
>
>     Long live power in the hands of the soviets of workers' and soldiers' deputies![74]

As this resolution indicates, concern with keeping the factories running and fear that strikes could be turned into lockouts were another source of restraint on the wage issue (which contrasted sharply with the growing militancy over issues concerning production itself). But this too was tied in the workers' minds to the need for state power.

# 4 On the Eve

At a meeting of the Bolshevik CC on 16 October, Zinoviev, a member of the party's moderate wing which was opposed to an insurrection, stressed that 'the mood in the factories now is not what it was in June. It is clear that there is not such a mood as in June.'[1] The previous day at a closed session of the Bolshevik PC, Latsis, party organiser in the Vyborg District and a consistent leftwinger, reported: 'In the coming out [*vystuplenie*] the organised apparatus must be in the fore; the masses will support us. It is totally different from before.'[2]

On this point, at least, there was agreement: in contrast to the pre-July period, one could not now expect initiatives from the rank-and-file workers in overthrowing the government. It was the turn of the party, grown accustomed, as Latsis put it, to acting as a fire hose, to light the fuse itself.

In attempting to describe and explain the workers' state of mind on the eve of the insurrection, one must be careful to identify the issues as they were debated at the time and not as they have come to be seen in retrospect, as so often occurs in the historiography. The first problem that the workers had to face as the Soviet Congress drew near was whether the soviets should take power at all or whether it made more sense to await the Constituent Assembly (elections for which, after several postponements, were finally set for mid November) in the expectation that its majority would decide on an exclusively revolutionary-democratic government. This second option once again held out the alluring prospect of a peaceful transition of power and the avoidance of political isolation. On the other hand, to wait at least several more weeks meant to allow the present impossible economic and military conditions to deteriorate further.[3]

In essence the debate was whether violence and civil war were inevitable. The moderates—LSRs, Menshevik–Internationalists and moderate Bolsheviks (the defencists, who continued to support the coalition, had little worker support and can be ignored for the moment)—argued that a soviet seizure of power, a violent overthrow, were unnecessary (and, in any case, unlikely to succeed) and would only alienate potential allies within revolutionary democracy and lead to civil war. The left countered that some degree of civil war was not only unavoidable but already existed. Even if the Constituent Assembly were to declare itself for a revolutionary government, Kerenskii would certainly not yield power without a fight. Besides, what guarantee was there that the Constituent Assembly would ever meet? Actions, not marking time, would win over the rest of revolutionary democracy.

These issues were set out clearly in the political debate at the All-Russian Conference of Factory Committees in Petrograd on 18 October. Trotsky's report on the 'current moment' was received enthusiastically. Not surprisingly, the major part of his speech was devoted to showing that in Russian conditions civil war was unavoidable. Those who compared Russia to the France of 1789, he argued, were blind. France had only the embryo of a proletariat, while in Russia

> our working class represents a developed organised type of revolutionary class . . . On the other side stands organised capital. This has determined the high degree of class strife. Conciliationism would have a basis if class antagonisms were not so acute . . . There are two extreme wings, and if the revolutionary parties were to draw back from civil war now, the right wing would all the same carry out its attack on the revolution and all its achievements. Desertion by the parties would not avert the civil war. It would merely unfold in an unorganised form, in a haphazard and scattered manner and, one may assume, to the greatest benefit of the propertied classes. Civil war is imposed upon us by the economic situation and by the course of our history.

Trotsky then turned to the question of the workers' isolation and noted that 'between the landowners and the peasantry a civil war is already in progress'. Peasant petitioners were arriving daily at the Petrograd Soviet to ask for help against the government's punitive expeditions. Meanwhile, the soldiers at the front were telling the Soviet in no uncertain terms to take power and avert a spontaneous mass desertion at the first snowfall. As for the Constituent Assembly, the bourgeoisie was undermining it by every means it possessed.

> Only through the seizure of power can the genuinely revolutionary class, the proletariat, and the army that is gravitating towards it, and the insurgent peasantry struggle for the Constituent Assembly . . .
>
> You cannot artificially direct historical development along a peaceful path. We must recognise this and say openly to ourselves that civil war is inevitable. It is necessary to organise it in the interests of the working class. This is the only way to make it less bloody, less painful. You cannot achieve this result by wavering and hesitation; only through a stubborn and courageous struggle for power. Then it is still possible, there is still a chance that the

bourgeoisie will retreat. By conciliationist wavering you will achieve just the opposite. We cannot allow the demoralisation of the working class through wavering.[4]

Kamkov, speaking for the LSRs, agreed with Trotsky that the workers, soldiers and peasants all wanted to replace the coalition with census society by a revolutionary-democratic government. The question was: how do you go about organising such a government? 'Is it possible, is it permissible to organise it through the revolutionary pressure of a single city?' He reminded the delegates of what had taken place on 3–5 July.

We consider a coming out in the given circumstances the greatest political mistake. The conditions are not now favourable for an open battle with the bourgeoisie. If it were a question at present of either staking all or perishing, then we would follow the example of the Paris Commune. But in fact, the opposite is true. The revolutionary wave is growing in strength daily as ever new masses rally to the proletariat ... Power will not slip away; there is no one to take it from.

Rather than take power through the congress, which is being convened 'despite the sabotage of the TsIK',[5] the workers should use it to guarantee the convocation of the Constituent Assembly.[6]
The conference voted by 53 against 5 (9 abstentions) for the following resolution:

The government of the counterrevolutionary bourgeoisie is destroying the country, having demonstrated and itself understood its total inability to wage war, which it is dragging out for the sole purpose of smothering the revolution. It does nothing for the struggle against economic dislocation. Just the opposite—its entire economic policy is directed at aggravating the dislocation in the aim of starving the revolution to death and burying it under the debris of general economic ruin. The salvation of the revolution and the goals put forward for it by the toiling masses lies in the transfer of power to the hands of the Soviets of Workers', Soldiers' and Peasants' Deputies.[7]

This conference reflected the dominant sentiment in the factories of Petrograd. On 21 October, the general assembly of the Admiralty Shipyard met to discuss the 'current moment'. Pakhomov, a Bolshevik worker and the factory's delegate to the Petrograd Soviet, spoke first:

At this time we should not at any price support the government which tries to dupe the people and by every means ruin the revolution, [a government] thanks to which the army is perishing along with the revolutionary navy in an unequal battle, which is trying to hand over the workers of Petrograd to the apprenticeship of the German capitalists. [I] propose that we demand that power be transferred to the Soviet of W[orkers'] and S[oldiers'] D[eputies].

Turning to the issue of an insurrection, he stated:

All this talk of a coming out by the Bolsheviks is being circulated for one reason only—to test the cowardly and to give a reason for sending a new Kornilov to Petrograd to put down the Bolsheviks once they have come out; yet it is necessary to take power. And therefore he declares that he is not calling you out into the streets but proposes to be ready 'to die with honour or live with shame'. That means that if a coming out becomes necessary, then it will be criminal to sit on the side.

Pakhomov was answered by Zakharenko, a defencist worker.

He expresses his doubts about why the lefts are acting in such a risky manner. He proposes to be cautious, and if the lefts talk of socialism, then let them show what socialism is; about peace he said that in the trenches they are waiting for peace more than here and if the soldiers are brought to that point, they will not be soldiers but bands shooting peaceful citizens. On the coming out Z. spoke of it as unarmed crowds coming out in a duel with an armed army which will unconditionally demolish us. On land he said that anarchy has begun in the villages, but why he did not say: because the land is not equally well-situated in different places in our Russia and you can't give power to the soviets because they represent a minority since only the Petrograd proletariat follows the soviets and the villages totally ignore the soviets.

In what had become the main tactic of the defencists, Zakharenko devoted most of his speech to playing on the workers' fears of isolation. He offered no rebuttal of the Bolsheviks' criticisms of the government but merely stated that a soviet seizure of power would fail. His position was further weakened by his failure to propose an alternative to soviet power or the Provisional Government.

Kharitonov, another Bolshevik worker, replied to Zakharenko:

Since when have we had in Russia a majority of capitalists and landowners who all this time have been in the government from which the Bolsheviks are now proposing that the entire people free itself and give this power to the soviets as chosen by the people? He spoke of Rodzyanko's intention to surrender Petrograd and read the speech of General Brussilov at the Moscow Conference.

Following the discussion, the meeting resolved unanimously:

We, the workers of the Admiralty Shipyard, Galernyi ostrovok, having heard a report on the current moment, declare that the government, as a [government] of the bourgeoisie and landowners, is a government of bourgeois–landowner dictatorship and civil war and is conducting a policy of betrayal and deception of the people. The government is preparing to desert Petrograd for Moscow and by this, together with Rodzyanko, to surrender Petrograd to the Germans. In this counterrevolutionary undertaking we see an insolent challenge to the workers and a new conspiracy against the revolution, one more dangerous than Kornilov.

We declare that all to the last man will fight for the power of the soviets of WS and PD, for only in this lie peace, land and freedom.[8]

Dozens of resolutions passed at factory meetings on the eve of the insurrection leave no doubt that when asked to choose between waiting for the Constituent Assembly and seizing power at once through the soviets, the Petrograd workers as a whole were almost as unanimous as those of Admiralty.[9] In fact, a careful search of the press as well as published and unpublished archival material, revealed only one resolution clearly supporting the internationalists' call to use the Soviet Congress not to take power but to prepare the Constituent Assembly. It was passed by the Obukhovskii workers.[10]

Even among workers who voted for LSR candidates, there was a strong tendency nevertheless to support the call for immediate soviet power. Thus, although the Admiralty resolution was passed unanimously, in recent elections here the LSRs had received over one-quarter of the vote.[11] The SR organisations of the Petergof District and of the Sestroretsk Arms Factory themselves called on the congress to take power![12]

The fact was that the workers could simply wait no longer, as the Menshevik–Internationalist and LSR leaders themselves admitted. 'Our speeches seemed doomed to us', recalled Mstislavskii, a prominent Petrograd LSR.

True, at meetings the workers and soldiers applauded our orators, but we felt that they were applauding the voice, the sound, but not the sense of the words—they went on thinking their own thoughts as before. And in face of this 'their own', what force could our ideas on a 'system of power', 'priority of the social', 'transitional period' have in comparison with the battle cries of Lenin, so resonant and comprehensible to the masses?

A few days before the insurrection, Mstislavskii wrote in *Znamya truda*:

> Of course it is difficult for the masses, exhausted by the sense of 'dead end', to stand ground before the lure of a slogan that solves so simply and radically, with one wave of the hand, all our difficulties, the economic ruin, the 'accursed questions'. To all desires, one reply—rise up! In a word, one short moment of decisiveness, a new upsurge of energy, intense street fighting—and we will have crossed the frontier before which we have been lingering for months.[13]

Any lingering doubts about this were laid to rest on 22 October, the 'Day of the Petrograd Soviet', the half-year anniversary of the February Revolution. The Petrograd Soviet called for a peaceful review of soviet forces through mass meetings, and eye-witness accounts all concur that the response was overwhelming.

'The day surpassed all our expectations', recalled Lashevich, a Bolshevik soldier activist and delegate to the Petrograd Soviet. 30 000 showed up at the People's House.

> Anyone present at that meeting will never forget it. The enthusiasm of thousands of workers and soldiers was so great that one direct appeal and that entire human colossus would have left with empty hands for the barricades, for death.

When Trotsky spoke, 'one could actually feel the electricity in the air'.[14]

Although the reference to the barricades should perhaps be taken with a grain of salt, that the mood was positive is beyond doubt. Testovskii, another Bolshevik who spoke at two factories on Vasilevskii ostrov, notes: 'We spoke frankly before the masses of the coming seizure of power by us and heard only words of encouragement.'[15]

Non-Bolshevik observers, hostile to the insurrection, confirm this. According to Mstislavskii,

> The Day of the Soviet took place amidst a tremendous upsurge of spirit. Trotsky so electrified the crowd by his speech that thousands of hands rose in a single outburst of emotion at his call, swearing loyalty to the revolution, to struggle for it—to the mortal end.[16]

Sukhanov found the People's House

crammed with an innumerable throng. It overflowed the theatrical halls waiting for the meetings. But there were crowds in the foyers too, in the buffets and corridors ... [The mood] was definitely elated. Trotsky began to heat up the atmosphere. He described the suffering in the trenches. It was all a matter of mood. The political conclusions had long been known ...

Around me was a mood close to ecstacy. I felt as if the crowd would rise on its own and sing some religious hymn. Trotsky formulated some brief resolution, something like: we will stand for the cause of the workers and peasants to the last drop of blood. All as one raised their hands. I saw these raised hands and the burning eyes of the men, women and youths, workers, soldiers and typically philistine figures. 'Let this be your oath—to support with all your energy and by any sacrifices the Soviet, which has taken upon itself the great burden of carrying through to the end the victory of the revolution, of giving land, bread and peace!' The hands were still in the air ...

With an unusually heavy heart I watched this truly majestic scene ... And all over Petrograd it was the same thing. Everywhere final reviews and final oaths. Strictly speaking, this was already the insurrection. It had already begun.[17]

Even the defencist *Rabochaya gazeta*, which for months had been writing of the 'disillusionment' and 'apathy' of the masses, had to face the reality:

And so it has begun. The Bolsheviks gave the signal for the 'insurrection'. At the Sunday [22 October] meetings, the masses of soldiers and workers, electrified by the 'revolutionary' speeches of the Bolshevik leaders, vowed to 'come out' at the first call of the Soviet.[18]

On the face of it, it is hard to accord this with the appraisal of the mass mood, common to both right and left wings of the Bolshevik Party, that 'there is no such mood as in June', that the workers were not exactly tearing into the streets. Indeed, despite the resolutions and the enthusiasm of 22 October, they were to all appearances patiently awaiting an initiative from above.

The explanation lies partly in the changed circumstances that confronted the workers after the July Days. In setting out to demonstrate in early July the workers had in mind a peaceful transition of power to the soviets. It was a matter of pressuring the TsIK to declare itself the legitimate government. As Stankevich had told the Soviet back in April, all that was needed was a phone call from the TsIK, and the Provisional Government would be no more.[19] But after July no one could doubt that the transfer of power would require armed struggle, some degree of open civil war. Kerenskii would not hesitate to open fire, as he had clearly shown in July. He would try to disperse any Soviet Congress that decided to take power. This situation called for the deployment of armed forces, which in turn required planning, coordination and leadership. It could not begin spontaneously 'from below', as had the July demonstrations. At the start of October the entire Vyborg District had only some 5000 poorly trained and armed Red Guards. This then was not a time for the mass street scenes of February, April, June and early July. In July, the worst the workers expected was to return empty-handed. But in October all the cards were being played—failure meant a revolution drowned in their own blood.

The Bolsheviks, on their part, were doing everything to dissuade the workers from independent initiatives, warning at every possible turn against premature, unorganised actions. The Soviet had decided to observe 22 October in indoor meetings because it feared that even peaceful demonstrations could turn into a premature and bloody confrontation.

But this is still not the complete picture. The Bolsheviks were obviously not complacent about the workers' mood. Had it been merely a question of changed objective circumstances, they would not have shown such concern that the mood was 'not that of June'.

True, the workers were more united than ever in their desire for the Soviet Congress to take power. But desire alone would not establish soviet power. The workers would have to seize it by force from the Provisional Government and then fight to defend it. A closer analysis of the workers' attitudes reveals that the virtual unanimity displayed at the meetings did not necessarily signify a uniform readiness to act. For many workers, the problem posed by the July Days had still not been resolved.

One can discern at least four different 'moods' among the workers in relation to the insurrection. *Novaya zhizn'* caught something of this in an editorial comment on agitation being conducted in the factories calling on the workers to prepare to come out in active support of the soviets:

> The mood of the masses, in so far as one can judge it, is not characterised by any definiteness. A certain part apparently is prepared to come out. Another part is not in an especially militant frame of mind and is inclined to refrain from active steps. Finally, there is another group which has a negative attitude toward the coming out or a totally passive one. It is hard to say what the correlation among these three groups is. But the active group is hardly a majority.[20]

The hesitators indeed seemed to be the largest group, strongly for soviet power but with equally strong memories of July and little taste for bloodshed. They would not act until circumstances left no alternative. Hence Trotsky's stress on the inevitability of civil war and the generally defensive tone of Bolshevik agitation regarding the necessity of eventually 'coming out'.

On 21 October, Sukhanov was called out to speak at a meeting in the Petergof District. He arrived to find about 4000 workers standing in the yard of the Putilov Works under the autumn drizzle listening to a succession of speakers. Martov told him that they had barely allowed him to finish his talk. 'The mood is very strong. Of course, only a minority is active but it is enough to spoil the meeting.'

> I saw myself that the mood was strong. An SR, true, totally untalented, was unable to get even two consecutive words out. It was undoubtedly a minority acting, and even a small one at that—the local Bolshevik youth. The majority stood silent with a 'vigilant [*vyzhidatel'noe*—from *vyzhidat'*—bide one's time, literally, to wait out] and concentrated' look. The bearded ones were shaking their heads in a puzzled or distracted manner.
>
> These were the same Putilovtsy who had come out 30 000 strong on July 4 to give power to the soviets. They all without exception hated and despised the *kerenshchina* [Kerenskii's régime]. But they understood how the July Days had ended. Power to the soviets—an excellent thing. But a coming out? . . .

Sukhanov, who was well known to the workers from his articles in *Novaya zhizn'*, artfully began with a fierce attack on the coalition government. But no sooner did he state that a 'coming out' was unnecessary, than pandemonium broke loose, and he had to give up.

> Yes, I confirm that the mood was conditional, ambivalent. The majority were ready 'in their hesitation to abstain'. But the minority, capable of putting together an impressive fighting force, was undoubtedly eager for battle. At any rate, the fruit was ripe. No reason to keep waiting, not to speak of there being any possibility of doing so. The mood could not be better but it could decline. A ripe fruit should be picked. At the first success, the flabby mood would harden. If it does not end up in wild scenes of senseless bloodshed, all will support.[21]

Reports from the districts at the 15 October Bolshevik PC meeting give a similar impression of a large group of indecisive workers. Several speakers began by stating that 'the mood is extremely complicated' or 'it is difficult to appraise the mood'. The representative from

the Narva District (which in party circles included Petergof) agreed
with Sukhanov: 'The general picture is that there is no striving to come
out. Where our influence is great the mood is brisk [*bodroe*] and
vigilant [*vyzhidatel'noe*] ... The level of activity [*samodeyatel'nost'*] of
the masses had fallen.' In the Petrograd District: 'Where our influence
is strong, the mood is vigilant.' Rozhdestvenskii: 'The mood is vigilant.
If there is a coming out on the part of the counterrevolution, then we
will give a rebuff. But if there is a call to come out, then I don't think the
workers will go.' Vasilevskii ostrov: 'Military training is being conducted in the plants. There is no mood to come out.' And finally, the
report from the trade unions:

> There is almost not a single union where the mood in our favour has
> not grown. One does not observe any definite militant mood among
> the masses. If there is an offensive on the part of the counterrevolu-
> tion, then a rebuff will be given. But the masses on their part will not
> take the offensive. If the Petrograd Soviet calls for a coming out, the
> masses will follow the Soviet.[22]

The picture, in these districts at least, was clear: the worker rank and
file would not take the initiative but would respond if attacked.

Of course, as several speakers indicated, it was not easy to gauge
these attitudes, particularly since the possibility of an offensive action
was not being directly raised before the workers. In fact, until the
Bolshevik CC met on 16 October, no decision on an insurrection had
yet been taken. And even after it was decided, it seems that a large part
of the party rank and file was not informed. As for the Bolshevik
leaders, they continued rather demagogically to speak of a 'coming
out' largely as a necessary response to a possible (or very likely) attack
against the soviets or the Congress. Only Lenin did not mince words.
He directly called for an immediate insurrection in his letters published
in the Bolshevik paper on 19–21 October.[23] As Mstislavskii aptly put
it, while Lenin said 'necessary!', Trotsky said 'inevitable'.[24] Undoubtedly the defensive tone of party agitation was based upon the leadership's evaluation of the popular mood.

The traumatic memories of the July Days, when the Petrograd
workers suddenly found themselves isolated (even from a part of their
own comrades) and defeated by the support of moderate democracy
for the government, were a major factor in this indecisive mood. A
basic issue for the workers was how much support they could count on
in an action against the government. The left wing of the Bolshevik
Party was at pains to show how much the situation had changed in
three months: all the major soviets had been won over, the army was
just about ready for peace at any price and the peasant war was shifting
into high gear. The 'conciliators' were hanging in the air.

The moderate Bolsheviks and other internationalists, on the other hand, emphasised the workers' continued isolation from the rest of democracy, which was waffling to the left but could be frightened into the arms of reaction by a premature insurrection. Responding to rumours of an impending action, *Novaya zhizn'* warned the workers that the counterrevolution would do everything in its power to make it even bloodier than July. It would be a repeat of the Paris Commune. There would be no food. Furthermore, a bloody civil war would make it impossible to solve the problems facing the revolution.[25] Even among the workers and soldiers of Petrograd, the paper warned, only a small hot-headed group would come out. Support would be even weaker in the provinces and at the front.[26]

If the moderate internationalists believed that defeat was inevitable, though perhaps only after a protracted civil war, the defencist and census papers were so confident that a rising would be handily crushed that some even dared the Bolsheviks to try.[27] These ubiquitous Cassandra calls, which poured salt onto the still open wounds of July, took their toll of the workers' confidence. Sokolov, a Red Guard in the Petrograd Pipe Factory's detachment (and thus not one of the 'waverers'), recalled the night of 23–4 October when the Red Guards were placed on alert. They decided to spend the night at the factory.

> But I did not feel like sleeping. Many thoughts raged through my head, much was still not understood that is so clear now. The July Days stood out too vividly before my eyes. The hissing of the philistine crowd shook my certainty in victory.

The previous afternoon there had been a review of Red Guards at the factory. Among the speakers was a Menshevik who

> tried to frighten the workers with the untimeliness of the action. This time they listened more calmly than usual—all felt the gravity of the moment. The speaker, encouraged by this, said that the mass of workers would not come out. Finally the workers shouted: 'Enough!' And they shouted him off the platform.[28]

Sukhanov also emphasised the burden of the July experience:

> It was specifically in these weeks more than ever that . . . I went to the factories and spoke before the workers. I have a definite impression: the mood was ambivalent, conditional. The coalition and the existing conditions could be borne no longer. But should we 'come out' and should we carry out an insurrection? They did not know firmly. Many remembered well the July Days. It should only not happen again . . .[29]

The other major cause of hesitation was the economic situation. Naumov, a metalworker from the Vyborg District, told the Bolshevik PC on 15 October: 'The mood is depressed, there is a hidden dissatisfaction in the masses with the wage rates, the evacuations, the factory dismissals. The mood is exceedingly complex.' 'The mood has declined', it was reported from the Rozhdestvenskii District, 'in connection with the mass dismissals resulting from the evacuation of the factories.'[30] Schmidt made the same point in his report on the trade unions to the Bolshevik CC:

> The mood is such that one should not expect active [as opposed to defensive] comings out, especially in view of the fear of dismissals. Up to a certain point this is a restraining factor. In view of the existing economic conditions one can expect in the near future colossal unemployment. In this connection the mood is vigilant. All agree that outside the struggle for power there is no way out of the situation. They demand power to the soviets.[31]

The influence of the economic crisis was, thus, twofold. While it lent great urgency to the demand for soviet power, the fear of a general lockout and the rise to prominence of the workers' most basic material concern—their very livelihood—inclined them towards caution and away from bold initiatives.

Aside from the temporisers, another segment of the working class, drawn particularly from among the women, the unskilled and the recently arrived workers, was withdrawing from political life, growing indifferent to the seemingly futile debates surrounding state power and falling under the influence of anarchist direct-action agitation.[32] In a report at the end of September, the Narva District Menshevik organisation noted:

> In the worker milieu the interest in political phenomena has declined. Something like disillusionment is beginning: the masses are already not satisfied with Bolshevism. One observes a growth in the influence of the maximalists and the anarchists. In the worker masses there is not a trace of discipline.[33]

Kollontai, who was active among the women workers, warned the All-Russian Factory Committee Conference in October:

> I consider it my duty to make a declaration here on what is taking place among the women workers of Piter, as the most backward and undeveloped part of the working class ... Fear that indifference which now exists in the midst of the women workers.[34]

But the situation was in reality much more complex. Other reports from factories and districts whose workers had previously not shown particular militancy and who until recently had been strongly SR-defencist noted increasing political interest and activism and a 'brisk' (*bodroe*) mood regarding the seizure of power and possible 'coming out'. According to the Bolshevik PC representative from the Moscow District, where only the workers of the large leather and shoe factories had participated in the July Days: 'The mood is daring [*besshabashnoe*]. The masses will come out on the call of our party. The organs created in the Kornilov Days have been maintained.' In the Nevskii District, which had almost completely abstained from the July demonstrations: 'The mood is in our favour. The masses are beginning to prick up their ears.' And from the Obukhovskii Factory:

> Earlier ... [it] was a pillar of the defencists. Now a turning point has been reached in the mood in our favour. At meetings that we organised, 5000–7000 people came ... The factory will uncondi-tionally come out on the call of the Petrograd Soviet.

A similar report came from Kapsyul'nyi Factory in the Porokhovskii District, where 'until the Kornilov Days they had a preponderance of Mensheviks and SRs. Now the mood is ours ... The factory committee is fully prepared, in case of a call to come out, to lead the masses behind it.'[35]

Among the originally SR-defencist, and largely unskilled, workers, the time of their conversion to soviet power appears to have played an important role in determining the pre-October mood. Those like the unskilled workers in the Narva–Petergof District, who had partici-pated in the July Days, were becoming increasingly disillusioned with the political struggle. But others who had supported the coalition in July were showing new enthusiasm and energy. Here the movement for soviet power was still fresh. It had no directly experienced defeats or disappointments behind it.

This also helps to explain the generally more militant and decisive mood of Moscow's workers. Few workers had participated in the July Days in Moscow, which passed by scarcely noticed. But in October Moscow's new-found militancy presented a striking contrast to Pet-rograd. In Moscow the workers' resolutions spoke openly of the coming insurrection as an offensive action. No effort was made to tie it to an initial attack by the government or the counterrevolution or even to the opening of the Soviet Congress.

On 9 October, a meeting of Moscow Textile Workers' Union delegates and representatives of the factory committees voted for a general textile strike. Immediately afterward, the entire assembly proceeded to the Moscow Soviet, where it declared its readiness to come out to do battle for soviet power at the first call.[36] On 15 October a city-wide meeting of delegates of the Moscow Metalworkers', noting that the bourgeoisie was out to crush the revolution by means of an economic crisis and that the workers had to take upon themselves the task of organising the economy on a national scale, declared: 'All this taken together poses the following task before the proletariat: the seizure of power by means of an organised coming out through the soviets jointly with the poorest strata of the village.' The same meeting called on the Moscow and Petrograd Soviets to exert their revolutionary authority to end immediately all strikes, satisfy the workers' demands by decree and legislate the right of control over hiring and firing by the workers.[37]

The mood was similar among the Moscow rank and file. A delegate from the Gyubner Mill told a union delegates' meeting on 15 October that the plant's workers had mandated him to say that the Gyubner workers 'do not want to conduct an economic strike. But for political gains they are unanimously prepared to come out.' Another delegate proposed that the union at once break off negotiations with the owners and if necessary the workers should 'defend our rights on the barricades'.[38]

There were, of course, other reasons for this contrast between Moscow and Petrograd. For one thing, the Moscow Bolshevik leadership was speaking more forthrightly and was less subject to the waverings of the Bolshevik CC (located in Petrograd). In addition, events in Moscow did not bear the same national significance as those in the capital, where, for example, a decision by the Soviet to satisfy all striking workers' demands would have already meant an insurrection. But the parallels between Moscow's workers and the recently radicalised segment of Petrograd's working class suggest that the newness of the movement and the absence of the July experiences were more crucial factors.

But among the skilled workers of Petrograd, the great majority of whom had been converted to soviet power before July, there was also a significant resolute segment, again centred mainly in machine-construction and other skilled metalworking shops and factories. Although the mood in the Vyborg District (a centre of machine construction) was 'totally different from before', it was far from unfavourable to an immediate seizure of power. The PC report noted that 'in the masses one observes serious concentration and work. In the district a centre was organised without the knowledge of the district [party] committee. Its organisation occurred from below.'[39] With 18 per cent of Petrograd's industrial workers, this district put forth one-third of its Red Guards.[40] In the Kolomna District, with its three large shipyards, 'the mood is better than July 3–5'.[41] And among the

Finnish and Lettish workers, a largely skilled, urbanised group, 'the mood is cheerful ... The [Lettish] comrades will come out not on the call of the Soviet but of the PC. In the July Days our line was left.' 'The Finns feel that the sooner the better.'[42]

Many of these workers, in fact, demanded of the Congress of Soviets of the Northern Region (representing Petrograd, Moscow, Kronstadt, the Baltic Fleet and other northern towns) meeting on 11–12 October to take power immediately itself. On 12 October, the Kolomna District Soviet resolved to consider

> as a task that cannot be postponed, the immediate transfer of power to the hands of the Soviet W. and S.D. [The District Soviet] considers any delay in this a most serious crime against the revolution and proposes that the Congress of Soviets of the Northern Region put this slogan into practice.[43]

*Novaya zhizn'* reported that three delegates from the soviet appeared before the congress proposing that 'the Congress, having taken power into its hands, not adjourn'.[44]

At the 2 October session of the Petrograd Soviet, the delegate from the Russko-Baltiiskii Wagon-construction Factory read out the protocols of the plant's general assembly. According to *Novaya zhizn'*,

> From the protocols it is clear that the workers demand that the Petrograd Soviet explain to the proletariat and the garrison that the counterrevolutionary government of the bourgeois dictatorship is consciously challenging the workers to come out into the streets. They demand the immediate creation of a Soviet of the Northern Oblast', around which Finland, Kronstadt, etc. could unite.[45]

On 12 October, 2000 workers of the Old Parviainen Machine-construction Factory in the Vyborg District boldly announced: 'We will go out into the streets when we find it necessary ... We are not frightened by the battle which is near at hand and we firmly believe that we will emerge from it as victors.'[46] The workers of the Baranov-skii Machine-construction Factory in the same district on 11 October urged the Petrograd Soviet itself to 'take full military and civil power into its hands at once and declare the conspirators headed by Kornilov, Kerenskii and Co. to be outside the law and arrest them'.[47] These and other factories that showed similar decisiveness were often the same that had been the first to call for soviet power in the spring of 1917.[48]

Among the workers prepared for immediate decisive action, the Bolshevik workers undoubtedly constituted the largest single group. A month before the October Revolution the Petrograd organisation counted 43 000 members, of which Stepanov calculates that 28 250 were workers (and 5800 soldiers belonging to the Military Organisation).[49] Their attitudes towards the seizure of power can be gauged from the October meetings of the PC and from the Third City Conference of 7–11 October.

Opinion in the PC had completely changed since early September, when the majority had felt that the situation called for a peaceful route. Kalinin, who chaired the 5 October session, observed that the 'militant line of the majority striving for power is characteristic'. Even those who opposed an insurrection admitted there was no alternative. They argued rather that the time was not yet ripe, the chances of success not favourable.[50]

But these moderate voices were severely criticised by most speakers. 'I thought we were all revolutionaries here. But when I heard comrade Volodarskii and Lashevich [who opposed an insurrection], my opinion wavered.' 'The opinions expressed by comrades Volodarskii and Lashevich', commented another, 'are valuable, but there is something negative in them. They have become infected with the spirit of the Smol'nyi Institute.' (The reference is to the Bolshevik CC, which was consistently rejecting Lenin's urgent appeals to prepare an insurrection.) The delegate from Vasilevskii ostrov summarised the position in favour of an insurrection:

We can no longer say that we are in some sort of indefinite period. Our task: to find a line along which we can go with unfurled banners ... We are holding a course towards a socialist revolution. I remember the opinion expressed at the [July] Petrograd Conference, when it was said there will be attempts and also defeats. Why, we have built our entire tactic on the enthusiasm of the worker masses. Remember how, basing ourselves upon the workers, we overthrew the [Tsarist] yoke? You close your eyes to this. You speak of Lenin forcing events. You are wrong. Our aim is neither conspiracy nor to force events, but in any case we can achieve nothing through passivity. We ourselves do not depend upon our own will ... Forcing events is when you say: plan for the 20th. [Mentioning no dates, Lenin called to seize the most opportune moment.] The greatest mistake is not to pay attention to the counterrevolution. They are trying to provoke an unorganised movement. While we sit here and do not know whether or not to enter the pre-parliament, they are conducting pogrom agitation ... Events have unfolded in an historically inevitable manner. Our task is once more to raise the banner and go into battle. Otherwise they will call us out to battle, and then the outcome will be in doubt.[51]

While the record of the political debate at the City Conference has been lost, the resolution passed leaves no doubt as to where the conference stood. It concluded: 'All these circumstances say clearly that the moment of the last decisive battle which must decide the fate not only of the Russian but of the world revolution has arrived'.[52] Similarly, a meeting of Petrograd party activists at the time of the Congress of the Northern Region resolved:

> The continuation of the policy of 'amassing forces' ... would only lead to the disillusionment of the masses in the party of the re-volutionary proletariat and would lead not only to their refusal to further support the Bolsheviks ... but also to unorganised comings out by the masses, and in conditions of extreme atomisation and of general disorganisation ...
> Hopes attached to the Congress of Soviets are not well founded, inasmuch as solutions to the basic tasks of the revolution are expected from resolutions and not from the struggle of the masses ... As for the Constituent Assembly, even the most left composition of the Constituent Assembly cannot change anything without the direct and active support on the part of the worker and peasant revolution ...
> A defensive policy is incorrect. An offensive is needed to im-mediately root out the seeds of the counterrevolutionary government.[53]

Thus, while as late as 16 October the Bolshevik CC was still debating the issue, the Petrograd organisation had for some time already been insisting on an immediate insurrection. In his theses for the Petrograd City Conference, Lenin noted that 'in the *verkhy* [the upper levels] of the party, unfortunately one can observe a wavering, as if there is a "fear" of the struggle for power, a tendency to replace it with resolu-tions, with protests'.[54] He specifically appealed to the *nizy*, the lower party ranks, to put pressure on the leaders. Copies of his letters to the CC (which the latter kept secret) were distributed to the PC, the Vyborg and other district organisations. The Moscow organisation was of the same mind as that of Petrograd. Its 10 October City Conference instructed the MC 'to bring the revolutionary forces into battle readiness'.[55]

Of course, there were doubts among the party rank and file too. Malakhovskii, commander of the Vyborg District Red Guards, re-called:

> These [Lenin's] articles, this incandescent atmosphere, had the same effect on everyone. However, even in our district there were those who wavered, were cautious, wanting to appear prudent. Before the insurrection one of these waverers, comrade A. F. Kornev [a turner at Baranovskii], started dropping by for chats. Zhenya Egorova flew into a tizzy, fearing that he might sow confusion among us. But I

firmly assured her that the devil himself could not change our minds.[56]

Everyone was apprehensive about the prospects of an uprising. But these fears did not paralyse the will of the more militant workers.

The other organisation whose members were solidly on the side of bold action was the Red Guards. Sukhanov, who repeatedly insisted on the indecision of the 'average rank-and-file workers', felt compelled to add:

> This did not mean that the Bolsheviks were not able to put together, call out and send into battle as many revolutionary batallions as were necessary. Just the opposite. They were undoubtedly able to do this. They had sufficient numbers of developed active cadres ready for sacrifice. The most dependable were the workers and their red guards. Then the sailors were a fighting force. Worse than the others were the garrison soldiers ... There was enough fighting material, but only a part of the masses who followed the Bolsheviks were good quality fighting material. On the average the mood was strongly Bolshevik, but rather flabby and unfirm concerning a coming out and insurrection ...
>
> They had to place their hopes in the workers' red guards. But one could only depend upon their spirit. The fighting abilities of the men, who had never smelled powder or seen a bullet, were more than doubtful.[57]

Mstislavskii concurs that 'the sailors, the guards regiments and the red guards—particularly the red guards—rushed to the job'.[58]

This attitude among the Red Guards is not surprising. Membership was voluntary and at the time offered few advantages and many risks. Given the overwhelmingly negative assessment of the insurrection's chances in society, there is very little ground to suspect opportunistic motives among the ranks. Skorinko, the Putilov worker, was emphatic on this:

> The conduct of the red guards was above criticism. It is a lie and insolent slander that the red guards got drunk during searches, raped and looted. This did not occur. For at the time, being a red guard promised no material benefits. Just the opposite—given the growing strength of the reaction, it threatened serious troubles. Only conscious workers, dedicated body and soul to the interests of the revolution, joined its ranks.
>
> Just how highly the factory workers valued their red guards and looked out for their purity is shown by the fact that in certain shops of the Putilov Factory workers were elected by the general assembly

The author of these lines, not without pride, recalls how he was one of the delegates of the turret shop to the red guards.

And if a comrade was found whose presence in the red guards or whose casual conduct shocked everyone, he was expelled from their ranks in disrepute. Of course, I will not speak of the conduct of the red guards afterwards, when a mass of foreign elements [i.e. foreign to the working class] wormed their way into its honest ranks.[59]

Skorinko recalls waking up on the morning of 23 October to find his father, just returned from work, on the floor cleaning his rifle. He had tears in his eyes. Skorinko's mother was about to explode with anger.

'Your father in his old age has signed up with the windchasers. He won't beat his son for that. And now look what he is up to! Cleaning his rifle. What are you going to do, kill somebody?' my mother asked spitefully ... 'Everyone in the courtyard is laughing at you.'

Turning a deaf ear to these taunts, the father told Skorinko that Kerenskii had just shut down the Bolshevik press and was threatening to disarm the workers.

Accompanied by the weeping and the admonitions of my mother and the ironic looks of the other tenants, my father and I, our rifles over our shoulders, set off for headquarters, where we found extraordinary excitement.

At the headquarters under the tables, on top of the tables and next to the tables we saw a mass of workers whose interests had previously been limited to their family circle now fondly cleaning their rifles, barely keeping themselves from going to the centre to win their workers' power.

Everywhere conversations were in progress. But there were none of the arguments which are a necessity in conversation. To argue at such a moment, when unification was taking place on the other side of the barricades, this the workers felt to be dangerous. Among the hundreds of red guards, among whom there were both Mensheviks and SRs, there was such a community of interest on that day that my father, embracing me, remarked: 'Today I feel especially brave. And if everyone feels like me, then tomorrow there will be soviet power, that is—our own.'

'And if the next day we have to give it up?' jokingly remarked a company commander as he ran past.

'Never! But damn it, even for a day, but it will have been ours,' shouted my father, shaking his rifle and evoking enthusiasm from the crowd. 'If only for one day, we would show them how we take care of our property ...'

In the morning came the soviet's order to get into battle readiness.

During the reading of the declaration, I knew that to show our resolve to struggle for a communist society, we, the armed workers, would do anything. We were high spirited then and madly bold. Who now can doubt that?[60]

Ivan Peskovoi of the Shchetinin Aircraft Factory recalled that the mood of the plant's Red Guards was

so militant that each of us could hardly wait for the coming out. As for our military preparation, it was at the time beneath all criticism. Despite the fact that we had to move against trained soldiers, our revolutionary spirit conquered all.[61]

It was not certainty of victory that moved the Red Guards, but the conviction that there was no other way, mixed with a large dose of revolutionary enthusiasm and class pride, to die with honour, if need be, but not to live in shame.

The Soviet historian Startsev has analysed 3500 dossiers on Petrograd Red Guards compiled in 1930 for pension purposes. Although, as he himself admits, the sample is far from perfect—some had died by then, others had joined only in the days following the rising, and many members of the moderate socialist parties in 1917 would have preferred to report themselves as unaffiliated—nevertheless, the dossiers do provide valuable, if only approximate, information on the organisation's composition.

About three-quarters of the members were metalworkers. This figure appears less significant in light of the fact that about three-quarters of the male industrial work force were metalworkers.[62] The women who participated in the insurrection served largely as medics.

More interesting are the data on party affiliation. Although 69 per cent of the command positions in the sample were occupied by Bolsheviks, members of that party were actually a minority in the organisation as a whole—44.3 per cent.[63] The participation of non-Bolshevik workers is confirmed by much other contemporary evidence as well as worker memoirs.[64] It cannot, therefore, be claimed that the insurrection was strictly a party affair or that the Red Guards were acting out of party discipline.

Almost three-quarters of Startsev's sample were under thirty-one years old, 52.2 per cent were under twenty-six and 26.4 per cent under twenty-one.[65] 'As always', recalled one worker, 'the youth was in front, happy and satisfied.'[66]

The youth were indeed in the van. (This was true of the youth of all classes and their struggles in Russia.[67]) But it would be wrong to see the

Red Guards as a gang of young leather-jacketed toughs. For one thing, there was a very sizeable contingent of older workers. A little over one-quarter of Startsev's sample was over thirty-one years old and almost half were twenty-six and over.[68] Skorinko's father was forty-eight, married, with a grown son, his own apartment and even a lodger—hardly a shiftless adolescent. 'It was interesting', noted Peskovoi, 'to look at the composition of the detachment. In it were young workers about 16 years of age and old ones of about 50. Such a mixture made for great cheer and fighting spirit.'[69]

As for the moral character of the Red Guards in this period, besides Skorinko's testimony cited earlier, there is the account of V. Pavlov, commander of a detachment that left Petrograd for the civil war front in the south at the end of 1917.

The majority of red guards fought like devils. The quartermaster sergeant and the cooks left their kitchen during the battle to take up rifles. One of the cooks even commanded a platoon ... They fought amazingly bravely but were unable to adapt to local conditions. For example, they preferred to shoot when under enemy fire and did not take care against encircling movements or superior enemy numbers.

At first the red guards were very jealous of the honour of their organisation. They banished looters from their ranks, were very generous to prisoners, even to white guard officers and Junkers. But in the course of time, as they came into contact with the old army, this sense of honour gradually declined, the concept of 'war booty' appeared, shooting of prisoners—true, rarely, and on suspicion of espionage.[70]

This sense of proletarian and revolutionary honour sometimes manifested itself in strange ways. Malakhovskii, a soldier, paid tribute to the Red Guards' fighting spirit and daring, which he claimed even infected the reluctant soldiers. But from a military viewpoint they were totally unsuited for open battle.

On the attack and while running, many did not crouch down sufficiently, which caused many unnecessary casualties. We, the soldiers, in teaching them pointed this out. They replied that to bend over while running and to shoot while lying flat—these were a disgrace for revolutionaries and showed cowardice. We had to explain during instruction that there was no sense in volunteering one's forehead to the enemy.[71]

Militarily, such attitudes were a liability. But politically they were indispensable to the revolution. For without them this leap into the unknown could not have occurred.

This, then, was not the mob of lumpen elements so often portrayed in hostile accounts. Without citing sources, Melgunov (in 1917 a Popular Socialist, close to the Kadet left wing) writes:

It was not revolutionary cohorts of Bolsheviks that forced their way into the [Winter] palace but an ill-sorted mob, in the full sense of the word, with a mob's interests, excesses and violence, a mob aroused by the martial atmosphere of gunfire, powder and bursting shells. Hooligan elements looted the palace, elements which probably gathered at the palace with the whole demoralised 'okhlos', which some researchers of the revolution are inclined to place at the forefront of the events of October.[72]

Yet three pages later, he concedes:

Five days later a special commission of the City Duma established that the loss of valuable works of art had been small ... We must be objective. All the rumours of violence and reprisals that appeared in the socialist press and were later recorded in the journals, should be attributed to overwrought nerves ... This was corroborated by the Duma investigation.

Adamovich, who had been among the workers on the Palace Square on Bloody Sunday 1905, found himself in the same place on the night of 25 October. This time, however, he was a Red Guard and himself doing the shooting.

We burst into the palace, ran down the stairs along some sort of corridor. We entered a room—entered and gasped. We had never seen such splendour and luxury. Mirrors, gold, silver. One lad reached his hand toward a clock. He was yanked away. Someone gave him a box on the ear. Laughter and sorrow. We had entered a room and did not know how to get out. Worse than in the deep woods. We were lost and from behind new workers were pushing. We barely made our way out.
    A shot. What? From whom? By the wall, behind the sofa, a woman was lying—from the [Women's] Battalion of Death. We were already inside the room, and she is taking pot shots, the lout. We ran to the sofa, grabbed her, and she is biting and scratching like a wild kitten. There were ten more of them in the next room. Some in the closet, some under the table, one by the fireplace. They fell to their knees, shaking: 'We went for the sake of a crust of bread.' We let them get the hell out.[73]

Estimates of the number of Red Guards in Petrograd on the eve of the insurrection vary wildly from 10 000–12 000 claimed by a Soviet author in 1938[74] to 40 000 reported by Uritskii at the Bolshevik CC meeting on 16 October.[75] On the basis of archival and memoir materials, Stepanov offers the figure 34 000,[76] which tends to be supported by reports from the districts made to the Bolshevik PC.[77]

But even exact figures would not tell what proportion of workers were prepared to take up arms. The scarcity of arms remained a serious problem right up to the insurrection. A worker from the Schlusselburg Powder Factory told the Bolshevik PC on 15 October: 'Our red guard is organised, but people sign up unwillingly since there are few arms.' This complaint was general.[78]

Even so, there was no intention at this time of making Red Guard service universal. The constitution of the Admiralty Shipyard's Red Guards, passed at a general assembly, called for a detachment of only 200–300. The factory employed 2100 workers. Moreover, all Red Guards had to be without criminal records and 'as far as possible, literate, of irreproachable conduct, familiar with military matters and not younger than 18 years old'. It also stipulated that 'as far as possible', all 300 should be armed.[79] And, as Skorinko noted, in some places Red Guards were actually elected.

The mood among Petrograd's workers on the eve of the October Insurrection, as Naumov had observed, was indeed complex. The very keen desire for an end to coalition politics and for soviet power was practically unanimous. But a large part of the skilled workers, disheartened by the deepening economic crisis, hesitated before the harsh odds, the threat of political isolation and the spectre of defeat in a civil war. Many of the unskilled workers, especially among those who had demonstrated and tasted defeat in July, had grown weary of a political struggle that yielded no tangible results. They seemed indifferent to the entire debate.

In these circumstances, the presence of a resolute minority willing and able to take the initiative was critical. All that was required was for them to begin, to force the issue, to inject a new dynamism into the movement and to make it impossible to procrastinate further. The others would rally. Sukhanov was right: 'It was all a matter of mood. The political conclusions had long been known ... At the first success, the flabby mood would become firm.'

But without this initiative, the very powerful, commonly shared yearning for revolutionary change would have had little real impact. Political stagnation and economic misery would have completely demoralised the workers paving the way for the counterrevolution. In October the Bolshevik concept of the revolutionary party as the authentic vanguard of the working class was to be put to the crucial test.

# 5 The October Revolution and the Demise of Revolutionary Democracy

Technically, the insurrection began on the morning of 23 October as a response to government measures against the Petrograd Soviet and the Bolsheviks. (The immediate impulse behind the government's moves was the order of the Soviet's MRC (Military Revolutionary Committee) placing the garrison under its command.) On the night of 23–4 October the government shut down the Bolshevik papers *Rabochii put'* and *Soldat* for inciting to insurrection and issued orders to arrest Bolsheviks involved in anti-government agitation and to begin criminal proceedings against the MRC. At the same time, Kerenskii summoned troops from outside the capital (the garrison was fully under Bolshevik influence), posted Junkers (officer school cadets) at strategic points, ordered the bridges to the workers' districts raised and sent the cruiser Aurora, docked for repairs at the Franko-Russkii Shipyard, out to sea on a 'training cruise'. Telephone lines to Smol'nyi (which housed the Petrograd Soviet and the Bolshevik CC) were cut.

The MRC immediately went into action, beginning by reopening the newspapers. By the afternoon of 25 October, the entire capital, except for the Winter Palace, seat of the Provisional Government, was in the hands of the MRC acting in the name of the Petrograd Soviet.

At 2.35 p.m. Lenin made his first public appearance since the July Days, addressing the plenum of the Soviet.

Comrades! The workers' and peasants' revolution, the necessity for which the Bolsheviks have been speaking all this time, has been accomplished ... We will have a soviet government, our own organ of power with no participation whatsoever of the bourgeoisie ... The Third Russian Revolution must in the final analysis bring about the victory of socialism ... To end this war, intimately tied up with the current capitalist system, it is clear to all that we must defeat capital itself. In this we will have the aid of the world labour movement, already beginning to develop in Italy, Germany and France ... We must immediately publish the secret treaties ... We will win the trust of the peasants by a single decree which will destroy landlord landed property . . . We will establish genuine workers' control over production . . . Long live the world-wide socialist revolution![1]

This speech was received with a prolonged ovation, and a resolution of full support for the 'workers' and peasants' revolution' was passed.[2] Arsen'ev, a Menshevik–Internationalist delegate to the Soviet Congress from the Crimea, recalled that meeting:

> When Trotsky informed the Soviet that 'power had passed to the people', a thunder of applause followed. Then Lenin and Zinoviev came out. Such a triumph. Especially Trotsky's speech carved itself into my mind‚ . . . Each word burned the soul . . . , and I saw that many people were clenching their fists, that an unshakeable determination was forming in them to struggle to the end.[3]

The insurrection itself ended with the capture of the Winter Palace and the arrest of the Provisional Government after a siege lasting into the night. It was during this siege that the Congress of Soviets opened. Shortly afterwards, the defencist delegates walked out in protest over the insurrection carried out 'behind the back of the Congress'. They retired to the City Duma, around which a Committee for the Salvation of the Revolution and the Country was formed, consisting of representatives of the Duma, the old TsIK, the EC of Peasant Soviets, the defencist parties, the pre-parliament and some front army committees. This became the principal centre of organised resistance to the new régime.

While it is true that the insurrection began before the congress could pronounce itself, the defencists' sincerity in citing this as their reason for leaving is rather suspect. The TsIK had, after all, gone to considerable lengths to sabotage the congress, which it itself had called, and the defencists had practically disowned the soviets well before the congress. If their conduct at the Congress of Soviets of the Northern Region (which they also left) is any indication, they would have left in any case because they rejected outright the idea of a soviet government, regardless of how it came about.

In view of this, one is on very shaky ground in arguing, as some have, that the insurrection (and particularly its timing) was a major factor leading to civil war and dictatorship, which otherwise could have been avoided through peaceful political compromise.[4] On the other hand, it seems quite plausible that one of Lenin's reasons in insisting that the insurrection should begin before the congress was to present that body with a *fait accompli* to ensure there would be no wavering as well as to make certain of a split between the Bolsheviks (hopefully, along with the other internationalists) and the defencists. For Lenin, a coalition with defencists would be totally unworkable.

But one also cannot ignore purely military-tactical considerations, which were surely at least as weighty. Everyone, including Kerenskii, was quite certain the congress would meet with a Bolshevik majority and in all likelihood decide to take power. With power still in the Provisional Government's hands, the congress would have been a sitting duck. Of course, in retrospect the government appears to have been almost powerless. But this was far from the contemporary perception. In fact, outside of the Bolshevik Party and working-class circles, the common expectation was of an even bloodier and more permanent repeat of the July defeat.

In any case, it was a relatively small minority that left the congress. Remaining from the original 650 delegates were about 390 Bolsheviks, 90 LSRs, the Menshevik–Internationalists grouped around *Novaya zhizn'* (Martov's group voted fourteen against twelve to leave) and several smaller groups. (About eighty Mensheviks (of all shades) and sixty SRs had been elected to the congress.)[5]

After a recess, the congress reconvened on the evening of 26 October and passed a 'Decree on Peace', which proposed an immediate, democratic peace to all governments, at the same time summoning the world's workers to action, and a 'Decree on Land', abolishing private landed property for the exclusive use of the actual cultivators. Finally, the congress confirmed the new government, the Sovnarkom (Council of People's Commissars) consisting exclusively of Bolsheviks, the LSRs and Menshevik–Internationalists refusing to participate without the defencists (who at this point would not even hear of a government that included Bolsheviks). The congress closed in the early morning of 27 October.

### Attitudes towards the Insurrection[6]

Once the insurrection had become a fact from which there was no turning back, the workers gave it their overwhelming support. Their earlier hesitation and doubt had not been over the principle of a violent seizure of power. It sprang rather from fear of bloodshed and defeat. Therefore once it was underway, there was no question in the minds of the great majority of workers where their sympathies lay.

But it is perhaps easiest to deal first with the opposition. The extreme rarity of resolutions opposing the insurrection attests to its remarkable weakness.[7] Not unexpectedly, the main worker opposition came from the printers, traditionally a moderate voice among the skilled workers. The immediate issue they raised was freedom of the press, the MRC having closed the capital's non-socialist papers. But behind this lay a rejection of the insurrection's very legitimacy. On 27

October, the Delegates' Assembly of the Printers' Union resolved by a vote of 173 to 60:

> Taking into account that freedom of the press is an inalienable right of the proletarians and all citizens, that freedom of the press was won by the entire Russian people for the whole nation, that restriction of freedom of the press deprives the other parties, including the socialists, of the right to express their views, that the abolition of freedom of the press by sham representatives of the working class opens the way for counterrevolutionaries of all shades and makes pre-election agitation for the Constituent Assembly impossible—this meeting of delegates mandates the executive committee of the union to defend freedom of the press by all means up to a general strike.[8]

Resolutions refusing to recognise the 'Bolshevik government' were passed by the workers of the State Printing House,[9] the press of the Ministry of Internal Affairs, the Bulletin of the Provisional Government, *Delo naroda* and the Ekateringof Printing House, as well as by the Executive Committee of the Union of Cardboard Workers[10] and the workers of the Municipal Power Station on the Fontanka.[11] This exhausts the list of hostile resolutions.

However, what these resolutions signified in practice was revealed by events at the State Printing House (which, in addition to printers, employed a large number of unskilled paper workers). According to a report in *Pravda* in early November, at this plant 'part of our comrades have still not freed themselves from Menshevik–SR illusions about the "unity of all vital forces" '.[12] S. Gavrilov, a typesetter, recalled that 'from the first days of the revolution . . . Mensheviks and SRs sat firmly. Of 1200 workers, there were one or two Bolsheviks and a group of sympathisers.'[13] When the MRC sent S. Arbuzov, a Bolshevik carpenter, on 26 October to replace the Provisional Government's commissar at the plant, the workers and white-collar employees refused to recognise him. (According to Arbuzov, it was only a minority of workers, led by the clerical employees.) The factory committee requested time to discuss the matter and promised a response the following day. Arbuzov left.

But on 27 October, he received a report that Kerenskii's appeal to the population against the soviet government was being printed at the plant. He arrived to find twenty-three workers and the old commissar, the Menshevik Rybakov, with the stereotypes and 600 printed copies. These were seized and destroyed, touching off a strike. A meeting resolved

To consider this government not a government of revolutionary democracy but one of the Bolshevik Party of the Petrograd Soviet[!]. Considering the government illegitimate, we will support by all our forces the Committee for the Salvation of the Fatherland and the Revolution, in which all of revolutionary democracy is participating.[14]

According to Arbuzov, only 60 to 90 workers supported the strike. *Novaya zhizn'*, which was hostile to the new régime, at least partially confirms this:

As is known, dissatisfied with the insurrection, [the factory] decided to strike. One of the shifts on Saturday evening ended work early. The engineers decided not to work at all on Monday. After listening to speeches of many orators [on the need] not to intensify the split within democracy by isolated strike actions, both meetings [the factory committee and the Paper Workers' Union local] rejected the strike as a means of struggle against the adventurists . . .
    The attitude towards the government is most varied. There is no unity in this opportunist plant.[15]

On returning to work after lunch on 28 October, the workers (the white-collar employees stayed out until 30 October) resolved:

We, the workers, find the strike of white-collar employees [*sluzhashchie*] impermissible, since the lack of credit will call forth anarchy in the country, will further intensify the ruin and accelerate the collapse of the country.[16]

The significance of this incident readily emerges in a comparison with the conduct of the educated elements of revolutionary democracy, who embraced the strike as a legitimate weapon against the new régime. The worker opposition saw things differently. For them, actively to fight the new government meant not only to support the coalition government, for which they had little love, but also to aid the counterrevolution. For as the July Days had shown, a defeat of the Bolsheviks would also be a defeat of the working class and would pave the way for the counterrevolution. Indeed, at that very moment Kerenskii was on his way to Petrograd with an army of Cossacks led by General Krasnov, a known Kornilovist. Even the most hostile workers had to reject active opposition as harmful to their own interests.
    The same logic was at work among the railroad line workers, among whom a significant number were also opposed to the rising (in contrast to the workers in the railway depots and workshops). At the Moscow

Conference of Main Railroad Committees on 13–15 November, the representative of the Samara–Zlatoust Railroad reported:

> I will not say that our line consisted of Bolsheviks. In the majority it is against the Bolsheviks, but a collision is taking place – those who are against the Bolsheviks have to defend a government which does not satisfy us.[17]

The representative of the Libavo–Ramenskœ Railroad concurred:

> The first despatch from Petrograd was met by us in the most negative sense ... To suppress the rising of Bolsheviks we were prepared to come out with arms in hand. At the same time, a new government was being constructed, and we were not at all sure that the Committee of Salvation represented an organ that would save the revolution rather than the counterrevolution. If Kerenskii had received reinforcements and made war on Petrograd, we would not be meeting here now—we would be walking around at home up to our knees in blood.[18]

This was also Sukhanov's feeling about the Committee of Salvation. One of its 'sensible' members, a member of the old TsIK, proposed 'to assemble some troops and clear out those bastards [i.e. the Soviet Congress]':

> This was not just a mood, it was the programme of the Menshevik–SR wreckage ... Under the flag of the 'Committee of Salvation', the Mensheviks, united with the almost-Kadets Avksent'ev and Shreider [rightwing SRs], began work on the restoration of the *Kerenshchina* ... All these elements, a microcosm of the Democratic Conference without the Bolsheviks, were loyal allies of Kerenskii, who was marching on Petrograd in a Kornilovist offensive ... The *Kerenshchina* was realisable only through a *Kornilovshchina*. This, however, would have meant a real military dictatorship and the end of the revolution. But they refused to understand this.[19]

The main opposition to the insurrection from within revolutionary democracy came not from the industrial or even non-industrial workers but from the 'democratic intelligentsia'. Besides the employees of the state bureaucracies and the banks, especially the higher and middle levels (only a part of whom, of course, would have seen themselves as part of 'revolutionary democracy'), the following were some of the groups that came out against the insurrection and the new régime: the

Union of Draughtsmen, the administrative personnel of the Murmansk Railroad, the office workers of the Baltic Shipyard, the office workers of the DEKA Factory, the Executive Bureau of the Socialist Group of Engineers, the Council of the Petrograd Society of Journalists, the General Assembly of Teachers and Students of the Petrograd Teachers' Institute, the United Students of Petrograd and the Students of the Women's Higher Courses.[20]

The resolution of the Executive Bureau of the Socialist Engineers gives a sense of the intensity of the left intelligentsia's hostility towards the October Revolution:

> A band of utopians and demagogues, utilising the fatigue and dissatisfaction of the workers and soldiers, by means of utopian appeals to social revolution, through deliberate deceit and slander of the Provisional Government, has attracted to it the benighted masses [!] and, despite the will of the huge part of the Russian people, on the eve of the Constituent Assembly has seized power in the capitals and in certain cities of Russia. With the aid of arrests, violence against the free word and press, with the aid of terror, a band of usurpers is trying to maintain itself in power. The Bureau of the Socialist Group of Engineers, decisively protesting against this seizure, against the arrest of the people's ministers, against the order to arrest Kerenskii, against murders, violence, against the closure of newspapers, and persecutions and terror, declares that the acts of the usurpers have nothing in common with socialist ideals and destroy the freedom won by the people ... True socialists cannot give the slightest support either to the usurpers of power or to those who will not decisively and firmly break with them.[21]

One would be hard pressed to find such belligerence among even the most defencist workers.

The demand for a break with those who refused to break with the Bolsheviks (i.e. the vast majority of workers and soldiers, the 'dark masses') illustrates the political chasm that now divided even the left wing of the intelligentsia from the working class. In reaction to the October Revolution many state and public organisations in fact, split between the *verkhi*, who went on strike, and the *nizy*, who condemned their superiors as saboteurs. Such condemnation was expressed, among others, by the Union of Junior Personnel of State, Educational and Other Organisations; the workers and employees of the City Duma; the Union of Commercial and Industrial Employees; the Junior Employees of the Ministry of Education.[22]

It would be wrong, however, to attribute the widespread opposition of the left intelligentsia towards the seizure of power solely to the manner in which it took place. For like the defencist politicians who walked out of the congress, the vast majority of the socialist intelligentsia were opposed to soviet power *per se*, a position that expressed profound political differences with the workers dating back far beyond 25 October. In this regard, V. Polonskii's survey article on Russian *zhurnalistika* (journalism and periodic literature) as 'that collective physiognomy that until recently reflected the soul of our so-called intelligentsia, our spiritual aristocracy' is extremely revealing, all the more so since Polonskii himself was a Menshevik–Internationalist, hostile to the 'madness of Bolshevism'.

One could hardly find another group of people apart from the intelligentsia in whose thoughts and moods the revolution has wreaked such havoc. I have before me a pile of newspapers, magazines, brochures. Among the current material one most often finds the theme which is most prominent in our intelligentsia's consciousness: 'the intelligentsia and the people'. And as one reads, the picture that emerges is most unexpected. Until recently, the predominant type of *intelligent* was the *intelligent-narodnik* [populist], the well-wisher, sighing sympathetically over the lot of our 'smaller brother'. Now, alas: this type is an anachronism. In his place appears the malevolent *intelligent*, hostile to the *muzhik*, the worker, the entire dark toiling mass. 'Today's' are no longer striving, like the previous type, to fill in some sort of abyss separating them from the *muzhik*. Just the opposite: they want to set themselves apart from the *muzhik* by a clear and impassable line ... Such is the portentous and sudden shift that one observes. In literature it expresses itself exceedingly clearly. In a large number of articles devoted to the people and the intelligentsia, the people are treated as a benighted, brutal, greedy, unbridled mass, rabble; and their present leaders – as demagogues, worthless nullities, emigrés, careerists who have taken as their motto that of the bourgeoisie of old France: Après nous, le déluge ... If you recall what yesterday's defenders and advocates of the people have been writing lately about the rule of the mob [*okhlokratiya*], the extremely alarming fact of our present situation becomes indisputable: the intelligentsia has completed its departure from the people. The intelligentsia had just enough energy left to bid good night to the 'one who suffers all in the name of Christ, whose rough eyes do not cry, whose sore lips do not complain'. And it was enough for that eternal sufferer to rise to its feet, mightily to shrug its shoulders and take in a deep breath for the intelligentsia to feel itself disillusioned.

And it is not the excesses of the October Days nor the madness of Bolshevism that are the cause of this. The departure of the intelligentsia, the transformation of the 'populists' into 'evil-wishers', began long ago, almost on the morrow of the [February] Revolution.[23]

Although devoted mainly to the cultural intelligentsia, this article could easily be describing any segment of the socialist intelligentsia, including the scientific-technical and political. Of course, there were important exceptions in every group, but as a general characterisation, Polonskii's portrait was very much on the mark.

The great majority of Petrograd's workers greeted the news of the insurrection unconditionally. Resolutions supporting the action came from every type of factory – from long-time supporters of soviet power in the machine-construction plants of the Vyborg District to the relatively recent converts in the textile mills, the Nevskii District and even a significant number of printing plants.

Typical of the first group was the unanimous resolution of the Rozenkrantz Copper Foundry in the Vyborg District, which greeted

> the Revkom [MRC] of the Petrograd Soviet of W and SD for its steadfast struggle and also the Petrograd Soviet of W and SD and the All-Russian Congress, which has taken the path of struggle and not conciliation with the bourgeoisie – the enemies of the workers, soldiers and poorest peasants ... Comrades, take this path, as hard as it may be. On this path, together with you, we will die or be victorious.[24]

Of greater interest, however, was the support of the state factories that had been known as 'defencist strongholds'.[25] At the Promet Pipe Factory (whose work force was only about one-third adult male[26]), elections to the Petrograd Soviet held on 17 October gave the Bolsheviks 963 votes and the Mensheviks and SRs 309 and 236 respectively. Yet the general assembly of the day shift on 27 October resolved unanimously (with 18 abstentions) to

> greet the new popular socialist government and express our full confidence in it and promise it our full support in its difficult work of carrying out the mandate of the Congress. We protest against the formation by the SD Mensheviks and the SR Defencists of the National Committee of Salvation as an obstacle to the execution of these measures, which the broad masses of workers, soldiers and peasants await with growing impatience, and we express our full condemnation of the Committee of Salvation.[27]

The railroad workshops, long SR supporters, responded to the insurrection in the same way[28] as did factories in the largely female textile, food and rubber industries.[29]

Most telling perhaps was the considerable rank-and-file opposition to the stand of the Printers' Union. A joint meeting of the workers of the Orbit and Rabochaya pechat' Presses on 28 October declared:

We are deeply angered by ... [the resolution of the meeting of union delegates] and consider it unworthy of printers and protest against it in the strongest manner. We declare that a delegates' council that passes this sort of resolution cannot express our will but only that of the bourgeois oppressors of the people. Therefore we express our total lack of confidence in the Executive Committee of the Union, which purposely did not inform us of the meeting, and also in the Delegates' Council for its resolution, and addressing the proletariat of Petrograd we declare that we are together with you and not with this sort of Executive Committee and Delegates' Council.

Long live the Soviet of W. and S.D! Long live the revolutionary people! Away with traitors to the working class, such as the Rubins [who introduced the resolution at the delegates' meeting] and their likes.[30]

A revealing incident occurred at the plant where *Novaya zhizn'* was printed. The paper's 29 October edition published a protest by the editors against the action of the typesetters, who had prevented the publication of an order by Kerenskii as well as an address by General Krasnov to the Cossacks and a report of the City Duma. (The Menshevik–Internationalist position was one of neutrality.) The editors explained that they had not been present, and when the technicians objected, the typesetters summoned the district commissars.

On 30 October, the general assembly of the paper's printers, along with the workers of the Paris Printing House, resolved to condemn the conduct of the union leadership as 'unworthy of conscious workers and a disgrace', particularly its spreading 'false information on the activity of the MRC and calling the men and women workers to sabotage the decisions of the revolutionary government of workers and peasants, which forbade the publication of declarations of a purely pogrom character'.

We brand with disgrace the criminal activity of the 'executives', which leads to a split in our proletarian midst and which will aid only our class enemies ...

At a moment when the people are destroying the rotten roots of the capitalist system and giving power to the true representatives, we, the printers, cannot use our labour to print the 'orders' of Kerenskii, overthrown by the people, and therefore we recognise the activity of our comrade typesetters as correct. And if in the future our aid is required by the Revolutionary Committee, we are always ready to give it.[31]

Mounting dissatisfaction with the defencist majority of the executive soon led to their replacement with Menshevik–Internationalists and for a brief period after that with Bolsheviks.[32]

Despite the massive support among the workers for the insurrection, the defencist papers continued to write of the weakness and the isolation of the new régime: 'Look at the streets', wrote *Rabochaya gazeta* on 27 October. 'They are empty in the working class districts. There are no triumphal processions, no delegations to meet the victors with red banners . . . The Bolsheviks will hardly last a week.' Melgunov argues that 'mass participation by genuine [!] workers in the operation of October 25 cannot be claimed. Thus, on the morning of the uprising, work at the factories did not stop.'[33]

Yet not even the most biased Soviet historian writing under Stalin ever thought to claim that the workers were pouring out into the streets. There seems to be an implicit comparison here between October and the mass street scenes of February, a comparison that does not sufficiently take into account the very different circumstances of the two revolutions. February was a spontaneous movement that pitted masses of unarmed workers against armed soldiers and police. The role of the workers had been crucial as a *moral* force in winning over the soldiers and giving them direction. Once this was done, the revolution had practically been accomplished. For the most part actual street fighting was confined to the last two days and involved disarming the police, a relatively minor task. By contrast, in October the armed forces of the Provisional Government in Petrograd had already been won over to the Soviet before the rising. The insurrectionists' task was to occupy buildings and disarm the last supporters of the old régime. There was no room here for mass actions. Just the contrary: they might have provoked unnecessary bloodshed, which after the experience of the July Days could have had a seriously demoralising influence.[34] Moreover, given the eight months of frustration and disappointment, the disastrous economic and military situations, given the fact that October was to a significant degree an act of desperation, should one really wonder at the absence of triumphal processions?

But even more important, those who insist on the lack of mass participation choose to ignore that the leaders of the insurrection did not want the workers to come out. They actually made great efforts to ensure that the workers would remain at work. (25 October 1917 fell on Friday.) For example, the delegates' assembly of the Petrograd Woodworkers' Union unanimously voted, in view of the insurrection, to end their strike.

Each worker in these days must be at his place and in this way prove his dedication to the new régime. Order, restraint, calm and vigilance! We must go to work and at the first call of the new government come out to do battle with the enemy.[35]

An appeal to the workers signed by the Petrograd Soviet, the Petrograd Trade Union Council and the CS of Factory Committees appeared in bold type on the front page of *Pravda*:

> Strikes and demonstrations by the worker masses in Petrograd do only harm ... Production in the factories and in all enterprises is needed by the new government of soviets because any disorganisation of work creates new difficulties for us, and we have enough as it is. Everyone at his place! The best way to support the new government of soviets in these days is to do one's work. Long live the firm restraint of the proletariat![36]

Many writers hostile to the October Revolution are unable to reconcile themselves to the absence of the outer trappings of a popular rising. Yet the October Insurrection, perhaps best of all, shows that a planned, military-like operation can be a popular insurrection in the sense that it was embraced by the masses as their own even if their direct participation was not called for. Apart from the resolutions one really need look only as far as the 424 000 votes (45 per cent, up from 33.4 in August) cast for the Bolsheviks in mid November in the elections to the Constituent Assembly in Petrograd. And this was virtually repeated two weeks later when the Bolsheviks received 359 684 votes in elections to the City Duma.[37]

Sukhanov, whose editorials on the new régime were often harsher than those to which he had treated the Provisional Government, noted in his memoirs how for months after the insurrection the defencists continued to comfort themselves with the thought that it had been a military conspiracy and not a popular insurrection. But he points out that the broad masses

> had nothing to do on the streets. They did not have an enemy which demanded their mass action, their armed forces, battles and barricades ... This was an especially happy circumstance of our October Revolution, for which it is still being slandered as a military rising and almost a palace coup.
>
> It would be better if they asked: Did the Petrograd proletariat sympathise or did it not with the organisers of the October insurrection? Were they with the Bolsheviks? Or did the Bolsheviks act independently of their will? Were they on the side of the accomplished insurrection, were they neutral or against it?
>
> There are no two answers here. Yes, the Bolsheviks acted on the mandate of the Petrograd workers and soldiers. And they accomplished the insurrection throwing into it as many (very little!) forces as were necessary. No, excuse me. Through carelessness and clumsiness, the Bolsheviks threw in much more than was necessary.[38]

Some authors have pointed to the absence of ferocity and even the gentleness of the Red Guards towards their enemies as indications of the half-hearted support for the enterprise among even its active participants. This was indeed one of the most remarkable characteristics of the October Insurrection. An army officer, one of the defenders of the Winter Palace, gave this account of the 'storming':

> Small groups of red guards began to penetrate the palace [for the purpose of agitation among the defenders]. While the groups of red guards were still not numerous, we disarmed them, and this disarming was accomplished in an amicable way, without clashes. However, these red guards grew more and more numerous. The sailors and soldiers of the Pavlov Regiment made their appearance. A disarming in reverse began—of the Junkers, and once again it was done in a rather peaceful fashion ... [When the actual storming began] large masses of red guards, sailors, Pavlovtsy entered the Winter Palace. They did not want bloodshed. We had to surrender.[39]

Recalling the Red Guards' lenient treatment of White prisoners captured in the fighting at the end of October outside Petrograd, Skorinko wrote:

> Executions were alien to us. We looked upon demands for them with loathing. The workers and peasants had to pay for this later with their blood. General Krasnov, released on his word of honour, ran off to the Don and repaid our nobility in a manner befitting a general.[40]

Melgunov also reports a 'certain kindly attitude and embarrassment' in the relations between the arrested government ministers and the workers and sailors escorting them to jail. 'Guards and prisoners exchanged comments that developed into conversations ...' 'How will you manage without the intelligentsia?', Tereshchenko reportedly asked a sailor. [41]

Sukhanov and Melgunov interpret this as a lack of fighting spirit and determination. But this is to misread the atmosphere of the period. The main argument in the arsenal of the socialist opponents of the insurrection had been that it would lead to bloodshed and civil war. This had been the essence of the charge levelled at the Bolsheviks after the July Days. The forces of the insurrection had every reason to avoid unnecessary violence in order not to frighten away the wavering elements of revolutionary democracy. In their speeches on 25 October Lenin and Trotsky both made a point of stressing the 'exceptionally bloodless' character of the act.

Flerovsky, a Kronstadt Bolshevik on board the *Aurora*, recalled how on the fateful night of 25 October the crew 'decided to wait just another quarter hour [before firing on the Winter Palace], sensing by instinct the chance of a change of circumstances.' But Trotsky, who insisted on the popular nature of the rising, had little patience with this interpretation: 'By "instinct" it is necessary to understand here the stubborn hope that the matter would be settled by mere demonstrative methods.'[42]

That tolerance and even gentleness towards the foe could be, and were, combined with resolve to lay down one's life for soviet power is evident from the following episode at one of Moscow's hospitals. In Moscow, in contrast to Petrograd, the fighting had been protracted and the scales were tipped only by the arrival of worker reinforcements from the suburbs and nearby towns. One of the participants told the Moscow Soviet in early November that he had been mandated by 100 wounded fighters in Byelostok Hospital to insist firmly that the soviets take power. He then proceeded to thank

the Military Aviation School for the wine they sent us, which is being distributed [and] although it was meant only for the fighters for freedom, but since the Junkers and officers are lying among us, and in the hospital we say there can be no party distinctions, we decided among ourselves to distribute the wine and show the Junkers that the Bolsheviks are not so terrible. And when the doctor came and asks: What? Should I give some to the Junkers? We decided to do it, so that in case the Aviation School makes inquiries they should not have cause to complain against the hospital for giving presents to the Junkers.[43]

The terror and savagery of the civil war still lay ahead. Despite the intense class struggle, October appears as a period of remarkable tolerance.

### The Debate over a 'Homogeneous Socialist Government'

Any illusions that may have existed among the workers about the possibility of settling down to peaceful constructive work soon came up against a harsh reality. On the morning of 27 October, Krasnov's armoured train mounted with artillery arrived at Gatchina in the approaches to Petrograd. Meeting no resistance there, he proceeded the following day to Tsarskoe selo, less than an hour from the capital, where his forces easily scattered the Red Guards who had arrived from Petrograd. The 16 000-man local garrison, with no will for fighting, remained neutral. That night, in conjunction with Krasnov's campaign, the Junkers rose up in Petrograd. Also on 28 October Vikzhel, the Menshevik–Internationalist led All-Russian Executive Committee of the Railroad Union, presented the government with an ultimatum threatening a general railroad strike unless a 'homogeneous socialist government', a coalition of all socialist parties, was formed. Meanwhile, Moscow reported much bloodshed and an insurrection in serious trouble.

The fortunes of the October Insurrection seemed to have hit bottom. Malakhovskii, commander of the Vyborg District's Red Guards, recalled:

From the morning of the 28th news of our defeats at the [civil war] front began to arrive. There was an uprising of Junkers in Petrograd. For several moments despondency reigned at headquarters. The spectre of defeat appeared. Then we shook ourselves out of it. It was—it wasn't. At least there is something to remember, at least for four days we chased out the capitalist ministers.[44]

It was at this point that the issue of the Bolshevik government's isolation became the subject of very lively debate in the factories. 'Everywhere in the working-class districts', observed *Novaya zhizn*', 'in almost all the factories and mills, the current political events in connection with the creation of the Bolshevik cabinet and Kerenskii's troops approaching Petrograd are being heatedly discussed.'[45] The Menshevik–Internationalists and LSRs were particularly active in organising meetings in favour of a socialist coalition to pressure the Bolsheviks and the defencists to come to terms.[46]

It is worth stressing at the outset that not even the Bolsheviks, Lenin and Trotsky included, insisted on an exclusively Bolshevik government (though many, including these two, would have nothing to do with the defencists). Just the opposite is true: Petrograd's workers' organisations, by now virtually all Bolshevik-led, including the CS of Factory Committees, the Petrograd Soviet and the Trade Union Council, all urged the formation of a unified socialist government.

The problem was the vagueness of the word 'unity'. Although much bandied about, it left crucial questions unanswered: On what basis unity? And at what price?

Only two positions, both allowing for a coalition, had any real following among the workers. The one, advocated by the Menshevik–Internationalists and the LSRs, called for a 'homogeneous revolutionary democratic government' of all socialist parties from Popular Socialists to Bolsheviks. The other, that of the Bolsheviks, insisted on a soviet government, responsible to the newly elected TsIK. (The defencists were demanding that power be given to the Committee of Salvation or the City Duma until the Constituent Assembly. But they had very few takers among the workers.)

Although the Bolshevik position was quite straightforward, there was considerable confusion over the internationalists' demand. The internationalist leaders intended it not as a modified version of the existing government responsible to the TsIK but as an alternative to soviet power. They consistently argued that the soviets represented only a part of democracy. Significant elements were not attached to the soviets but organised around other bodies such as the cooperatives, dumas, etc. That part of democracy represented by the soviets was too narrow a base for a revolutionary government. It would be a dictatorship of one part of democracy against another.[47]

A related motive behind the internationalists' position was their rejection of a Bolshevik-dominated government. *Novaya zhizn'* made this clear in its comments on the Bolsheviks' decision to allow representatives of the parties that had left the congress as well as of Vikzhel, the Post and Telegraph Union and the socialist fractions of the Moscow and Petrograd Dumas to enter a broadened TsIK. These additions would, nevertheless, have left the Bolsheviks with a majority.

> The TsIK is the only source of power, with insignificant additions that guarantee Bolshevik predominance ... If it is merely a question of having as many Bolsheviks as possible, why change the government at all? Either the government is strong enough to rule in the desired Bolshevik direction—and then, why water down the 'proletarian dictatorship' with petty bourgeois?—or it is not. In that case there is need of an honest coalition with the 'philistine elements', at least on an equal basis.[48]

In sum, the Bolsheviks represented only the urban workers and even if they could obtain the passive support of the peasants, the régime could not survive on such a social basis. Moreover, this exclusively working-class base would inevitably push the régime into socialist experiments that would be disastrous in Russian conditions. But if the soviet government enjoyed the active support of the workers and the passive support of the peasantry, who was still missing? According to *Novaya zhizn'*, a revolutionary government had to have the support of the 'philistine elements', the middle strata of society, the urban petty bourgeoisie and the wealthier peasants, but above all, the intelligentsia, which had rallied to the defencist parties. Just as the defencists feared a break with census society, so the internationalists feared a break with the defencists around whom most of the 'middle strata' were grouped.

> At present, a purely soviet government can be only Bolshevik. But with each day it becomes clearer that the Bolsheviks cannot govern—they issue decrees like hot cakes and cannot carry them

into practice. Why cannot a government supported by the broad masses of workers and soldiers rule? The Bolsheviks say: sabotage of the intelligentsia led by the defencist parties. That is not quite exact. There is also the striking ignorance of the Bolsheviks in legislative affairs and state administration. Decrees read more like newspaper editorials. They do not tell what to do to achieve the desired goal ...

But let us admit that it is sabotage. Thus, even if what the Bolsheviks say is true, that the socialist parties do not have any masses behind them but are purely intellectual ..., even then large concessions would be necessary. The proletariat cannot rule without the intelligentsia ... The TsIK can be only one of the basic components of the institution before which the government is to be responsible.[49]

Among the Bolsheviks there was no disagreement over the soviet nature of the government or the necessity of vigorously pursuing the civil war currently raging outside Petrograd and in Moscow. (Menshevik–Internationalist neutrality was denounced as collusion with the counterrevolution.) But while the party's left wing began from the position that the defencists would sabotage any revolutionary programme and therefore negotiations should be rejected out of hand, the moderates and the centre insisted on giving them a chance.

The internationalists' demand for a homogeneous government (not responsible to the soviets) and an immediate end to the civil war (for which they tended to blame both sides equally) found support largely from three sources in the working class: small factories, mostly metal-working and printing; large state factories (mostly ordnance production); and a number of other factories employing mainly unskilled labour.

The workers of the small factories (up to 300–400 workers) had been among the less active and more moderate elements throughout 1917 partly for the same reasons as the printers, whose plants rarely employed over 150 people. The situation of these workers fostered in them a mentality that made it difficult for them to come to terms with the new régime's isolation from the 'middle strata' and to accept a civil war involving elements of democracy on both sides. The general assembly of the Atlas Foundry and Pipe Factory (with about 400 workers) resolved (with only five abstentions) towards the end of October:

1. We demand an end to this fratricidal war which goes on thanks to inter-party disagreements, which are leading the revolution to ruin.

2. We demand the creation of a homogeneous socialist government from the Bolsheviks to the Popular Socialists.

3. We protest against the seizure of power by the single party of Bolsheviks, whose tactics, along with those of the defencist parties supporting a coalition with the bourgeoisie, have brought the country to civil war.[51]

The large state factories in question all belong to the Main Artillery Authority—Arsenal,[52] Orudiinyi,[53] Patronnyi[54] and Kapsyul'nyi.[55] All had been traditionally moderate and only recently had abandoned defencism. The resolution at Kapsyul'nyi was sponsored jointly by the local Bolsheviks, LSRs and Menshevik–Internationalists and demanded a united socialist government and the end to civil war within democracy. The Arsenal workers declared that they would consider counterrevolutionary any party that refused to enter into such an accord. A meeting on 30 October at Patronnyi elected a delegation to the Vikzhel-sponsored negotiations and mandated them to demand an end to the fighting and an immediate accord. In vain the Bolsheviks attempted to persuade the meeting to specify the basis for such an accord, i.e. the composition of the body before which a coalition would be responsible. (This, of course, was the chief bone of contention at the negotiations.)

The remaining resolutions were from three paper mills, Vargunina, Shapovskaya and the Belgian Paper Mill,[56] the Pal' Textile Mill,[57] Nevskii Stearine Works[58] and the Siemens–Shukkert Electrotechnical Factory[59] (built during the war and producing mainly artillery ordnance). Three of these factories, Vargunina, Pal' and Nevskii Stearine (as well as Atlas, mentioned earlier), were located in the Nevskii District, which became the centre of opposition to the soviet government in the spring of 1918.

If those resolutions are any measure—and all sides went to great efforts to publish the statements of their supporters—support for the internationalist position on power was rather modest. Moreover, not even all of these workers were able to embrace the internationalists' neutrality. While the Odner workers insisted on a government 'resting on the Bolsheviks, Mensheviks and SRs', they added that 'a victory of Kerenskii's troops would have a ruinous effect on the revolution's achievements'. The Arsenal resolution concluded: 'In view of the movement of Cossack troops against Petrograd, we consider the most energetic defence of Petrograd to be necessary.'

The main reason for this weak response was that the internationalists' appeal for unity—which did indeed strike a responsive chord among the workers—was not premised upon soviet power: unity at the expense of this most basic demand was simply meaningless to most workers. During the discussion in the Bolshevik CC over whether to allow the inclusion of elements not represented at the Soviet Congress into an enlarged TsIK, the PC's representative insisted that 'for the masses the issue of this plan has already been decided, and there is no need to speak of any broadened soviets'. He recommended that the CC keep the will of the masses in mind and reject any changes in the TsIK.[60] Proshyan noted the same thing when the LSRs' TsIK fraction met to discuss Vikzhel's proposals (which would have given the defencists a slight majority): 'This plan is the result of intellectual flabbiness, a retreat before the horrors of civil war, which they are trying to stop at any price.' He insisted, however, that a coalition was still possible on the basis of responsibility to the soviets, 'since the mood of the workers should make the defencists ready for greater concessions'. He was seconded by Levin and Emel'yanov:

> The masses would see this [Vikzhel's] accord as a rejection of their slogan and would get the impression that everything they have been fighting for is being ceded without a struggle by the leaders of the movement.[61]

In an editorial entitled '2×2=5' in *Novaya zhizn'*, Bazarov recognised that the workers most often coupled the call for unity with insistence on soviet power. But he misinterpreted this as confusion resulting from a lack of political sophistication.

> At certain factories at the present time, resolutions are being passed which demand simultaneously a homogeneous democratic government based upon an accord of all socialist parties and the recognition of the current TsIK as the organ before which the government should be responsible.
> The Bolsheviks, who have overwhelming influence among the Petrograd proletariat, never bothered to teach them political arithmetic. The basic rule of parliamentary arithmetic is that the executive power belongs to the party that predominates in the institution to which the government is responsible or else it is formed by all the parties in that institution proportionately to their representation there ... At present, such a government can be only Bolshevik.[62]

There does appear to have been some confusion among the workers, particularly those demanding a homogeneous socialist government. But it was of a different sort than Bazarov imagined. For there was still a quite widespread belief that the split between the socialist parties was the product of personal and organisational rivalries involving only the leaders and having little to do with issues of principle. A worker from the Schlusselburg Powder Factory took 'our socialists' to task in *Znamya truda* for continuing to fight over who should be given power, the Bolsheviks or the SR Defencists, disregarding what is taking place around them, where the best forces of the workers and soldiers, who have decided to die or achieve victory, are perishing while you, the 'leaders of the Russian Revolution', continue to haggle. It is time that you came to your senses and end the strife ... Where is the rest of revolutionary democracy, the revolutionary proletariat, the toiling peasantry and soldiers, who, exhausted, sit in their dugouts? ... That is where power should be, but not in the current parties, not in the discord of their 'leaders'. And you should recognise this if you are true socialists and say sincerely to the people: yes, we were wrong. The Soviet of WS and PD should take power ... and you must carry out its will in the specified direction.[63]

The brunt of this letter is nevertheless directed at the defencists.

On 31 October, the general assembly of the Obukhovskii Factory sent a delegation to the Vikzhel negotiations to demand an end to the fighting. According to Kamkov, who witnessed the incident, the delegation presented an ultimatum stating that 'if by the morning an agreement is not reached, the workers will start fighting amongst themselves but will first knock off [*pereb'yut*] all the leaders'. It then read out the general assembly's resolution:

> The meeting discussed the situation and found that there could be absolutely no return to the old coalition government in this country. We resolve to consider such a state of affairs [the split in revolutionary democracy] criminal and propose to all workers, regardless of party affiliation and political convictions, to influence their political centres in the direction of an accord among all the socialist parties and the formation of a socialist government on a proportional basis and *responsible to the Soviet* [my emphasis] on the basis of the following platform: (1) immediately propose peace; (2) land to the local land committees and abolition of private property in land.[64]

There was nothing here, in fact, that the negotiators on the Bolshevik side objected to. (On the other hand, as already noted, this was not Lenin and Trotsky's position. They had purposely absented themselves from the CC session that decided to participate in the negotiations.) There is no reason to doubt the sincerity of Kamenev's response:

> Tell the Obukhovtsy that the TsIK [with its Bolshevik majority] stands on the same platform as you are proposing. The TsIK stands for an accord and therefore it sent its representatives to the Vikzhel conference, and if the first groups [the defencists] agree that the

government should be responsible to the TsIK of the All-Russian Soviet, then an agreement can be reached.[65]

Besides the workers' attachment to soviet power, another source of weakness in the internationalists' position was its neutrality in the civil war, which few workers would tolerate, let alone support. The workers in Petrograd's railroad workshops and depots simply labelled their union executive as counterrevolutionary. A meeting of 1090 workers of the locomotive workshops of the Nikolaev Railroad resolved unanimously

> to express our lack of confidence in Vikzhel for its clearly counter-revolutionary policy [and] to express full confidence in the All-Russian Congress of Soviets of WS and PD, the true expression of our interests and which fully defends the happiness and power of the people. The meeting calls on all our comrade railwaymen to rally around their proletarian organisations and sends its greetings to the Petrograd proletariat, which is shedding its blood, and says: Comrades! We are with you![66]

This, and other resolutions like it, were not mere words. The workers were quite prepared to act. At the Conference of Railroad Committees in mid December 1917 (a body on the whole hostile to the Bolsheviks), the delegate from the Nikolaev Railroad reported on a meeting of the workers of the First and Second Districts which resolved:

> Upon full clarification, we recognise the activity of the main railroad committee as supporting Vikzhel and hence Kerenskii ... If in its activity it does not enter into the struggle against Kerenskii's troops, then we will arrest it.

The delegate continued:

> Certain people at the meeting insisted that it was necessary to support Vikzhel's position and thus spare the fatherland from bloodshed. And the workers of the workshops arrested them.[67]

The delegate from the Moscow Committee reported that

> In the workshops and among the workers we saw a force such that if we did not adhere to the Bolsheviks, then a settling of scores would take place with the main railroad committees. On certain lines there was an attempt by workers, having organised into Red Guards, to take active steps toward arrests and even executions.[68]

Neither actually took place, however, because Vikzhel's threatened strike met with very little response in Petrograd and Moscow, not least, according to the conference speakers, because the railroad committees feared the workers.

In reality, the main and truly consistent support for the internationalists' position came not from the workers but from the soldiers and white-collar (clerical, technical and managerial) employees and certain non-industrial unions that included white-collar (and managerial) personnel. Towards the end of October, a strong movement arose in the Petrograd garrison aimed at forcing an end to the civil war outside the capital through negotiations between the belligerents. Various units urged the MRC to allow them to send delegations for talks with Krasnov's troops.[69] Except for the Guards' regiments, there was little stomach for fighting.

In contrast to those workers who supported the internationalists, the white-collar employees' neutrality was heavily weighted against the Bolsheviks. For example, the draughtsmen at the Putilov Works passed the following resolution:

> As involuntary witnesses to the seizure of power by the Bolsheviks and to the fratricidal war that is taking place, we express our strong protest against that party which has led to this bloodshed and we join those socialist parties that stand for an immediate end to the civil war and the formation of a socialist government on an equal basis for all socialist parties.[70]

The Vyborg District Soviet put forth a vision of unity and the means to achieve it that was very different from what was being offered by the Menshevik–Internationalist and LSR leaders, and, as it turned out, much more in keeping with the workers' own inclinations. Significantly, this resolution was endorsed by all three party fractions in the soviet.

> Steadfastness, courage, unity! Comrade workers! We ... consider it our duty to address you with an appeal to end party quarrels and strife – this is not the time for it, when the blood of workers who stand behind the same lathes as you is flowing, when discord among us is a mockery over their bodies ...
>
> Why do we create hostile camps in our worker family? Who of us does not understand that discord among us is necessary for the counterrevolution? Who among us has not made clear to himself that the bourgeoisie, having enlisted the support of *those who have broken away from the revolutionary proletariat* [emphasis added], is leading the suppression of the revolutionary movement? No one, of course. Comrades, among us there are not and cannot be enemies of

the working class, enemies of themselves; among us there are not and cannot be traitors, because that would mean to betray oneself . . .

Think well. Do not attach any significance to trivialities such as party disputes at the present moment. It is not a matter of parties now but of the fate of the revolution, the fate of the proletariat; it is a matter of securing for ourselves an end to the world slaughter; it is a matter of ourselves and our families not swelling up and dying of hunger – that is what the counterrevolutionaries who oppose us want. Thus, can it be that you will help them to ruin our children? No, a thousand times no! The worker is not as dull-witted and stupid as the traitors think. He has suffered. Suffered too long. But the cup of patience is overflowing. We have no more strength to stand as silent witnesses to our ruin, no more strength to waste time on talk when it is actions that are needed . . .

All as one defend our just workers' cause and we will win, we will win despite the net of treachery cast before us, we will win despite the gnashing of our enemies' teeth, we will win if we have unity of the socialist forces of the proletariat.

Away with fratricidal strife! Long live the united working class! [Signed] Fraction: SRs, SD Mensheviks, SD Bolsheviks and the Vyborg District Soviet of W and SD.[71]

This too was an appeal to unity, but unity from below and on the soviet side in the civil war. And there is no doubt who the 'traitors' who have 'broken from the revolutionary proletariat' were.

The great majority of Petrograd's workers rejected neutrality and gave unconditional support to the new soviet government. But while the more moderate of these workers expressed the desire for a socialist coalition that would include the defencists (but would nevertheless be responsible to the soviets), others limited themselves to urging the internationalists to join the government or were totally silent on the need for any change.

Typical of the first group was the following resolution:

We, the workers of the Putilov Shipyard, numbering 3600, having heard reports by comrade Pavel Suvorov, member of the Soviet of W and SD, on the current moment, have reached the following decision:

Considering an agreement of the socialist parties desirable, we . . . declare that an agreement can be reached on the following conditions:

[1–3. Dismissal of anyone participating in the political strike or refusing to submit to the MRC; that the government's programme be based upon the Congress decrees on land and peace and the draft decree on workers' control.]

4. We ask all those who stand for the workers', soldiers' and peasants' cause to censure those leaders who from purely factional and personal motives abandoned the Congress of Soviet on October 25, thus desiring to splinter and split the united front of workers, soldiers and peasants. Therefore, having decided that henceforth there should be no party or fractional disagreements in our midst, we all, as one, will defend to the last drop of blood our new Revolutionary Government—the Congress of Soviets of WS and PD and the MRC created by it; and all other organisations, such as the Committee to Protect Public Safety and party groups that do not desire to submit and work in close unity with the All-Russian Congress of Soviets, do not enjoy even the smallest degree of our support and will meet in all their actions opposed to the Congress of Soviets with our decisive and unanimous resistance. Having abandoned the Congress, they have gone against the workers, soldiers and peasants. Instead of the slogan of unification, they try to introduce fragmentation and internal strife.

5. We ask all democracy to struggle mercilessly against the counter-revolution (Kerenskii, Kornilov and Kaledin).

6. We ask all democracy, in the name of the liberation of the people, to recognise the Second All-Russian Congress of Soviets of W and SD with the participation of the peasants as the sole source of power.

7. We demand a government responsible solely to the TsIK.

8. Total rejection of representation in the TsIK of organisations that are not represented in the soviets.[72]

Judging by the PC reports from the districts on 29 October, this position was especially prevalent in the Nevskii, Porokhovskii and Narva Districts. In the first, the general mood was the following:

1. For an agreement with the socialist parties on a socialist government proportionate to the representation in the TsIK formed by the Congress of Soviets, responsible to the soviets and with our slogans.

2. Take measures to liquidate the civil war in a peaceful manner. At present, defence against the attack of the troops led astray by Kerenskii.

In Porokhovskii, 'one observes a certain desire for an agreement, but not at the cost of retreats from our demands ... They unswervingly demand a government of soviets, no concessions.'

In the Narva District

signs of a certain fatigue are beginning to show. Blood is completely unmentioned, as its shedding is considered normal in war. There is bitterness toward the Cossacks. The attitude toward an accord is seen from the viewpoint of safeguarding the gains of the October Revolution. Given the smallest possibility of conceding anything and the attitude is strongly negative. There exists a significant desire for an agreement, inasmuch as it will end the [civil] war while keeping our gains.[73]

To sum up these reports, there was a significant amount of sentiment in these districts for a socialist coalition and for a quick and peaceful end to the fighting, but not at the expense of soviet power. In the meanwhile, however, support for the existing government was unconditional.

But not all workers were still disposed to cooperate with the defencists. The report from the Moscow District went:

The attitude toward a coalition with the internationalists is positive, inasmuch as the latter stand firmly on the platform of the Second Congress. With the defencist element—negative. There is some sentiment for, but all the same on the platform of the Congress.[74]

and Rozhdestvenskii:

The mood is very enthusiastic about the new government as long awaited. If the government conducts negotiations with the defencists and at the same time the forces of the enemy regroup, then the workers will take a negative attitude toward everything. The position on a coalition—only with the internationalists.[75]

'In the localities', reported the delegate from the Petrograd District, 'they are angry at the negotiations with the Mensheviks and SRs.'[76]

The defencists' action in leaving the Soviet Congress lost them what credit they had managed to retain among the workers. To workers who identified so strongly with the soviets, this was tantamount to a break with the working class. The defencists' participation in the Committee of Salvation only seemed to confirm this. The Petergof District Soviet, while noting the desirability of sharing governmental responsibilities with other parties, was firm on this point:

At the same time we condemn in the most categorical manner all those who left the Congress, placing themselves in the position of deserters from the revolution and new allies of the hidden and over revolution.[77]

Many meetings, however, were totally silent on the desirability of a coalition. This could scarcely have been an oversight since all the workers' organisations were calling for a coalition and the loca internationalists would certainly have raised the issue. Yet the list of such resolutions is quite impressive.[78]

In view of the predominantly defencist attitudes among the women workers before July, their strong representation in this group is quite striking (although much of the internationalists' support also came from women workers). In fact, the rank and file of the Textile Workers' Union had a spirited run-in with their executive over the latter's less than unconditional support for the new government during the crisis at the end of October. Along with the Petrograd Trade Union Council, the Executive of the Textile Union had published a resolution calling for a socialist coalition 'from Bolsheviks to Popular Socialists' responsible to the TsIK on the basis of the programme of the Congress. An angry meeting of union delegates on 26 November took their executive to task, not so much for demanding a coalition with the defencists (though they were clearly not happy about that) but for its failure to give the Sovnarkom its full support while the negotiations were going on. In particular, it had failed to hand over the 4000 roubles collected in the mills at the start of November for the MRC and the new TsIK. 'While we decided to give the money of that part of the proletariat that had declared a merciless struggle against capital', declared one delegate, 'the executive committee found it too difficult to give the pennies collected from the workers to [the representatives] of this proletariat'. 'Shame for this conciliationist policy!' admonished another.

For its part, the executive explained that its resolution had included all the basic demands of the workers. As for the call for a coalition of all socialist parties, this was made at a time when an accord seemed possible. It was an attempt to pressure both sides to unite against the counterrevolution. Now that an agreement was clearly impossible, it unconditionally supported the government. The money, it was rather lamely claimed, had been held up because the first meeting of the executive had lacked a quorum, while the next meeting decided to postpone discussion of the issue.[79]

The preparatory meeting of the Conference of Women Workers on 5 November, whose 500 delegates claimed to represent 80 000 workers, also censured the Bolshevik and internationalist leaders who had withheld full support from the new government and in particular condemned the Bolshevik leaders who had resigned their posts. (On 1 November, the Bolshevik CC reversed its decision to participate in the Vikzhel negotiations, resolving to bring the talks to an end on the grounds that they were impractical. Five of its members who were People's Commissars as well as several minor officials resigned their posts, vowing to carry their position to the masses. A few days later Zinoviev wrote: 'We left the party to force an agreement, but the other side refused. We received much criticism from comrades and worker delegations.'[80]). The meeting called on all socialist internationalists not to sabotage the peasant [!] revolution, to work in a united revolutionary front in all soviet organisations, and it declares to the People's Commissars and the internationalists who have left that the proletariat will not forgive desertion from the field of battle when the worker–peasant government needs a total effort for the great battle with the capitalists.[81]

A part of the workers, at least, was well to the left of the leaders.

The Petrograd Bolsheviks themselves reflected the same gamut of opinion as the worker masses, although the party rank and file on the whole tended more unanimously towards outright rejection of the defencists as coalition partners and of any concessions on the composition of the TsIK. Thus, without directly challenging the CC, the general assembly of the Vyborg District organisation of 1 November declared: 'No conciliationism nor agreement with parties and groups that strive to undermine the proletarian–peasant revolution by conciliationism with the bourgeoisie.'[82]

This resolution by the Vyborg District closely echoed the position taken by the PC on 29 October when it discussed the decision to participate in the Vikzhel talks. There was strong opposition at this meeting to the CC, and the resolution it adopted insisted on a soviet government, passing over in total silence both the issue of the negotiations and the desirability of a coalition.[83] When the PC reconvened on 2 November to discuss the latest developments, particularly the defencists' rejection of governmental responsibility to the soviets, it was reported that representatives from the Moscow Committee were meeting with the CC and still insisting on an accord with the defencists. Moreover, the LSRs were threatening to withdraw from the TsIK if a coalition were not formed. (When the TsIK hardened its position on 1 November, voting 40 to 31 against the inclusion of delegates of organisations not represented in the soviets, the remaining Menshevik–Internationalists walked out and the LSRs presented their ultimatum.) The meeting, fearing that the CC, which was anyway too moderate for its liking, might cave in and reverse its decision to end the negotiations, immediately despatched a delegation to the CC to warn against any retreat from exclusive soviet power. Fenigshtein summed up the majority sentiment:

The fact that the Menshevik Internationalists left yesterday and today the LSRs threaten to leave does not change the issue. It is not a question of an accord, but of the character of the Russian Revolution . . . If we accept an accord with the defencists, they will introduce changes that will be directed against a worker-peasant government. By their entire conduct they demonstrate [that they believe] it is necessary to bridge between the proletarian–peasant revolution and the bourgeoisie.[84]

The meeting voted to support the TsIK's position (opposing the inclusion of non-soviet elements in the TsIK).[85]

The PC, however, was not unanimous. At a meeting of the Bolshevik committee of the Second City District on 4 November, it was reported that under the impact of the LSR ultimatum, Kamenev had succeeded in persuading the TsIK to retreat and agree to the inclusion of fifty new members from among the socialist deputies of the Petrograd Duma and the reduction of the Bolsheviks to 'at least 50%' of the portfolios in a coalition government. This latest development had divided the PC, some members fearing the isolation of an all-Bolshevik government and others refusing to retreat from soviet power.[86]

The lower ranks of the party, however, were much more unified. Of the ten who spoke at this meeting of the Second City District (at least half of whom were workers), all rejected concessions on exclusive soviet power.[87] Other districts responded in the same way. The general assembly of the Narva District Bolsheviks justified the party's 'finding itself in power [alone]' by the defection of the defencists and the LSRs' refusal to enter the government. Any accord that might undermine the party's platform and the revolutionary activity of the government was decisively rejected. Turning to the moderate opposition in the CC, the meeting resolved:

> No wavering on the part of the leading bodies of the revolutionary party. We declare to the commissars and members of the CC, Kamenev and Zinoviev, who have resigned, that the working class will not forgive this desertion from responsible posts in so grave a moment.[88]

The resignations were also condemned by the party organisations of the Rozhdestvenskii, Lesnoi and Liteinyi Districts, though the latter two, which were small and non-industrial, favoured a broad coalition.[89]

A special Fourth City Conference of Petrograd's Bolsheviks that met on 4 November sided squarely with the left of the CC:

> Our party needs not the cooperation of the petty bourgeois groups but the unreserved support of the toilers. Such support is guaranteed to our party on the condition that its leading institutions, while drawing into the soviet government and organs all vital elements standing outside the party, at the same time categorically rejects unprincipled conciliations with political and professional élites [*verkhushki*], whose interests are totally inimical to the proletarian–peasant revolution.[90]

As before October, the lower ranks of the party were to the left of the CC (and, for that matter, of the PC). And as in April and on the eve of the insurrection, the left minority of the CC was able to carry the majority with it not so much because of Lenin's great authority or 'charisma' (which had not prevented the CC from suppressing his letters before the insurrection), but because of the pressure of the rank and file. Lenin was not bluffing when he again threatened to appeal to the party masses against the highly placed 'deserters'. The ranks indeed had little sympathy for them.

The issue of a 'homogeneous socialist government' was finally laid to rest in the workers' minds by the realisation (for those who still had doubts) that party differences involved issues of principle that could not be resolved through pressure. Once this had sunk in—and for this the Vikzhel negotiations had been crucial—accusations of 'Bolshevik intransigence' and references to the 'personal vanity' of the leaders ceased to be heard. No doubt the victory of the soviet forces outside Petrograd and in Moscow also helped to allay fears of isolation and defeat, which had been so acute at the end of October.

On 6 November, the Petrograd Soviet once again discussed the negotiations. Speaking for the Bolshevik fraction, Sokol'nikov explained that the defencists were in effect demanding a new pre-parliament, one in which the TsIK would have only minority representation and the defencists a majority. Thus, the army's representatives would not be elected by the soldier masses (as were the army's TsIK delegates) but by the army committees elected back in the spring when the great majority of soldiers were defencist. Furthermore, the defencists wanted an unconditional end to all repressions, particularly the reopening of all non-socialist papers and the freeing of political prisoners, including the (non-socialist) ministers and the Junker participants of the 28 October rising. Such 'pleading for the bourgeoisie', according to Sokol'nikov, was disgraceful. And to boot, the defencists were insisting that all armed forces be subordinate to the City Duma, the core of the Committee of Salvation. This meant disarming the revolution.

Sokol'nikov concluded that the soviet government could negotiate only with the LSRs, who should join a coalition. The commissars who had resigned claimed that their wavering reflected the will of the masses. 'Is that true?' he asked. Shouts of 'No!' 'Who can justify those who left, let them raise their hands.' No hands were raised. With one opposing vote and twenty abstentions, the Soviet resolved:

> Power must remain in the hands of the soviet and cannot be given away to any pre-parliament ... in which Mensheviks and SRs want to form a majority of supporters of Kerenskii. The Petrograd Soviet demands a complete end to negotiations on an accord with the traitors, the Mensheviks and SRs, and at the same time proposes to

the LSRs to adhere decisively to the workers and peasants and enter the Sovnarkom.[91]

This Soviet, it should be recalled, had urged an all-socialist coalition at the end of October. A similar shift occurred in factories that had done the same. For example, on 31 October a meeting of 1500 workers at the Admiralty Shipyard decided unanimously to condemn

the conduct of the leaders of the socialist parties who led to a split of the proletariat and of all revolutionary democracy that will undoubtedly result in the destruction of the entire revolution.

And they went on to demand an accord of all socialist parties from Bolsheviks to Popular Socialists to form a government responsible to the soviets on the platform of the congress.[92] On 7 November, however, after a lengthy debate and speeches from the different party fractions, the general assembly against only two dissenting votes resolved to

speak for full and undivided soviet power and against conciliation with the parties of the defencist conciliators, who by their policies have led the country to the edge of ruin. We demand of our workers' and peasants' government a strong, decisive and merciless policy toward those who sabotage and by other means try to undermine the power of the workers and peasants.

We have sacrificed much for the revolution and we are ready, if it is necessary, for new sacrifices, but we will not give up power to those from whom we have taken it in a bloody battle. No wavering. No hesitation. With complete faith in our forces and in the success of our just cause—onward![93]

The LSRs, the only other party still enjoying significant worker support, underwent a similar evolution. On 8 November *Znamya truda* admitted that time had passed by the slogan of a homogeneous socialist government. The problem was that people who call themselves socialists turn out to be merely 'bourgeois democrats'.

Even if we had achieved such a 'homogeneous government', it would have really been a coalition with the most radical part of the bourgeoisie. The error was soon clarified in the heat of events. Once both sides realised the mistake—and the defencists realised it first, taking from the start an irreconcilable position—the accord fell away of its own.

While the Menshevik–Internationalists continued to push for a broad coalition, themselves remaining outside the government but participating in the TsIK,[94] the LSRs' shift opened the way for their entrance into a coalition with the Bolsheviks as the only parties standing for unadulterated soviet power. Since the LSRs' real popular support was in the countryside, this coalition can with some justice be viewed as a worker–peasant alliance.

An Extraordinary All-Russian Congress of Peasant Deputies ('extraordinary' because not all peasant soviets sent delegates) took place in Petrograd on 10–25 Nov. Against the wishes of the old Peasant EC, delegates were chosen from the *uezd* (county) and not *guberniya* (province) level and were therefore much closer to the peasants' current mood and more to the left. Accordingly, the party breakdown was 110 LSRs, 50 SRs, 40 Bolsheviks and 15 sympathisers, and 40 non-affiliated. (The defencists walked out soon after the opening.) On 15 November, the congress endorsed the platform of the Second Congress of Soviets of W and SD and decided to merge its EC with the TsIK.

It seemed that the strategy of the Bolshevik left had been vindicated—the policies of the new régime on land and peace had won it the support, if not of all the peasantry, then of a substantial part. When it was reported at the Peasant Congress that the Russian troops had concluded a ceasefire agreement on all fronts, 'something indiscribable took place. The first moment—silence, after which loud and stormy unending applause broke out. The majority of delegates rise and, standing, continue to applaud.'[95] When the Bolshevik speaker on the land question admitted that the Soviet Congress's Decree on Land had received much justified criticism, adding: 'We leave it to you, the peasants, as you see best', the alliance was as good as sealed.

The merger of the two ECs was met enthusiastically by Petrograd's workers, still worried by their isolation. 'Having heard the report of the Soviet of W and SD on the unification of the three socialist parties: Bolsheviks, Menshevik–Internationalists[!] and LSRs, declared the workers of the Putilov forging press and cutting shops,

> We, the workers, as one, greet this unification as long desired and we send our warm greetings to all our comrades working on the platform of the Second All-Russian Congress of the toiling people, of the poorest peasants, workers and soldiers. Unanimous.[96]

Accompanied by orchestras and an honour guard, the Peasant Congress proceeded en masse to Smol'nyi for a joint session with the TsIK. 'The mood is jubilant', wrote *Znamya truda.*

> The atmosphere exalted, joyous. One indeed feels that something great is taking place. Spiridonova [one of the most venerated of LSR

leaders, who had served many years at hard labour for the assassination of the subduer of the Tambov peasants] opened the meeting declaring that this was the 'first act toward the union of the toilers of the entire world'.[97]

Unlike the July Days, the workers in October had not been isolated and crushed. Unity was being achieved, but of a different sort than originally envisaged by those who had called for an all-socialist coalition. It was unity from below (not complete, to be sure, but sufficient for now) from which the vast majority of the intelligentsia, including its socialist segment, was absent. 'It is curious to note', wrote *Znamya truda* of the LSR Congress at the end of November,

> that all those reporting, when speaking of the lefts and rights, state that it was chiefly the intelligentsia that went with the right, thus forming small groups. But the masses followed the LSRs and the Bolsheviks.[98]

It was a sign of the times that the Conference of Railroad Workers (*rabochie*—manual workers, convened to counter Vikzhel, which included administrative personnel) met on 13 November with an 'almost total absence of intellectuals. Even the praesidium consists almost completely of rank and file.'[99] It was becoming difficult to find intellectual spokesmen for the workers' positions. The conference, whose composition was two-thirds Bolshevik, the rest LSRs with a smattering of Menshevik–Internationalists, voted by 154 against 22 to condemn Vikzhel as the 'elite [*verkhushka*] of an organisation that by no means reflects the revolutionary will of the proletariat'.[100] The LSR Levin expressed the view from below, which was very bitter towards the intelligentsia:

> At the moment when the old bourgeois chains of state are being smashed by the people, we see that the intelligentsia is deserting the people. Men who had the good fortune to receive a scientific education are abandoning the toiling people, who carried them on their exhausted and lacerated shoulders. As if that were not enough, in leaving they mock their helplessness, their illiteracy, their inability painlessly to carry out great transformations, to attain great achievements. And this last is especially painful to the people. And inside it, instinctively grows a hatred for the 'educated', for the intelligentsia.[101]

The October Revolution finally forced the workers to accept the split in revolutionary democracy, resolving in its own way the problem posed openly for the first time by the July Days. October was the final stage in the polarisation that had for years been eating away at Russian society. It was now split irrevocably into two irreconcilably hostile camps. In this respect October appears as the antithesis of February, which for a brief moment had papered over the cracks in the social edifice. But February had really resolved nothing. It required only eight months for the social contradictions fully to work their way through to a new revolution, a revolution of the *nizy* of society against the *verkhi* and the first act of a bitter and prolonged civil war that the workers had wanted so much to avoid.

# 6 The Constituent Assembly and the Emergence of a Worker Opposition

## The Elections

The weeks following the insurrection were undoubtedly the high point of working-class support for the Bolsheviks and the new régime. Not since February had the workers shown such a degree of political consensus as in the elections to the Constituent Assembly on 12–14 November.

Though the electoral campaign was brief and not especially intense, particularly on the Bolsheviks' part,[1] 78 per cent of the 1 205 737 eligible voters went to the polls.[2] Of these, 45 per cent cast their vote for List no. 4, the Bolshevik slate, a significant rise over the 33.4 per cent the party received in the 20 August duma elections.[3]

As before, this vote drew heavily on the working class (see Table 6.1). *Novaya zhizn'* observed that in the Vyborg District,

> populated chiefly by workers and numbering up to 95,000 voters, the elections took place in a lively yet calm manner ... The largest and exclusively proletarian sector here is the fourteenth ... Here during the two days 70% voted. With few exceptions it is the Bolshevik list ...
>
> The fifteenth sector in the Kolomna District is working class, and List 4 is popular ...
>
> The workers and employees of the Moscow Tram Depot vote only for List 4 ...
>
> The fact has to be admitted: the workers of Petrograd have recognised the Bolsheviks as their leaders and the spokesmen for their mass opinion in the Constituent Assembly also.[4]

(The correlation between $\dfrac{\text{no. industrial workers employed in district}}{\text{no. eligible voters in district}}$

and the relative size of the Bolshevik vote in each district was $r = 0.7744$ at a significance of $p(F) < 0.0005$. While only a very rough

343

TABLE 6.1:    *District Breakdown of Constituent Assembly Election Returns in Petrograd (per cent of total district vote)*

| District | Men. Bol. % | Men. Int. % | Men. Men. % | SR % | Kadet % | Other[a] % | Total no. votes cast |
|---|---|---|---|---|---|---|---|
| Admiralty | 23.0 | 0.5 | 1.4 | 17.7 | 43.4 | 13.8 | 13387 |
| Aleksandr-Nevskii | 48.5 | 1.0 | 1.4 | 19.4 | 21.0 | 8.7 | 59713 |
| Kazan' | 19.9 | 1.2 | 2.1 | 14.0 | 48.2 | 14.7 | 22475 |
| Kolomna | 35.8 | 1.2 | 2.3 | 14.5 | 34.0 | 12.3 | 37951 |
| Lesnoi | 47.4 | 2.2 | 2.6 | 12.8 | 27.6 | 7.3 | 21107 |
| Liteinyi | 19.7 | 1.1 | 2.4 | 13.7 | 47.4 | 15.7 | 48731 |
| Moscow | 26.2 | 1.4 | 2.5 | 12.2 | 44.6 | 13.0 | 67706 |
| Narva | 48.4 | 1.0 | 1.6 | 18.9 | 20.5 | 9.6 | 91608 |
| Nevskii | 41.3 | 0.7 | 1.3 | 39.0 | 10.7 | 6.9 | 43736 |
| Novaya derevnya | 45.7 | 1.7 | 2.3 | 14.4 | 25.8 | 10.1 | 12567 |
| Okhta | 45.7 | 0.8 | 1.4 | 19.6 | 23.9 | 8.6 | 20841 |
| Petergof | 68.2 | 0.6 | 0.8 | 18.7 | 6.6 | 5.0 | 42144 |
| Petrograd | 39.1 | 1.8 | 3.2 | 12.4 | 33.7 | 9.9 | 115623 |
| Polyustrovo | 57.7 | 1.2 | 1.2 | 24.3 | 10.0 | 5.5 | 23357 |
| Rozhdestvenskii | 28.2 | 1.4 | 3.1 | 14.3 | 38.4 | 14.6 | 54505 |
| Spasskii | 29.5 | 1.0 | 1.0 | 9.7 | 40.1 | 18.6 | 35202 |
| Vasilevskii ostrov | 48.1 | 1.0 | 1.5 | 15.3 | 24.4 | 10.3 | 94549 |
| Vyborg | 67.9 | 1.0 | 1.3 | 12.8 | 11.7 | 5.3 | 47821 |
| Garrison | 77.0 | 0.5 | 0.6 | 11.3 | 5.6 | 5.0 | 88197 |
| All Districts | 45.0 | 1.2 | 1.8 | 16.1 | 26.2 | 9.6 | 942333[b] |

[a] Includes votes for religious parties (4.5% of total), right socialist groups (3.2%) and a few others.
[b] The column actually adds up to 941 220. The discrepancy with the published figure is due to the exclusion of five lists from the district breakdown.
Source: *Nasha rech'* (17 Nov. 1917).

indicator, the high correlation reinforces the other evidence brought here. The same correlation in the August elections was r = 0.6878, p(F) < 0.01.)

By now the mood of the garrison was at one with the workers. The soldiers had all but abandoned their former attachment to the SRs, casting 77 per cent of their 88 197 votes to List no. 4.[5]

Table 6.2 shows the deepened polarisation of Petrograd society since May and August. The extremes, the Bolsheviks and Kadets, grew at the expense of the moderates, the 'conciliators', although Bolshevik gains since August outstripped those of the Kadets on the order of two to one. In August the SRs had won majorities or pluralities in ten districts, the Bolsheviks in six and the Kadets in two. In November the SRs did not lead in a single district; the Bolsheviks carried twelve and the Kadets six.

TABLE 6.2: *District Breakdown of Returns in Petrograd Elections to District Dumas[a] (27 May–5 June[b]), Central Duma (20 August) and Constituent Assembly (12–14 November 1917) (percentage of total district vote)*

| District | | Bol. % | Men.[c] % | SR % | Socialist Bloc[d] % | Kadet % | Other % | Total number votes cast |
|---|---|---|---|---|---|---|---|---|
| Admiralty (19761)[e] | M | 15.8 | | | 58.7 | 23.8 | 1.8 | 18931 |
| | A | 35.7 | 2.2 | 35.8 | | 21.3 | 5.0 | 11865[c] |
| | N | 23.0 | 1.9 | 17.7 | | 43.4 | 13.8 | 13387 |
| Aleksandr-Nevskii (96472) | M | 12.8 | 10.6 | 60.5 | | 13.3 | 2.7 | 68318 |
| | A | 28.0 | 3.4 | 52.4 | | 13.8 | 2.5 | 43552 |
| | N | 48.5 | 2.4 | 19.4 | | 21.0 | 8.7 | 59713 |
| Kazan' (30043) | M | 10.1 | | | 41.9 | 42.5 | 5.5 | 22077 |
| | A | 17.1 | 3.5 | 29.9 | | 41.0 | 8.6 | 13375 |
| | N | 19.9 | 3.3 | 14.0 | | 48.2 | 14.7 | 22475 |
| Kolomna (58201) | M | 14.9 | | | 55.9 | 25.2 | 4.0 | 40626 |
| | A | 29.7 | 2.3 | 38.3 | | 26.2 | 1.5 | 23602 |
| | N | 35.8 | 3.5 | 14.5 | | 34.0 | 12.3 | 37951 |
| Lesnoi (33851) | M | | | | | | | |
| | A | 36.5 | 5.3 | 29.3 | | 24.6 | 4.3 | 15830 |
| | N | 47.4 | 4.8 | 12.8 | | 27.6 | 7.3 | 21107 |
| Liteinyi (64740) | M | 8.6 | | | 51.5 | 37.9 | 2.1 | 59423 |
| | A | 16.9 | 4.0 | 35.2 | | 38.5 | 5.3 | 31236 |
| | N | 19.7 | 3.5 | 13.7 | | 47.4 | 15.7 | 48731 |

TABLE 6.2:—*continued*

| District | | Bol. % | Men.c % | SR % | Socialist Bloc^d % | Kadet % | Other % | Total number votes cast |
|---|---|---|---|---|---|---|---|---|
| Moscow (100129) | M^f | 9.7 | | | 59.4^g | 31.0 | | 69942 |
| | A | 21.3 | 4.5 | 34.8 | | 33.0 | 6.3 | 39967 |
| | N | 26.2 | 3.9 | 12.2 | | 44.6 | 13.0 | 67706 |
| Narva (128294) | M | 17.1 | | | 68.9 | 11.9 | 2.1 | 106392 |
| | A | 33.3 | 3.2 | 50.2 | | 11.3 | 2.1 | 69973 |
| | N | 48.4 | 2.6 | 18.9 | | 20.5 | 9.6 | 91608 |
| Nevskii (59840) | M | | | | | | | |
| | A | 20.1 | 2.8 | 66.8 | | 8.5 | 8.5 | 30812 |
| | N | 41.3 | 2.0 | 39.0 | | 10.7 | 6.9 | 43736 |
| Novaya derevnya (18921) | M | | | | | | | |
| | A | 37.5 | 4.3 | 28.1 | | 28.5 | 1.6 | 9805 |
| | N | 45.7 | 4.0 | 14.4 | | 25.8 | 10.1 | 12567 |
| Okhta (30300) | M | | | | | | | |
| | A | 31.3 | 1.8 | 61.2 | | 4.7 | 1.0 | 10978 |
| | N | 45.7 | 2.2 | 19.6 | | 23.9 | 8.6 | 20841 |
| Petergof (59040) | M | | | | | | | |
| | A | 61.7 | 1.6 | 31.5 | | 3.4 | 1.8 | 27949 |
| | N | 68.2 | 1.4 | 18.7 | | 6.6 | 5.0 | 42144 |
| Petrograd (167071) | M | 22.6 | | | 54.1 | 21.8 | 1.4 | 134345 |
| | A | 38.0 | 5.4 | 25.9 | | 26.3 | 4.4 | 70515 |
| | N | 39.1 | 5.0 | 12.4 | | 33.7 | 9.9 | 115623 |

| District | | | | | | | | Votes |
|---|---|---|---|---|---|---|---|---|
| (…) | A | 39.0 | 2.3 | 47.7 | | 9.6 | 1.3 | 8592 |
| | N | 57.7 | 2.4 | 24.3 | | 10.0 | 5.5 | 23357 |
| Rozhdestvenskii (82987) | M | 5.0 | 32.1 | 28.2 | | 30.5 | 4.2 | 59358 |
| | A | 15.5 | 4.9 | 39.3 | | 33.6 | 6.6 | 34287 |
| | N | 28.2 | 4.5 | 14.3 | | 38.4 | 14.6 | 54505 |
| Spasskii (53201) | M | 13.2 | 3.6 | 39.7 | 44.8 | 29.0 | 13.1 | 37581 |
| | A | 16.8 | 2.0 | 9.7 | | 33.0 | 6.8 | 17970 |
| | N | 29.5 | | | | 40.1 | 18.6 | 35202 |
| Vasilevskii ostrov (116263) | M | 34.3[h] | 8.2 | 32.9 | 45.2 | 17.7 | 2.8 | 108975 |
| | A | 38.1 | 2.5 | 15.3 | | 17.7 | 3.1 | 64726 |
| | N | 48.1 | | | | 24.4 | 10.3 | 94549 |
| Vyborg (61134) | M | 58.2 | 3.5 | 23.9 | 33.4 | 6.9 | 1.5 | 58942 |
| | A | 63.0 | 2.3 | 12.8 | | 7.6 | 2.1 | 35711 |
| | N | 67.9 | | | | 11.7 | 5.3 | 47821 |
| All Districts (1205737) | M | 20.4 | 4.3[j] | 37.4 | 55.0[i] | 21.9 | 2.8 | 784910 |
| | A | 33.4 | 3.0 | 16.1 | | 20.8 | 4.0 | 549350 |
| | N[k] | 45.0 | | | | 26.2 | 9.6 | 942333 |

[a] Five outlying districts were incorporated into the city after these elections.

[b] Voting took place 27–9 May except in two districts where elections were postponed one week.

[c] In the November elections the defencists and internationalists ran two separate lists. The totals have been combined here. See Table 6.1.

[d] The Menshevik–SR bloc existed only in the May elections and not in all districts. In Kazan', Narva, Petrograd and Vasilevskii ostrov Districts the bloc included Trudoviki and Popular Socialists.

[e] Total number of eligible voters in the Constituent Assembly elections.

[f] Known to be incomplete.

[g] Includes Trudoviki and Popular Socialists though not here in bloc.

[h] This was a Bolshevik–Menshevik–Internationalist bloc.

[i] Includes Socialist bloc as well as Menshevik and SR votes where they ran separately.

[j] The Menshevik list in this election was Internationalist.

[k] Includes the soldiers' vote, not included in district totals for the CA elections. See Table 6.1.

Sources: Rosenberg, *Liberals in the Russian Revolution*, pp. 162, 220; *Delo naroda* (23–4 Aug 1917); *Nasha rech'* (17 Nov 1917).

All the Kadet victories, with the exception of the Moscow District (which was predominantly 'petty bourgeois'—white-collar employees, shopkeepers, artisans), were won in the central 'bourgeois' districts. The Bolsheviks took all the outlying industrial districts such as Vyborg, Petergof, Narva, Nevskii, Polyustrovo as well as the working-class sections of Vasilevskii ostrov and Petrograd.[6]

The centre, so strong in the spring, had collapsed in the capital. The Kadets had long enjoyed the near total allegiance of the propertied classes as well as a large part of the senior administrative and scientific-technical employees and professionals. Those who shifted between August and November were workers and soldiers and particularly the 'middle elements' of Petrograd society. The vast majority of the first two groups turned to the Bolsheviks. It is more difficult, however, to say which way the latter turned. In the Moscow District, which had a small industrial work force (21 000 in a total population of 194 000[7]), most went to the right. Elsewhere, however, especially where there was a strong working-class presence, such as in the Narva District (next to Petergof and heavily influenced by the Putilov Works), the opposite seems to have been true.

Of course, in Russia as a whole, an overwhelmingly peasant country, the population was not nearly as polarised, and the centre retained much of its strength: the SRs received 40.9 per cent, Mensheviks – 3.0 per cent, Bolsheviks – 23.6 per cent, Kadets and rightist groups – 8.4 per cent, national and Muslim parties – 20.1 per cent.[8] However, the urban soviet elections that took place all over Russia in the autumn as well as the party composition of the Second Soviet Congress leave no doubt that a large majority of Russian workers supported the Bolsheviks (and, to a much lesser extent, the allied LSRs). Nor was Petrograd exceptional among industrial centres in its polarisation. In Moscow the centre took only 11 per cent of the vote (SRs – 8.1 per cent, Mensheviks – 2.8 per cent), the Bolsheviks and Kadets receiving 48 per cent and 35 per cent respectively.[9]

It is also worth noting that the SR vote was not exclusively moderate or centrist. The LSRs split off (or rather, were expelled) from the SR organisation too late to run a separate list. However, judging by the Extraordinary Peasant Congress in November, they enjoyed substantial support in the countryside. Moreover, they had been very strong within the SR Party itself before the break. At the August SR Council, 40 per cent of the delegates adhered to the rapidly growing left wing.[10] Yet the left received only 40 seats of the 410 won by the SR list in the Constituent Assembly[11] because in constituting the list proportional representation had not been respected. The overall effect strongly favoured the right and centre.[12]

It is impossible, therefore, to know what part of the SR vote was intended for the left. In the larger cities many LSR supporters no doubt preferred to vote Bolshevik rather than support 'conciliators'. But in the countryside loyalty to the party of 'Land and Freedom' was strong, and knowledge of political developments very weak. One might note, however, that if one assumes that 40 per cent of the SR vote was left (the proportion of left delegates at the August Council), the LSRs would have had about 164 seats in the Constituent Assembly. Together with the Bolsheviks' 175 this would have given the two soviet parties a clear plurality (47.9 per cent) and very nearly a majority.[13] In any case, the strength of the centre is very much overstated if one takes the election returns at their face value.

In Petrograd most of the 152 230 votes cast for the SR list were defencist, since two weeks later in the duma elections, when the LSRs ran separately, they received only some 26 000 votes. On the other hand, the Bolshevik vote in the duma elections, 358 684, was not far from the result in the Constituent Assembly.[14] (The right and centre SRs boycotted these elections.) Who were the SR supporters in the Constituent Assembly elections? One observer noted that 'many who dream of leaving Petrograd for the land – cabbies, doormen, wartime workers, etc. – still believe that only the SRs can make land a certainty'.[15] But there was one district where the SRs were still a force to be considered. This was Nevskii, a moderate, traditionally SR working-class district with a large contingent of settled, small property-owning workers, many of whom found the implications of the October Revolution, particularly the break with the 'middle strata', with whom they felt a certain kinship, not to their liking.[16]

The majority of Menshevik voters also preferred the defencist over the internationalist wing (almost two to one, if one includes the 1823 votes for 'Edinstvo', Plekhanov's right social-democratic list).[17] The logic among the workers who had once supported the internationalists seemed to be that if one was going to vote left one might as well vote for the Bolsheviks, who at least consistently supported soviet power and so far had done what they said they would.

The Mensheviks' popular following in Petrograd was insignificant. Osokin, a Menshevik–Internationalist, commented on the state of the party in early December:

> The coalition enthusiasm of the Mensheviks has deprived them of any credit in the eyes of the working class – not only the newly arrived, temporary masses 'working for defence', but also among the cadres of the skilled proletariat ... Only a small old guard – the worker aristocracy, to a significant degree detached from the masses – remains in the ranks of Menshevism and even so, very characteristically, on its extreme right flank.[18]

But even the support of this 'aristocracy' was failing. The heaviest blow was the defection of the printers, who broke with a long tradition and elected a Bolshevik executive in December. It would prove rather short-lived to be sure, but Simonovich, a delegate from Petrograd to the All-Russian Congress of Printers at the end of December, was nevertheless able to state that 'the Petrograd printers have left the purely economic position of the defencists and have stood at the side of the proletariat with the election of a new executive'.[19]

But the vote of confidence the workers gave the Bolsheviks in the Constituent Assembly elections tells little about their views on the nature and role of that body in Russian political life. Certainly one should not conclude from it that the workers necessarily saw any opposition between the Constituent Assembly and soviet power. The Bolsheviks, for their part, had originally, at least, presented the Sovnarkom as a provisional government, one of whose chief tasks was the convocation of the Constituent Assembly.

There had been some fear among the Bolshevik leadership of apathy or boycottist attitudes among the workers towards the elections. On 10 November, Zinoviev told the Petrograd Soviet that 'in certain worker and soldier circles the idea is now spreading that the Constituent Assembly is not necessary since we have already secured full rights and freedom for ourselves and that when you have a good thing you do not go on looking'. But the Soviet itself decided with only four dissenting votes (ten abstentions) to summon the worker and soldier masses to the polls.[20] A representative of the Putilov Works at the Bolshevik PC reported that the workers were demanding elections. It was more often the soldiers who asked: why a constituent assembly if we already have soviet power?[21]

Although the campaign itself did not generate much passion, the turnout in the working-class districts equalled or slightly exceeded the city average, though in all districts it fell below that of the May elections, the first truly democratic elections Petrograd had known and therefore something of a novelty. This shows two things. On the one hand, the workers did consider the Constituent Assembly an important arena of political struggle. On the other hand, through their overwhelming support of the Bolshevik list they made known their desire for the assembly to confirm and continue the policies of the soviet government. The workers, in effect, wanted this body, elected by universal suffrage, to give an all-national seal of approval to the programmes and policies of the working class. Thus, the Conference of Women Workers of Petrograd and Vicinity, 500 delegates representing some 100 000 workers, voted by an overwhelming majority to call the workers to vote for the Bolsheviks, demanding unequivocally that the Constituent Assembly confirm all decrees of the soviet government.[22]

From a purely logical point of view, this position suffered from an internal contradiction. If the workers believed a class dictatorship was required in the interim, what basis was there to believe they could do without it once the Constituent Assembly met? Did it possess magical powers to overcome the acute class polarisation?

The explanation lies first of all in the still considerable emotional attachment to a slogan that the workers had fought and died for in two revolutions. More important perhaps was that the Constituent Assembly somehow still held out the hope, however faint, that the civil war could be halted. Even at this late date, many workers were unwilling to leave any stone unturned. And even for those who rejected such 'illusions', the assembly could not simply be ignored because of the legitimacy it still enjoyed among the peasantry and part of the working class. In any case, the Bolshevik Petrograd organisation itself called for the fullest participation in the elections.

**Dissolution of the Constituent Assembly**

Once the returns were in and the failure of the Bolsheviks and LSRs to win a majority throughout the country was evident, any hopes attached to the Constituent Assembly could no longer be sustained. The predominance of 'conciliationist' delegates promised to make it at best a slightly altered version of the Democratic Conference. It was at this point therefore, that the Bolshevik and LSR leaders and press began to state openly that the Constituent Assembly would be dispersed if it dared oppose soviet power.[23] Soon after, the government declared the Kadets 'enemies of the people', making their leaders subject to arrest.[24] At the Extraordinary Peasant Congress at the end of November Lenin explained that the composition of the assembly would not reflect the mood of the masses, that 'man was not created for the Sabbath, but the Sabbath for man' and that in the future the soviet régime would arrest all those who refused to recognise it.[25]

Against this background, some dissident Mensheviks (bucking the decision of their congress) and SRs organised a Committee for the Defence of the Constituent Assembly with the participation of workers, district duma members and party representatives. Demonstrations were called on 28 November and 5 January in support of the assembly.

At this stage, worker support for the Constituent Assembly came mainly from those factories that had espoused the internationalists' position in October. For example, the Petrograd Soviet delegate from San-Galli, a metalworking factory, was mandated by the workers in mid December to demand the inclusion of all socialist parties in the government and the immediate convocation of the Constituent Assembly.[26] These workers persisted in their refusal to accept the split in the socialist camp. Rejecting the inevitability of civil war, they insisted that the Constituent Assembly could save society from being torn apart. 'Only the Constituent Assembly can end the civil war', declared the workers of Reikhel', who added that the soviets must nevertheless be preserved, not as governmental bodies, but as the political organisations of the working class.[27]

At least part of two large state factories, the Shell Department of Patronnyi[28] and the Obukhovskii Factory[29] also came out in support of the Constituent Assembly. The meeting of '1500 workers (peasants) [!]' of the Obukhovskii Factory resolved to greet

> the Constituent Assembly as the ideal of the Russian Revolution, as the dream which we, the Russian people, have cherished and towards which all peoples, all toilers of the world strive . . .
>
> [There follows a list of demands, including: peace, the eight-hour day, minimum wage, land, workers' control as a transition to socialism, social insurance, universal education.] And for this, we demand of democracy, of the socialists in the Constituent Assembly, to remember that only the class struggle exists, the struggle of labour against capital, and there is no room for dissension in the Constituent Assembly, where the interests of the toiling people stand above all individual parties and there is no place for those who would forget the people and follow the lead of the bourgeoisie, and therefore we say:
>
> Down with division among the socialists! Down with hostility among party leaders! Long live the unity of all democracy as the guarantee of the victory of the toiling people! Long live the Constituent Assembly! Long live revolutionary socialism! Unanimous.[30]

And yet, these demands amounted to nothing less than the programme of the soviet government, demands that had been consistently ignored or sabotaged by the coalition parties, which formed a majority in the Constituent Assembly. Again one meets the belief, particularly tenacious in this factory, that since the popular masses all shared the same interests, there was no real basis for the split among parties purporting to be socialist and to represent the interests of the people and that somehow the Constituent Assembly would clear all this up.

On the whole, worker response to the campaign in defence of the Constituent Assembly was weak. *Novaya zhizn'*, a not unsympathetic observer, reported in detail on the demonstrations of 5 January, the day the assembly opened. By this time it was clear the government would not tolerate the body that would surely repudiate soviet power. It only remained to be seen what methods the government would use.[31]

> [Vasilevskii ostrov] By the start of the demonstration, about 1000 assembled, mainly school youth, many university students, students

from the Mining Institute, women students, etc. There are few workers in the demonstration, though there are banners from certain factories, such as Trubochnyi, etc. In the demonstration from this district small groups of soldiers and sailors also participate ... [The demonstrations from Vasilevskii ostrov and the Liteinyi District merge on the Palace Square.] Individual workers and soldiers accompanied the demonstrators with hostile shouts: saboteurs, bourgeois. The intelligentsia predominated in the large crowd: students, petty bureaucrats, etc. The groups of workers from the Vasilevskii ostrov District were small—in each group there were no more than a few dozen people. There were almost no soldiers ... From 10 a.m. the participants in the demonstration began to assemble on the Petrograd Side ... The crowd consisted mainly of intelligentsia, petty bureaucrats, many women. Rarely did one see small groups of workers. There were almost no soldiers ... [By 11 a.m. about 10 000 had gathered on the Field of Mars.] Especially imposing is the demonstration of the Aleksandr-Nevskii [apparently, the Nevskii] District, in which workers of the Obukhovskii Factory, Pal' and others participated. [In all 15 000 arrived.]

The demonstration arrived in front of the Tsarskoe selo Station at noon. Here is a group of workers from the Westinghouse Factory, employees of the Nikolaev Railroad, the All-Russian Railroad Union, socialist parties. There are also many students, government [white-collar] employees, employees of public and private institutions.[32]

Despite its own reports, *Novaya zhizn'* later attacked *Izvestiya* for claiming that the demonstration consisted of 'petty philistines and bureaucrats' and lacked workers, despite the presence of a 'whole series of factories that came out with banners'.[33] But Stroev, writing in the same paper, admitted: 'So it was that relatively few workers came out into the streets on 5 January to defend the united revolutionary front.'[34]

It is true that the soviets placed obstacles before the organisers from the Committee of Defence and that the leaders of the workers' organisations appealed to the workers not to demonstrate. These measures may have had some effect but they did not prevent other parts of the population from turning out in impressive numbers. And, of course, some workers did demonstrate, most notably from the Nevskii District.

The following resolution offers some insight into the reasons behind the failure of most workers to come out in support of the Constituent Assembly:

We, the men and women workers of the Treugol'nik Factory, having assembled on 1 December at a meeting in the cafeteria of the factory and having discussed the current political moment, declare:

1. The workers, soldiers and peasants, having won power at a fearful price, will not yield to anyone this power, which expresses itself organisationally through the Soviets of Workers, Soldiers and Peasants.

2. To all hypocritical attempts to undermine the power of the Soviets of workers and peasants under the slogan 'All power to the Constituent Assembly', we declare: We are also for the Constituent Assembly, but for a Constituent Assembly that truly reflects the will of the workers, soldiers and peasants, of all the oppressed and deprived. We are only for such a Constituent Assembly that will not oppose itself to the power of the Soviets, that will strengthen the policy of peace, the policy of the transfer of lands to the hands of the people without redemption, the policy of workers' control of production and distribution. But if in the Constituent Assembly, due to the abuses permitted during the election, the will of the toiling masses is so distorted that the Constituent Assembly stands as an obstacle on the path of the development of the workers', soldiers' and peasants' revolution, then we will oppose it with all the power and might of the workers, soldiers and peasants organised into their purely class organisations of Soviets of Workers and Soldiers ... In such a truly revolutionary Constituent Assembly there is no place for avowed enemies of the revolution, members of the Kadet Party, who mobilise their forces under the slogan 'All power to the Constituent Assembly' at the same time as they engage in an open offensive against the revolution with the aid of the Kaledins, Dutovs and Karaulovs [White generals in the initial stages of the civil war.] ... We repeat, the Constituent Assembly must be a Constituent Assembly that expresses the genuine will of the toiling masses, and the only guarantee of that and of safeguarding all the gains of the revolution is the preservation and the further consolidation of the power of the workers, soldiers and peasants, and therefore: Long live the power of the Soviets of Workers', Soldiers' and Peasants' Deputies.[35]

These workers made support for the Constituent Assembly conditional on the latter's support for soviet power. But the moderate socialist victory in the elections ruled this out.

Still, 5 January was notable as the first time workers came out actively against the new régime. More ominously, it was also the first time forces representing soviet power used violence against workers. The first clash occurred at 11 30 a.m. when 200 demonstrators crossing the Liteinyi Bridge were confronted by some fifty Red Guards and soldiers who fired into the air and seized their banners, which they then proceeded 'jubilantly' to burn in a bonfire. More serious was the confrontation with the Nevskii District demonstrators that resulted in two deaths and several wounded. Casualties occurred elsewhere too.[36] The Bolshevik leader Sverdlov told the Third Congress of Soviets in January 1918 that there had been twenty-one deaths, including two workers and one soldier.[37]

These repressions were the catalyst for the emergence of a much more significant opposition movement among the workers, whose centre was the Nevskii District. A series of factory meetings on 9 January devoted to the dissolution of the Constituent Assembly and the events of 5 January attracted large numbers of workers. 'It has been a while since one could observe so large an attendance', commented *Novaya zhizn'*. The largest meeting, with up to 8000 workers, took place at the Obukhovskii Factory, some of whose workers had been on the receiving end of the shooting. *Pravda's* distorted version of the events, which placed the blame fully on the demonstrators, caused particular indignation. The meeting decided by a large majority to protest against the dissolution of the Constituent Assembly and the shooting. It demanded the recall of all soviet delegates who did not protest against the actions of the Red Guards as well as the immediate return of the latter to their work benches. Similar resolutions were passed at the Nevskii Shipbuilding Factory, Vargunina Paper Mill, Aleksandrovskii Locomotive Factory, Pal' and Maksvel' Textile Mills and by the workers of the Nikolaev Railroad—all in the Nevskii District,[38] as well as by the workers of the Shell Department of Patronnyi, Siemens-Shukkert[39], Rechkin Wagon-construction,[40] Otto Kirkhner Printing House and Bindery and the Markus Printing House.[41] Almost all of these belonged to the group of factories that had supported the internationalist position in October.

One partial exception was Old Lessner, a metalworking factory in the Vyborg District, with a work force that was over 50 per cent female. (New Lessner, one of the most radical factories, was all male.[42]) Until August, these workers had tended more towards the SRs.[43] On 10 January the general assembly resolved 'to consider the Sovnarkom criminal and immediately to set new elections to the Petrograd and District Soviets'. Three weeks later, however, a report from the factory in *Pravda* attributed the resolution to the 'chance composition of the meeting' at this factory that had never 'fully followed the Bolsheviks, since the workers were of a petty bourgeois turn of mind'. After the Kornilov affair, the report explained, the Bolsheviks had managed to dislodge the SRs, but by January only one half of the original 1200 workers remained, and 60 of the factory's Bolsheviks were at the civil war fronts.

This report is lent some credence by the results of new elections held in mid January. Three lists ran: Bolshevik–LSR, Menshevik–SR and non-affiliated. Despite the participation of some 200 clerical employees, the Bolshevik Soviet deputy was re-elected. In the factory committee, the Bolsheviks won six places, the SRs three and the non-affiliated – two.[44] But even if the resolution only represented a fleeting mood, the changes in the composition of the work force and the political wavering at Old Lessner were a foretaste of things to come.

The campaign launched by the Mensheviks and SRs for new elections in the factories did yield some results. By 25 January, where the workers had decided to hold new elections (and this was far from everywhere), the Mensheviks, SRs and non-affiliated candidates managed to win about half the seats, the other half going to the Bolsheviks. As a result some 50 new non-Bolshevik delegates took their places in the Soviet – 36 SRs, 7 Mensheviks and 6–7 unaffiliated.[45] A serious worker opposition to the régime was beginning to emerge. But as the results of this campaign indicate, at the end of January, despite the dissolution of the Constituent Assembly and the repression, the Bolsheviks still clearly held the allegiance of a majority of Petrograd's workers (see below, pp. 390–413).[45a]

The protest movement that arose around the Constituent Assembly and especially the events of 5 January set a pattern for the following months. Although some Mensheviks were very prominent in organising the movement, the worker oppositionists preferred the SRs. As noted, the centre of the worker opposition was the Nevskii District, a traditional SR stronghold. Besides the party's ties to the peasantry and the land question which appealed to a part of the workers (particularly in the Nevskii District[46]), preference for the SRs may also have been related to the party's 'populist', non-class (in the sense of 'revolutionary-democratic') image. Workers who rejected civil war and the class dictatorship embodied by soviet power preferred a party that stood for the 'people' to a social democratic party whose very name (Russian Social-Democratic Workers' Party) labelled it as a working-class organisation.

Related to this is the characteristic counterposition of the Constituent Assembly to soviet power, of an all-national government (dominated, of course, by 'revolutionary democracy') to a class dictatorship, of democratic unity to civil war. This was not to be a 'loyal opposition' that aimed at a new soviet government with a non Bolshevik majority. The goal, at least of the leaders, was rather to replace soviet power as such.

Although the immediate background of the emerging worker opposition was political, it nevertheless owed very much to the increasingly disastrous economic situation. This was readily avowed by the Mensheviks: 'In worker circles, in connection with the dispersal of the Constituent Assembly and the food crisis, acute dissatisfaction ha arisen with the Petrograd Soviet.'[47] On 9 December, the bread ration was reduced to one-half funt (about one-half pound) and on 9 January it reached the 'truly hunger level' of one-quarter funt for the first time, dipping briefly to one-eighth on 18 January.[48] Typhus, the faithful companion of hunger, also made its appearance. Various food disorders broke out. In mid January, for example, a crowd broke into a storehouse of the Food Authority. Looting continued for three days.[49] Somewhat later, a crowd attacked and looted a food train until dispersed by Red Guards.[50]

As for the factories, those working for defence (the majority) closed down in mid December for a month to prepare for the conversion to peacetime production. But as the date for reopening drew near, it became more and more evident that most would not be able to resume work and certainly not with the same size work force.[51]

### The *Chernorabochie* and the Anarchist Upsurge

Yet another manifestation of oppositional sentiment, one that preceded the dissolution of the Constituent Assembly and had even stronger economic roots, was the continued growth of anarchist influence among the unskilled workers. The economic situation of the *chernorabochie* had been particularly undermined by the unbridled inflation. During the autumn, the workers' organisations struggled with increasing difficulty to restrain these restive workers, explaining that only the political struggle and soviet power could provide a solution. Now the unskilled workers looked to the new régime to improve their lot and bring their wages more closely in line with those of the skilled workers.

Of course, all workers were suffering badly. The secretary of the Sestroretsk Metalworkers' Local, which represented a quite skilled work force employed in the rifle factory, reported to the union executive that 'the masses are dissatisfied with the wage rates, since inflation is already making them too low. Only the authority of the union and the discipline of the masses hold them back. But they can't wait for long.'[52]

Elsewhere, discipline was not nearly as strong. In early December the Workers' Section of the Petrograd Soviet met with representatives of the unions and factory committees to discuss a conflict at the Metallicheskii Factory. The *chernorabochie* painters had beaten up and 'arrested' a representative of the Metalworkers' Union, refusing to release him unless he signed a paper granting them a 14-ruble daily increase retroactive from 5 June. According to Fedorov, a Bolshevik worker who chaired the meeting, antagonism between the skilled and unskilled workers had been simmering since the summer, when the

PSFMO rejected the union's demands for the unskilled workers while accepting those for the skilled. (The union was asking relatively less for the skilled workers in an effort to narrow wage differentials.) After the insurrection, the unskilled workers circumvented the union and, threatening violence, forced the administration to grant their demands. But on 1 December, the administration announced it was closing due to a lack of further military orders. Just as the factory general assembly was discussing whether to take over the plant, the unskilled workers burst in demanding an immediate reply to their demands. They refused to let anyone speak, even pulling speakers off the platform.

The Workers' Section decided to reject the demands as exceeding the collective agreement and to order payment stopped. Another meeting was set for a few days later to discuss 'the struggle against anarchy in the factories'.[53] At that time, a representative of the unskilled workers stated:

> You cannot forget the principles put forth by the October Revolution. In this hall you greeted the demands for equalisation of the material situation of soldiers and officers. Now the unskilled labourers want equalisation with the skilled workers. This is what the social revolution demands ... If the demands of the unskilled workers are not carried out, then the government of Lenin will fall just as the governments of Romanov and Kerenskii did.[54]

During these weeks the press reported a number of incidents in which unskilled workers, ignoring their organisations, resorted to violence.[55] Vasil'ev, chairman of the Putilov Factory Committee, told a meeting of the factory and shop committees:

> Of late, thanks to the agitation of certain elements who consider it their task not to solve the common proletarian class questions but rather to pursue purely personal egoistical aspirations, a movement has arisen that is disorganising the masses. Under the guise of political struggle and economic demands, a struggle of individual groups is being conducted against the workers' organisations and even against individuals. Arguments and conflicts arise on the basis of purely philistine, petty bourgeois desires. Here one can see the total absence of a sense of collectivism and the clear emergence of personal interests dictated by petty bourgeois swamp psychology.... The committee is accused of conducting the political struggle, having forsaken the economic.[56]

The situation became so serious that Shlyapnikov, Commissar of Labour, had to issue a special plea for unity: 'Chasing after the ruble only increases the dislocation. All demands are now actually addressed to the workers themselves.'[57]

But the anarchists, who took up the cause of the unskilled workers, portrayed the issues very differently—as a struggle of the unskilled against the privileged skilled workers, who staffed the organisations and were favoured by the Bolsheviks. An unsigned letter from 'a worker of Arsenal' published in the anarchist paper *Burevestnik* accused the Bolsheviks of abandoning socialist principles:

> We simple unskilled workers demand a rise [and] they point out to us that we are heavy labourers [*volovye*, from *vol*–ox] and therefore we must live as oxen. Is this socialism, comrade Bolsheviks? At Arsenal the Bolsheviks themselves protested against a rise for simple workers, and when this was achieved all the same, they gave the larger share to the skilled workers. The bourgeoisie divides the people into higher and lower categories, and the Bolsheviks also [divide us] into 'higher and lower workers'.[58]

This conflict was not merely over wage differentials. It was also a clash of consciousness, of differing conceptions of the October Revolution. Writing on the economic crisis, the Menshevik–Internationalist economist Bazarov concluded that work force reductions and increased productivity were necessary.

> But the *chernorabochie* masses will not recognise either of these needs, consisting as they do of occasional elements, new arrivals transformed into workers only during the war. And although skilled workers are usually elected to the factory committees and other elective worker 'collectives' since they are the most capable [*intelligentnye*], they are, in fact, powerless to do anything against the dull stubbornness of the demoralised and unskilled crowd. And in many cases they simply do not decide to reveal clearly and fully the true state of affairs.[59]

(One should note here in passing the mistrust and condescension towards the 'benighted' semi-peasant, unskilled workers, so characteristic of the Mensheviks, though not entirely absent among the Bolsheviks either.) 'Experienced observers', reported *Novaya zhizn'*, 'relate that the real orchestrators of all such [unorganised, violent, 'anarchistic'] acts are the peasants who entered the factories recently and who, having received several hundred rubles in one shot, quit and leave for the village.'[60] This was also the assessment of the leaders of the Metalworkers' Union:

> The composition of the working class, strongly diluted during the

war by an element only recently connected with the factory, organised only externally and not imbued with the spirit of genuine proletarian discipline and community of interest, in its backward part still sees the problem in individuals, does not recognise any obligations and is still incapable of rising up to socialist consciousness. [It] places its own interests above all else and wants the highest possible wage rise, even at the price of the destruction of production.[61]

What these leaders did not realise is that conditions of generalised want and even hunger were not fertile ground for the growth of this 'socialist consciousness', particularly among workers who lacked a strong commitment to the working class and its long-term goals. The mass of unskilled workers had been radicalised only after the July Days, when the effects of the growing economic crisis, abetted by governmental passivity and the entrepreneurs' 'lack of managerial enthusiasm', had begun to be felt tangibly in the factories. They entered the political struggle for soviet power largely because of the government's inability to deal with the economic situation (though they did, of course, attribute this incapacity to the 'counterrevolutionary' nature of the 'bourgeois government'). But even before October, many had begun to grow disillusioned with politics and turned to the anarchists and direct economic action. The October Revolution raised hopes in the political struggle again, but the new régime was really in no position to improve substantially the workers' material situation. Hence the accusation that the factory committees were neglecting the economic struggle for the political.

As a result, many unskilled workers again turned to the 'left', to the anarchists, who began to do very well for a time after October, now putting out two daily newspapers, *Kommuna* and *Golos truda*. One observer noted in mid November:

At first insignificant, now the anarchists are a force that will have to be taken into account. At one of the factories I accidentally expressed my opinion about the anarchists in strong words, calling them disorganisers of the labour movement, and I heard shouts from the audience: 'Enough! The anarchists are our friends!'[62]

But this phenomenon proved short-lived. Hunger, which arrived full force in January, put an end to the anarchist upsurge and caused a certain reaction in the opposite direction, towards the Mensheviks and SRs and the Constituent Assembly. More important, with the factory closures in mid December, many of the unskilled wartime workers left for the countryside. By the spring of 1918, very little was heard from the anarchists in Petrograd.

## The Lines Harden

Despite the growing significance of the opposition in the winter of 1917, it was still far from offering a serious challenge to the new régime. In particular it left practically untouched those workers who from the start had been the moving force behind the movement for soviet power. The consistently pro-Bolshevik workers of the Ya. M. Aivaz Machine-construction Factory responded to the events of 5 January in the following manner:

> We grieve for the blood shed on both sides ... But to the bourgeoisie and its agents, the RSRs and Mensheviks and all who are with them, in response to your hypocritical lamentations, we declare:
> You are to blame for the June offensive and the betrayal of Riga that cost the lives of hundreds of thousands of our brothers; you are to blame for the introduction of the death penalty for soldiers; you are to blame for the beatings, both in jail and outside, of revolutionary workers, soldiers and peasants; you tore to pieces comrade Voinov [an Aivaz worker] just because he was selling the paper *Pravda*; you, who did the shooting in the days of October and now on the Kaledin front, have absolutely no right to protest and to be indignant.
> The entire blame for the shedding of fraternal blood lies with those enemies of the people's revolution who have set as their task to return the bourgeoisie to power, not stopping before deception of the proletariat and peasantry. All blame lies with you.
> Peace to the fallen. Shame to the living who through deception have pitted brother against brother.
> Peace to the fallen. Glory to the living fighters for socialism.[63]

Soon after these events, the printers of *Novaya zhizn'* once again overruled the editorial staff by refusing to put out an edition of the newspaper. The following day the editors printed this explanation:

> The paper did not appear on January 12 because the autonomous commission [factory committee] of the workers of the State Printing Plant (formerly *Novoe vremya* [a non-socialist paper shut by the authorities]) took upon itself, without any order from the government, the role of censor and, declaring that the paper bore a 'pogrom character', halted its publication.[64]

Positions within the working class were hardening. It is against this background that the events of 5 January and the reactions to them should be viewed. The shooting does not appear to have been ordered by the government, which was hurt considerably by it. The action of the Red Guards was a low-level initiative. In this chaotic period, the soviets were having considerable difficulty controlling the Red Guards, who in one case even threatened a district soviet with arrest. But the ground for this bloodshed, inconceivable in the relatively tolerant atmosphere of October, was being prepared by the growing bitterness over the political strike ('sabotage' to the workers) of the educated stratum of society, the emerging civil war in the south and the rumours, as well as concrete evidence, of counterrevolutionary plots afoot in Petrograd. On 1 January, a car in which Lenin was riding was pierced by several bullets.[65] A week later, a large number of officers were arrested in connection with a conspiracy originally scheduled to coincide with the opening of the Constituent Assembly.[66]

On 4 January, the Petrograd Soviet discussed the attempt on Lenin's life. The worker Saulin's demand for 'a thousand heads for one' was greeted with vigorous applause. Sukhanov got up next to call for cool heads but was hooted down from practically all sides.[67] The shooting of the next day was in part an expression of this increasingly bitter atmosphere. Workers and soldiers on the sidelines hurled the epithets 'saboteurs' and 'bourgeois' at the demonstrators, and when news of the clashes reached the crowd outside the Tauride Palace, shouts of indignation on the part of the defenders of the Constituent Assembly were countered by 'that's just what they deserve!' from its opponents.[68]

When Sukhanov accused the Third Congress of Soviets in mid January of 'declaring civil war against all who do not agree with Lenin's principles', someone in the audience shouted: 'And we will go against our mothers and fathers too!'[69] At the Petrograd Soviet session which discussed the events of 5 January, Sukhanov narrowly escaped a beating at the hands of some of the delegates when he insisted on speaking against a proposed resolution despite the chair's refusal to recognise him. He was saved by Volodarskii who managed to calm the hall.[70] Similar scenes took place at the Congress of Soviets. During the discussion of 5 January, the Menshevik–Internationalist leaders Martov and Pobranitskii themselves were shouted down as 'Kornilovists' and 'saboteurs'. 'The majority cannot understand the essence of the objections of a small majority', commented Bazarov. 'They even see its very existence as something illegitimate and counterrevolutionary.'[71] All this was a far cry from the mood of the end of October when General Krasnov was released on his 'word of honour'.

There was an especially deep resentment towards the Menshevik–Internationalists among the worker supporters of the régime. The former had been bitter critics of the coalition but were now attacking the soviet government with equal vehemence. In late December, the workers of the Putilov cannon shop sent the following resolution to the editors and journalists of *Novaya zhizn'* in response to its criticism of a demonstration marking the ceasefire and start of negotiations at Brest-Litovsk:

[We] have decided to censure you, writers of *Novaya zhizn'*, as Stroev was once a writer and also Bazarov, Gimer-Sukhanov, Gorky and all the editors of *Novaya zhizn'* [.] your organ does not correspond to our present common life, you follow the lead of the defencists. But remember our workers' life of proletarians, do not criticise the demonstration that took place on Sunday, you did not organise this demonstration and it is not for you to criticise it. And in general our party is the Majority and we support our political leaders [as] genuine socialist liberators of the people from the yoke of the Bourgeoisie and capitalists, and in the Future if such counter-revolutionary articles are written then we workers swear [–] carve this on your foreheads [–] that we will close your paper, and if you desire inquire of your Putilov socialist so-called neutralist [.] he was at our Putilov Factory with his backward speeches [.] ask him if we let him speak or not, and soon you will be forbidden and your organ it begins to approach the same level as the Kadets, and if you bitter backward writers continue your polemics with the government [!] organ 'Pravda' also, then know that we will stop [its] sale in our Narva-Petergof District. [signed] Putilov Factory, Cannon Dept. Write a resp[onse] or there will be repressions.

Gorky replied characteristically that 'children who have read many books by Gustave Emar and imagine themselves to be terrible Indians reason with such ferocity'. He noted that he had been the recipient of many such 'angry epistles'.[72]

The Soviet régime still had firm support among Petrograd's workers. But the unanimity of the first weeks following the October Revolution was gone. Moreover, since the conditions that fostered these divisions continued to worsen, the opposition could only grow stronger. But in the winter of 1917–18 it was still quite weak and had not yet been compelled directly to confront the fundamental issue: when it came down to it, would the workers accept the Constituent Assembly as a realistic alternative to soviet power?

# 7 The October Revolution in the Factories

After the October Revolution, the factory committees moved with renewed vigour and militancy to establish full workers' control over production. In all the ensuing debates over the organisation of industry, the committees, supported by the factory masses, argued consistently for the broadest possible freedom of action *vis-à-vis* management. In this they came up against the opposition union leaders such as Lozovskii and Larin, many of whom were moderate Bolsheviks (and former Mensheviks), who accused the factory committees of anarcho-syndicalism.

On 26–7 October Lenin wrote a Draft Law on Workers' Control which gave the factory committees access to all documents, stores, etc. and made their decisions binding on management, subject to repeal only by the trade unions and conferences of factory committees.[1] After a discussion of the draft, the Sovnarkom set up a commission headed by Larin and Milyutin to work it out in greater detail. But the results of this commission were very disappointing to the workers and activists close to the factories. At a meeting between the Commissar of Labour and representatives of the unions and factory committees in November, the paragraph of the revised draft giving management parity with the workers in the controlling bodies was vehemently rejected. A whole series of speakers demanded revolutionary measures and emphasised the need for decisions of the factory committees to be binding on management.[2]

After much heated debate and compromise, on 14 November the TsIK finally passed a law on workers' control by a vote of twenty-four to none, with eleven abstentions. Milyutin, the rapporteur, responded to the major criticisms from the 'right'. He agreed that ideally the drafting of a general economic plan should have preceded the establishment of control. 'But life requires immediate intervention; and so we had somewhat to sacrifice systematic development.' As to the issue of organising control from above or below, it was decided to utilise the organisations that already existed, the factory committees and their CS, which would be supplemented with trade union and soviet representatives. Management would have three days in which to appeal any decision of the factory committee to this central council. In the interim, the committee's decisions were binding. Lozovskii, however, remained unconvinced, arguing that the decree was an anarcho-syndicalist deviation that did not guarantee the interests of the working class as a whole.[3]

With the law passed, the debate began to turn around the 'instructions' that were to guide the practical activity of the committees themselves. The Draft on Workers' Control of the CS of Factory Committees interpreted workers' control as broad power to intervene directly in management:

> Workers' control of industry, as an integral part of control over the entire productive life of the country, must be conceived not in the narrow sense of inspection [*reviziya*] but, on the contrary, in the *broadest* sense of *intervention* into the disposition by the entrepreneur of capital, inventory, raw materials, and finished goods belonging to the enterprise; [in the sense] of *active* monitoring [*nadzor*] of the correctness and rationality of the execution of orders [*zakazy*], the utilisation of energy and the work force, and *participation in the organisation of production itself* on a rational basis, etc. etc. [emphasis in original][4]

On the other hand, the draft instruction written by Larin specifically limited the functions of the factory committees to control narrowly conceived as 'passive' monitoring, leaving all executive authority with the owners:

> The control commission does not participate in the management of the enterprise and does not bear responsibility for its work and activity, which remains that of the owner ... The control commission itself can petition for sequestration but cannot itself seize and run the enterprise.[5]

This draft was endorsed by the All-Russian Council of Trade Unions and subsequently by the All-Russian Congress of Trade Unions.[6]

Needless to say, Larin's draft met with fierce opposition from factory committee activists. But not only from them. At a city-wide conference of the Delegates' Council of the Petrograd Metalworkers' Union and representatives of the factory committees, various speakers urged that it be rejected since it 'ties the hands of the workers, while the [CS's] Draft on Workers' Control allocates broad initiative to the workers and makes them the actual masters of the given factory'.[7]

Curiously, although the rapporteur himself began by defending Larin's draft, he concluded by proposing that both drafts be returned to committee for further work.[8]

The question was thus left open, and the Sixth Petrograd Conference of Factory Committees on 27 January 1918 resolved to exert pressure on the *verkhi* against 'those comrades on the right', who were lobbying the newly created VSNKh (Supreme Council of the National Economy) to endorse Larin's draft. But the conference went even further this time, calling for the government to begin at once to construct a technical apparatus to prepare the transfer of all enterprises to the state. These nationalised factories would be headed by workers' committees under the guidance of the local Sovnarkhozy (Councils of National Economy) because the state still had no special organ capable of doing this job and because 'the government of the workers, soldiers and peasants is strong because it is based upon the confidence of the toilers and their organisations'.[9]

It seemed as though the predictions of the industrialists and moderate socialists were coming true: that the seizure of power by the workers was leading to 'utopian socialist experiments'. Word had finally caught up with deed in the activity of the factory committees as they abandoned their pre-October refusal to participate in management and rejection of formal responsibility for production. Indeed, they were now even demanding full nationalisation, complete elimination of the capitalist administration in favour of management by the workers' committees.

Was this an expression of latent anarcho-syndicalist sentiment released by the soviet seizure of power, as has been traditionally claimed in the Western historiography? An examination of what was occurring inside the factories sheds much light on the true significance of this 'leftism.'

As noted earlier, workers' control before October had in practice been quite limited in scope and restricted largely to those factories directly threatened with cutbacks or closure. After the insurrection, however, workers in factory after factory moved to assert their right to control without, as they had consistently done before, bothering to justify their actions in terms of specific conflicts and policies (or the lack of them) on the part of management. Undoubtedly, then, the October Revolution gave a strong new impetus to the activity of the factory committees. But it would be wrong to see the post-October movement as the product of some entirely new motivation, for it remained fundamentally defensive. It was rather the depth and pervasiveness of the economic crisis and the sudden departure from the scene of a government hostile to the workers' initiative that explain the new upsurge.

Even after October, the workers did not reject cooperation with management if they felt this was in the interests of the factory. On 11 January 1918, the committee of the Erikson Telephone Factory gave an account of its activities to the CS. It noted that while management had been cooperating with the committee in the procurement of fuel and raw materials, since this did not directly threaten its prerogatives, it was resisting the committee in its efforts to establish financial and economic control. It refused to provide reports and even threatened the resignation of the entire administrative staff. The factory committee decided, therefore, not to press its legal right at this point so as 'to avoid premature complications that could cause a temporary stoppage'.[10] *Novaya zhizn'* commented approvingly:

> One should note that the factory committee at Erikson, acting in full contact with the administration, is utilising the decree on workers' control very intelligently while at the same time not overestimating its forces. Thus, for example, it froze all the financial assets of the joint-stock company and in this way prevented their intended removal from the enterprise and transfer abroad. At the same time, the factory committee in no way intrudes upon the economic rights of the administration. [11]

Similarly, at the Tentelevskii Chemical Factory an agreement was reached according to which the administration recognised the workers' right to control in return for workers' recognition of the administration's right to manage.[12]

But in practice, such agreements delimiting respective spheres of competence were seldom possible, since nearly all factories faced drastic cutbacks if not closure. From the workers' point of view this called not for 'passive' control as envisaged by Larin's draft but for the most active and continuous participation by the workers' representatives in management. For as a delegate to the November Conference of Factory Committees argued: 'how are you going to control factories that are closing?'[13] On 22 November, the director of Metallicheskii received the following note from the factory committee:

> In view of the persistent intention of the administration to destroy the enterprise, we, the workers and [white-collar] employees, are forced to defend our right to free labour and life and on the basis of the law have created a worker directorate (control-executive commission) for joint management with the administration.[14]

The defensive attitude is still very evident.

However, even the broad and active interpretation of workers' control advocated after October by the factory committees was proving untenable and, in practice, turned out to be the final stage before the total elimination of the old administration and the end of workers' control as a form of factory dual power. It was, after all, the perceived passivity and negligence of the administration that had originally moved the committees to go beyond control in the narrow sense of monitoring to direct intervention in management. If monitoring had failed, then there was even less chance that the workers' participation in management would rekindle the enthusiasm of the administration.

And, in fact, the administrations most often refused to cooperate and were finally eliminated, in some cases sooner than others. The official position of the PSFMO was that owners should abandon factories where the workers asserted the right of control over the administration.[15] In his report on the VSNKh to the Metalworkers' Union Congress in late June 1918, Larin, one of the most prominent 'comrades on the right', himself admitted:

> We tried in many cases to put off the moment of full management of the enterprises and to restrict ourselves to control. But all our efforts led to nothing. In the present situation not one of the existing forces can—and sometimes they do not even desire to—manage the economy ... Now there is but one way out: to move forward or go down. We have to abandon the idea of workers' control and, whether we like it or not, shift to a system of full management of the enterprises and leadership of the economy of the country.[16]

Soon after the October Revolution, as the industrial crisis deepened, appeals began to reach the government in ever increasing numbers for sequestration or nationalisation of particular factories. They cited various reasons. In some cases it was a question of the administration's refusal to recognise workers' control. But this was most often coupled with the assertion that the administration was heading for a shutdown or had already closed the factory. On 12 December, the committee of Robert Krug informed the general assembly that the administration had rejected the draft on workers' control and had expressed its intention to stop operations. The meeting decided that the workers should take the factory into their own hands and remove the five top administrators. That very day, the entire administrative staff disappeared taking with it the plant's current operating funds. 'As a result of this criminal sabotage', the committee informed the CS, 'we were placed before the necessity, in order to avoid stoppage of the factory, of calling a general assembly in which the grave situation was explained, and [it] decided to take the factory into its hands.'[17] This sort of report was quite common.[18]

Even where the assertion of the right to control itself was the immediate cause of closure, things were not as simple as they might seem. The PSFMO had indeed decided on a policy of non-toleration of workers' control, but when its representative, G. Kokoshkin, was asked at the 23 January meeting of the society's Leather Section how he envisaged in concrete terms the directive to abandon factories where the workers were demanding control, he explained: 'Leaving is conceivable for those enterprises that lack assets [*sredstva*], but in no case where the enterprises still represent some value for the owner.'[19]

In early February 1918 the Vulkan Factory Committee, whose conflicts with the administration in the summer and autumn (documented in Chapter 3) had moved the Provisional Government to step in and establish control over the administration with the cooperation of the factory committee and trade union, finally requested that the Sovnarkhoz of the North Region nationalise the factory. It was noted that the plant's finances were sound but the administration was placing insurmountable obstacles before the execution of 'active workers' control', continuing to view itself as the sole master of the factory. The only way out, it argued, was to transfer the factory to the state.[20] In a letter dated 23 March, the factory committee summed up the prevailing view from below on this issue:

The factory committee, having discussed ... the entire policy of the administration, has reached the following conclusion:

Since the entire policy of the administration, starting from July 1, 1917 to the present, has been and is being conducted with a definite view towards closing the factory (circulars of the administration) and that if the factory is not now closed the credit for supporting the life of the factory should be given to the energy of the factory committee, which in its activity, hourly encountering insurmountable difficulties, conducted its entire policy in an effort to support the life of the factory, the factory committee considers the [sort of] control that the administration is willing to accept to be a [mere] palliative, since the master of the enterprise will still be the administration, while responsibility for conducting the affairs in the factory will lie fully on the control commission, and consequently, dual power will not be eliminated—the factory committee sees the only way out in the nationalisation of the factory, and this petition once again affirms this.[21]

Here the immediate motivation for requesting nationalisation was the administration's refusal to recognise active workers' control. But an examination of the history of worker–management relations here reveals that this was merely the final act in a long and arduous struggle on the part of the factory committee to keep the plant running.

The attempt to demobilise industry after the ceasefire itself provoked a large number of demands for nationalisation. Very often the administration, and even the technical personnel, refused any part in this worker-initiated shift to peacetime production.[22]

There were, of course, also 'ideological' factors at play, the same ones that before October had prompted the factory committees to reject offers formally to assume responsibility for production. After the transfer of power, with the state in the hands of the soviets and supplying the factories with funds, materials and orders and with the workers in practice taking on more and more of the burden of running the enterprises, it made increasingly less sense to the workers to leave management in the hands of the capitalist administration, working for the enrichment of the private owners. Besides, in the circumstances, the latter's interest in profits seemed to have very little in common with the workers' concern with maintaining production.

The committee of the Franko-Russkii Machine-construction and Copper-rolling Factory explained the workers' decision to elect a new management in the following manner:

> The production and normal course of life in the factory are the main concern of the factory committee. In this direction the factory committee will take all necessary measures. Until now the role of the factory committee has been a very pitiful one: for the most part the factory committee served as a tool in the hands of the management, did not have a deciding vote, visited many institutions in order to obtain orders, fuel, materials and funds. It played the role of a middle-man between the administration and the workers, was silent when energy, money and materials were distributed, expended. Such a phenomenon, such a role is no longer admissible. The financing of the factory comes from the resources of the state treasury. Moreover, this money is given only with the cooperation of the factory committee. As this is the case, the workers, the factory committee should have a complete guarantee that these assets are not going to a bunch of exploiters for their enrichment at the price of [the workers'] labour but to the needs of those working at the factory. Productivity of labour and a conscientious attitude towards one's duties can exist only when people who all the toilers of the factory can trust are elected to the management. This will be the highest body in the factory. This management can and must put the life of the factory in order. Only this management, elected proportionately, is in a position to carry out the tasks which face the toilers of the factory.
>
> This is our plan at which we have arrived through our bitter experience of the past and in which we see the only way out of the situation that exists at the factory.[23]

On 23 February 1918, the general assembly elected a provisional management including one representative from the VSNKh, one from the Metalworkers' Union, one from the white-collar employees and three from the workers.[24]

Even here, however, the overriding concern was still the continued existence of the factory. And to this end, the committees expended truly herculean efforts. One of the most successful (relatively speaking) in this respect was the Opticheskii Factory Committee. In a document sent to the government in the early autumn of 1918 requesting nationalisation, it set out the entire saga of its struggle.

Real control began only after the October Revolution when the committee held up funds that the administration was attempting to transfer to the parent company in France.

> In the period of demobilisation and the threat from the German offensive [February—March 1918] and also in the alarming moments when dark and malicious elements were attacking the leading organisations, trying to intensify the disorder of national life, the factory committee had to assume the burden of the struggle to keep the factory from closing.

During the war, the optical department had been relegated to a relatively minor role as the factory took up production of grenade detonators. When it came time to demobilise in January, however, the Municipal Power Station cut back the supply of electricity to two days a week. The factory committee therefore decided to build its own power plant. It bought the machinery and completed it in three months. At the same time it took the initiative in preparing models of cinematographic equipment, running the factory legally two days a week and illegally at night for the rest.

Gradually, elements of the administration which refused to cooperate were dismissed. Among the workers too, a 'merciless purge' was conducted of the 'disorganising elements'. As a result, productivity had 'fallen less than at other plants'. When the Commissariat of Enlightenment finally placed an order for the projectors, the committee worked out prices and a contract was signed.

It was admitted that

> the factory committee and its control commission, taking into their hands the leadership of the enterprise, knew that they were going several steps beyond all the instructions issued by the higher governmental bodies charged with supervising the workers' organisation ... [But] feeling their strength, they confidently set to this great task and, after a stubborn struggle in every sense, were able to save the factory, create discipline, organise production on a new basis and spare the treasury of the People's State many millions in funds, which, had the workers' organisations not been up to the task, would have floated away, as happened in other cases, into the pockets of foreign imperialists, who, utilising these plundered millions, are trying to strangle our worker–peasant power ... Now it is time to remove superfluous obstacles. It is time to take fully into the

workers' hands the production they have put in order, [now] that they have prepared the workers for management.

One should add perhaps that this request was being made after the arrest of the owner and the flight of two members of the administration.[25]

In the majority of cases, however, the workers were much less successful. In view of the transport collapse and the scarcity of fuel and raw materials, their efforts often proved fruitless and, in the eyes of those charged with managing the whole of Petrograd's industry, even counterproductive. This, in fact, was a major argument of those who sought to limit the powers of the factory committees. Elected by, and therefore responsible to, the workers of the given plant, it was argued that the factory committees naturally had the interests of their own plant closest to heart and often pursued them at the expense of the general interest.

It was noted earlier that opposition to broad powers for the committees came particularly from the trade union leadership, in which moderate Bolsheviks such as Ryazanov, Lozovskii and Larin as well as Mensheviks played a very prominent role. This debate on the powers of the committees was really only the latest version of a long-standing conflict that dated back to the origins of the movement for workers' control in the spring of 1917. The opponents of broad control (the *Novaya zhizn'* group was especially prominent here) tended to portray the issue in stark black-and-white terms: the trade unions represent a centralising tendency; the factory committees – anarcho-centrifugal; struggle is inevitable. This attribution of inherently anarcho-syndicalist motives to the workers' control movement, as already noted, has passed largely unquestioned into later Western historiography.[26] However, this view had been and remained even after October a grossly oversimplified, not to say distorted, portrayal of the reality.

Not that accusations of 'mestnichestvo' (localism) directed at the factory committees were without foundation. In a widely publicised move, the Treugol'nik Rubber Factory refused to submit to the order of the CS to yield some of its oil reserves. It argued that it had worked hard on its own initiative all through 1917 to build them up and while they could keep Treugol'nik running for several more months, they would do little good distributed among several factories.[27] In a report in June 1918, the Metal Section of the Sovnarkhoz of the Northern Region took note of the zeal of the factory committees in keeping their plants open:

The Section also had run-ins with workers' organisations, especially with factory committees. The committees, not considering anything else, watch over the interest of their own parish striving to procure at once one subsidy or another, advances, although this money is given only after the most careful investigation of the enterprise. The committees try to revive the operation of closed enterprises no matter what, even though there is no objective basis for opening because of the lack of fuel or of a corresponding need for that type of production. The data we receive from the factory committees as well as from the administration are always one-sided ... The factory committees, not taking anything else into account, very often beseiged the authorities and institutions, snatched up orders, obtained advances and without sanction, without the approval of the Sovnarkhoz of the Northern Region, opened the factories. Unfortunately the majority of such orders turned out to be objectively unrealisable, not to mention the fact that they very much disorganise the work of the Section. They are unrealisable because many factories are unsuited for the given type of production ... The Metal Section will have to intervene in this work, take all orders under its control and, in accord with the interests of the general state mechanism, reorganise them. This is not going to occur without struggle of the workers' government against workers' organisations.[28]

There were also reports that some factories resisted demobilisation, demanding first new peacetime orders. At Old Lessner the workers rescinded their original decision to submit to the decree to close for demobilisation on 23 December after receiving unsubstantiated reports that other metalworking factories were not obeying. The general assembly decided rather to reduce operations to three days a week and in the meanwhile try to secure new peacetime orders.[29]

In this connection, one might also mention Lenin's letter of July 1918 (when the situation was admittedly much worse) to the workers of Petrograd exhorting them to leave for the countryside to organise the poor.

To sit in Piter, to go hungry, hang around empty factories, divert oneself with the ridiculous dream of resurrecting Piter's industry or saving Piter—that is *stupid* and *criminal*. The workers of Piter must break with this stupidity, kick out the fools who defend it, and go in their tens of thousands to the Urals, the Volga and the South, where there is much grain, where one can feed oneself and one's family, where they must help to organise the poor, where the Piter worker is necessary as an organiser, leader, commander.[30]

The factory committees did necessarily tend to look first to the immediate interests of the workers who had elected them. The problem was that in the bleak reality of 1918 these interests often clashed with the overall needs of the economy as perceived by the central economic bodies. This conflict and the 'leftism' of the committees in demanding broad powers against the administration have served to reinforce the view of them as anarchistically inspired organisations. To this way of thinking, the conflict between the unions and committees was one between 'orthodox Bolshevik centralisers' and anarcho-syndicalist workers.

But this interpretation contains some glaring inconsistencies. First, the CS, which supported the 'left' position, entered almost as a body the VSNKh, which was definitely a centralising force. On the other hand, some very prominent factory committee leaders, such as Levin and Vainberg, were at the same time important union leaders. These two, in fact, were elected by the Trade Union Congress as its represen-tatives in the TsIK.[31] Moreover, every conference of factory commit-tees had called for the closest cooperation with the unions and for eventual merger. If this was mere lip-service, its purpose remains obscure.

The merger of the Metalworkers' Union with the factory commit-tees of Petrograd's metalworking industry in the beginning of 1918 appears to have taken place painlessly, without visible conflict. Vain-berg, the union's secretary, wrote in *Metallist* that since the union was getting involved in the organisation of the economy, it was finding that the CS was duplicating its work. The proper solution was to merge the union and the factory committees, with the latter serving as the local apparatus for carrying out the policies set by the union. 'This view', he continued, 'is fully shared by the comrade members of the CS of Factory Committees, and on this basis a complete agreement has been reached with them.' In the new structure the highest body would be the conference of factory committees of the metalworking industry.[32] In early 1918, a conference of representatives of the Petrograd Trade Union Council, the CS, the Praesidium of the Sixth Petrograd Confer-ence of Factory Committees and the Petrograd Metalworkers' Union decided to abolish the old union delegates' council, approving the merger. The unions' new executive would be elected by the conference of factory committees.[33]

One of the first mergers took place in the Vyborg District in March at a meeting of delegates of the Metalworkers' Union and representa-tives of the factory committees. According to a report the biggest obstacle to this fusion had not been the attitude of the *nizy* but that of the central organisations. In fact, it had taken place almost as a surprise to these centres.[34]

The apparent ease of the merger indicates that there was no basic conflict of principle between the factory committees and the Metal-workers' Union over workers' control. However, the Metalworkers' Union was somewhat special in this respect as its leadership was more to the left than that of most other unions and more in tune with the sentiment in the factory committees. To understand the union–factory committee conflict it is necessary to look beyond the surface manifestations. True, the union leadership posed the problem as anarchism versus centralised 'orthodox' Marxist organisation. But there was more involved here than the distribution of power between the local committee and the central economic bodies. The more basic issue was the distribution of power between the workers and the owners. What was really being debated was how far the revolution should move in encroaching on the rights of capital. At issue was the social nature of the October Revolution.[35]

It was no accident that the top union leadership, drawn traditionally from the more moderate 'Western' type of social democrats, opposed broad powers for the committees: they did not feel Russia was ripe for 'socialist experiments'. On the other hand, the factory committees, whose main concern from the start had been to defend production, were not opposed to centralism *per se*. They had been demanding economic regulation on the national level for months and were quite prepared to cooperate with a centralised economic management that would proceed actively to organise the economy and would not be cowed by the sanctity of capitalist property rights.

It was certainly in these terms that the industrialists themselves viewed the union–factory committee debate. The rapporteur on workers' control at the 25 January session of the Petrograd Branch of the All-Russian Society of Leather Manufacturers concluded:

The struggle between the two currents in the worker milieu is still not over. On the one hand, we have to do with the anarcho-communist tendencies of the factory committees; on the other, a thought-out system of gradual transition to state socialism on the basis of the existing capitalist system. The second current is supported by all active members of the trade union movement. In evaluating the issue of who can save industry from total and final disintegration, one can without exaggeration state that at present the only ally of industry in this struggle between the anarchist element and the conscious workers is the organisations of these union activists.[36]

It should be obvious that the industrialists had no great preference for 'state socialism' over any other socialist model of industrial organisation. It was rather that during the transition to 'state socialism', which hopefully would be a very long one, their property rights would be respected. Not surprisingly then, the assembly was unanimous in its preference for Larin's draft on workers' control, since it was 'something we can live with'. And the rapporteur approvingly quoted

*Novaya zhizn'* (which argued that the revolution in Russia was bourgeois and private property had to be maintained[37]):

> In the given conditions it is possible to realise only state regulation of production with the participation of the workers in control but maintaining the private capitalist basis of the enterprises, i.e. private ownership of the means of production and profit.[38]

The 'leftism' of the factory committees can best be accounted for not by a lust for power, but by their belief that only the workers could save industry and that to do this they had to be free to act. The leaders of the Metalworkers' Union in Petrograd shared this view. The factory committees' insistence on broad powers was not directed against the centre. It was dictated first and foremost by practical considerations: in the first months after October there was still no working central state economic apparatus, and the committees were not about to sit around idly while one was being constructed—nor would the worker masses have let them.

A theme running through the entire Sixth Conference of Factory Committees was the 'lack of forces', not so much in the localities, as in the centre. On 23 January the work of the CS was discussed. The delegate from the Baranovskii Factory told of his shock when he found at the VSNKh only 'ten–twenty people where there should have been a hundred'. He complained that the conference had 'given work to the hands with a total fog in the heads of the hungry'. Zhivotov answered for the CS, admitting that all this was unfortunately true. There simply were not enough competent people. Even the members of the CS did not always show up to the meetings.[39]

The frustration with the disorganisation that reigned in the central state economic apparatuses that were only in the process of formation even gave rise to a certain sympathy among the factory committee delegates for the anarchists' criticisms of the government, if not for their proposed solutions. As one worker stated: 'Not being an anarchist, when I see the confusion at the centre, I involuntarily become one.'[40] Bazarov noted the curious phenomenon, where highly skilled workers, 'the cream of the proletariat', applauded anarchist critiques at economic conferences while staunchly defending the Bolsheviks and the government against attacks from the right. But he hurried to add that these skilled workers would never follow the anarchists, who were finding their support among the *derevenschchina*, the workers tied to the village. They were applauding the anarchists' 'no' rather than their 'yes'.[41]

The conflict between the factory committees and the trade union leadership was eventually resolved on a practical plane. In the end, even the 'comrades on the right' could not avoid the conclusion that there was no alternative but totally to remove capital from management of the enterprises. This undoubtedly helped to mute opposition to the merger outside the metalworking industry. It is again worth quoting the views of Bazarov, who was quite opposed to 'socialist experiments'. Writing at the end of January, he concluded that there were only two options in trying to restore industry:

> Either enter into a certain business-like agreement with the class of capitalists or organise production with the forces of state power. One must state that neither the first nor the second solutions to the task are feasible for this government: the first—for political reasons; the second—due to its factual impotence.[42]

This may have been a reasonable assessment of the situation in the early months of soviet rule. But the workers could hardly be expected to sit on their hands while something else was being worked out.

In a pamphlet entitled *From Workers' Control to Workers' Management in Industry and Agriculture* published in 1918, I. Stepanov outlined the dynamics of the process that had led the workers from control originally conceived as monitoring through control as broad powers of intervention into management, finally, to complete takeover of the administration and nationalisation. He concluded:

> Conditions were such that the factory committees became full masters of the enterprises. This was the result of the entire development of our revolution. It was the inevitable consequence of the unfolding class struggle. *The proletariat did not so much move toward this, as circumstances led it to it. It simply had to do what in the given situation it was impossible not to do.* [emphasis added]

This is an accurate reflection of the development of relations within the factory as seen from below.

But Stepanov went on to argue that it was taking too long to arrive at real control. The factory committees were often acting as heirs of the capitalists. It was, of course, natural for the committees to see their first task in helping the workers to live through these hard times. But in doing so they were often making it harder to deal with the crisis. Decisive measures on a national level were needed, and this, 'as terrible as it may seem to many', required the total removal of the capitalists from affairs.

> Yes, 'socialist experiments', as our opponents chuckle. Yes, we must say it directly: now what the working class of Russia has to do is remove the capitalists and resurrect all of industry on a new socialist basis. This is not a 'fantastic theory' or 'free will'. We have *no choice*,

and since it is done by the working class and the capitalists are removed in the course of the revolutionary struggle, it has to be socialist regulation.

This has to be said and said directly. Then what until now we did by dint of circumstances, hesitatingly, unsystematically, with inadmissible waste of effort and time, we will do consciously, in a systematic manner, looking further ahead.

'Will this be another Paris Commune or will it lead to world socialism?' he asked. That depended on international circumstances. 'But we have absolutely no choice.'[43]

The point had finally been reached when the essentially defensive, reactive nature of the social revolution, the revolution in economic relations, had to be abandoned for a more aggressive, forward-looking, planned approach. Consciousness had finally caught up with practice and, indeed, would soon overtake it as the revolution moved, into the stage of war communism in the summer of 1918. But even so, as Stepanov makes exceedingly clear, the origins of war communism are not to be sought in ideology but in perceived necessity: 'We have absolutely no choice.'

The power of the factory committees and with them of the rank-and-file workers in management of the enterprises was not immediately eliminated with nationalisation. In many cases the factory committees entirely took over management and with the sanction of the Sovnarkhoz continued to run the enterprises for many months. The Decree on Nationalisation of June 1918 itself gave one-third of the places in management to elected workers' representatives, the rest taken by appointees of the Sovnarkhoz.[44]

As for workers' control itself, it reverted to its original conception of monitoring by an elected commission totally independent of the administrative apparatus.[45] Unfortunately, by this time there was not much left to control.

# 8 Soviet Power for Better or Worse

## Dispersal and Transformation of the Petrograd Working Class

By the time the Decree on Nationalisation was issued, most of Petrograd's industry had in fact died, the victim of the economic crisis and political and military strife. It would be years before the working class of Petrograd could regain its numerical strength. But by then it would have been morally and physically transformed, a mere shadow of its former self.

Table 8.1 illustrates the catastrophic decline in the work force in the first eight months of 1918, most of it occurring between mid December and May. By 1 May 1918, little over one-third of the industrial work force of February 1917 was still employed in Petrograd's factories. The chief causes of this decline were the lack of fuel and materials, the result of the transport crisis and the civil war in the south, the demobilisation of Petrograd's swollen war industry and the evacuation in February in response to the renewed German offensive.

TABLE 8.1:   *Number of Employed Industrial Workers in Petrograd and Vicinity, 1 January 1917–1 September 1918*

|  | *1/I–17* | *1/I–18* | *1/V–18* | *1/IX–18* |
|---|---|---|---|---|
| Number of Workers | 406312 | 339641 | 142915 | 120553 |
| As percentage of I/17 | 100% | 83.5% | 35.1% | 29.7% |

Source: *Materialy po statistike truda severnoi oblasti*, vyp. v (Petrograd, 1919) p. 23.

But the remaining workers were far from privileged. A study of Petrograd workers' budgets in May 1918 concluded that the average industrial wage had fallen significantly behind the workers' basic material needs. To the extent that the difference was made up, it came from parcels sent from the villages, the sale of possessions, the sale to peasants of goods received as wages in kind, renting out of rooms and corners, loans and even begging. Wage rises, like the 30 per cent granted to the unskilled workers in June, utterly failed to keep pace with inflation: the cost of food alone rose 50 per cent in May–June.[1]

379

Even had the wages been higher, sufficient food, and particularly bread, the Russian staple, could be got only at free market prices, seven to eight times above state prices and beyond the reach of the workers. During the first half of 1918, Petrograd received only a little over one-third of the grain that had arrived in the corresponding period of 1917.[2] In mid January *Novaya zhizn'* came out with an editorial entitled 'Hunger':

> The long bony hand of hunger, with which Ryabushinskii had threatened democracy at the Moscow Conference, has already grasped Petrograd by the throat. The population of Petrograd has been put on a quarter-funt ration [funt = 409.5 gm, or about one pound]. For a quarter funt of bread (with straw) a day for an adult is the bread of unconcealed hunger, it is the harbinger of a hungry death, death from exhaustion, the harbinger of epidemics.[3]

Even during the lean years following the 1905 Revolution, the low-paid textile workers in Petrograd consumed on the average 1.9 funts of black bread and 0.7 of white.[4]

In May the Petrograd Soviet claimed that Petrograd was the worst off of all major Russian cities.[5] Malnutrition was a breeding ground for typhus, which made its first appearance in January, followed by cholera once the weather warmed up.[6] On 18 June, there were already about 800 reported cases of the latter. During that month, the Obukhov Hospital treated 177 cases of malnutrition and 30 in the first three days of July alone. Two-thirds of these were workers, the rest 'intellectuals'.[7]

Largely as a consequence of the uncertain and deteriorating economic conditions, labour discipline and productivity fell. Drunkenness and pilferage, particularly the use of work time and factory materials to manufacture articles for private sale, were on the rise.[8] General assemblies, factory committees, unions and government exhorted the workers to greater effort, introduced piecework, threatened merciless struggle against slackers, but to no avail, At the start of the summer of 1918 Strumilin wrote:

> As before, we face the issue of either raising wages [beyond the rise in June] or of reducing the prices of goods, and this must be resolved. For until then, until the worker receives the number of calories needed to work, all complaints about the low productivity of labour and all talk of raising it by intensifying 'labour discipline', including the Taylor system and other measures, will remain futile and idle talk.[9]

Life in Petrograd had become so hard by the summer that despite vast unemployment, the demand for skilled and even unskilled labour went unmet. On 1 September, the managerial collegium of the Izhorskii Factory in Kolpino, just outside Petrograd, wrote to the Sovnarkhoz of the Northern Region:

> Neither the local labour exchange nor that of Petrograd can supply the needed specialists or even ordinary unskilled labourers in sufficient quantity. And there is not even a faint hope that the situation will improve at the local labour exchange. The main reason for the absence of workers lies in the poor state of the food situation and the lack of desire among the unemployed workers who are still around to work in the factory [as they] prefer to engage in other things—trade, *meshochnichestvo* [speculative trading in food, from *meshochnik*—bagman], agricultural work, etc.[10]

It is sobering to recall the factory resolutions of 1917 condemning side activity in trade by workers as 'an indisputable evil, since the pursuit of gain introduces demoralisation into our comradely midst'.[11]

The decline in employment did not, however, affect all branches of industry and working-class strata to the same degree. The result was far-reaching changes in the composition of the working class with important consequences for overall political consciousness which hunger alone cannot explain. One can almost speak of a qualitatively different working class (see Table 8.2).

Metalworking was the hardest hit, retaining by May 1918 less than a quarter of the number of workers employed at the start of the revolution. It was still the largest industrial sector, but the metalworkers, from whom the majority of 'conscious workers' had issued[12] and who had been the most active supporters of soviet power, had lost their absolute majority and predominant influence. Textiles, food processing, paper and printing, least affected by the war and hence also by the demobilisation, now together accounted for almost half of the employed labour force. These workers had come to soviet power late in 1917 and in the case of printing and paper never completely or wholeheartedly.

But even within metalworking important changes had taken place. On the one hand, the demobilisation led to the departure of the great mass of semi-rural, unskilled wartime workers, who had numbered as many as 170 000 in all industrial branches. At the same time, however, a large part of the skilled urban workers, traditionally the most militant uncompromising element, had also gone. The 'Red' Vyborg District, the Bolshevik bastion and vanguard of the entire Russian working class in 1912–14 and 1917, virtually ceased to exist. By March 1918, a single large Vyborg metalworking factory, Nobel Machine-construction, was still in operation. By June, Arsenal, a moderate

TABLE 8.2:  Changes in Sectoral Distribution of Industrial Workers of Petrograd and Vicinity, 1 January 1917–1 September 1918

| Industry | 1 Jan 1917 | | 1 Jan 1918 | | 1 May 1918 | | 1 Sept 1918 | | 1 May 1918 as percent of 1 Jan 1917 |
|---|---|---|---|---|---|---|---|---|---|
| | Number of workers | Percent | Number of workers | Percent | Number of workers | Percent | Number of workers | Percent | |
| Metalworking | 249679 | 61.5 | 197686 | 58.2 | 57995 | 40.6 | 45525 | 37.8 | 23.2 |
| Textiles | 43272 | 10.6 | 44416 | 13.0 | 30173 | 21.1 | 27112 | 22.5 | 69.7 |
| Chemicals | 45029 | 11.1 | 42126 | 12.4 | 10495 | 7.3 | 7313 | 6.0 | 23.3 |
| Print and paper | 22044 | 5.4 | 23531 | 6.9 | 19776 | 13.8 | 19412 | 16.1 | 89.7 |
| Food processing | 14291 | 3.5 | 11924 | 3.5 | 10640 | 7.5 | 10278 | 8.5 | 74.4 |
| Woodworking | 4715 | 1.2 | 3027 | 0.9 | 1620 | 1.1 | 1206 | 1.0 | 25.6 |
| Leather and footwear | 11126 | 2.7 | 8413 | 2.5 | 6045 | 4.2 | 5747 | 4.8 | 54.3 |
| Mineral processing | 10237 | 2.5 | 2287 | 0.7 | 1429 | 1.0 | 1301 | 1.1 | 14.0 |
| Other | 5919 | 1.5 | 6231 | 1.8 | 4742 | 3.3 | 2659 | 2.2 | 80.1 |
| All industries | 406312 | 100.0 | 339641 | 99.9 | 142915 | 99.9 | 120553 | 100.0 | 35.1 |

Source: Materialy po statistike truda severnoi oblasti, vyp. 5, p. 23. See also Novaya zhizn' (26 May 1918) and Metallist, nos. 9–10 (1918) p. 10.

state factory, had also reopened. What had been Petrograd's largest industrial district in January 1917 with 69 000 workers (18 per cent of the capital's industrial work force and a quarter of all metalworkers) now employed only 5000 workers, including those in the small workshops.[13]

The list of twenty-one large factories (500 or more workers) still operating at the end of 1918 includes only five that had been strongly pro-Bolshevik in 1917—Aivaz, Lessner and Nobel (all machine-construction), the Sestroretsk Arms Factory, and the Cable Factory – as well as three tram depots. These together employed only 5500 workers out of the 45 000 in metalworking. The other sixteen were the much more moderate state factories, including Obukhovskii, Izhorskii, Patronnyi, Baltic Shipbuilding, Arsenal and the railroad workshops, as well as Nevskii Shipbuilding and the Putilov Works. Nevskii was now the largest industrial district with 25 000 workers, over a fifth of the industrial work force (as compared to its one tenth in January 1917).[14]

The factories lost the bulk of their most active and radical elements—the young workers and the Bolsheviks, who had emerged as the workers' natural leaders in the course of the revolution. Part of the youth went in the same wave of dismissals as the rural newcomers. A report on the Putilov Works in April noted that 'of the 39 000, there are now 13 000 working. During the reduction of the work force, those who had entered the factory later were the first fired. In this manner, the most revolutionary young forces left.'[15]

Others left voluntarily to take up work in the new state and economic administrations or to join the food detachments and the Red Army. The Red Army in particular took many of the young workers. Very few of the garrison soldiers joined, these peasants yearning only to return home as soon as possible.[16] Even before the formation of the Red Army in March, 8000 Petrograd Red Guards had left for the main fronts—the Ukraine, Don, Finland and the Western front. Two-thirds of Startsev's Red Guard sample were under thirty years old.[17] By 1 April, an additional 25 000 had enlisted in the Red Army for a total of 33 000.[18] This was still a voluntary army and ultimate victory very uncertain. Even if many of these were unemployed, it still would have been safer and easier to go to the countryside. One can assume, therefore, that these workers were among the most dedicated to soviet power.

Ivan Turunin, a Putilov worker, wrote in March 1918 that the workers had made a grave mistake during the German offensive of the previous month. 'We threw all our best worker–revolutionaries at the front and left the less developed [*malosoznatel'naya*] part of the workers to the enemies of the revolution, the opponents of Soviet power.'[19]

There was also a tremendous decline in the number of Bolsheviks in Petrograd. The Sixth Petrograd Bolshevik Party Conference in June reported only 13 472 party members, as opposed to the 43 000 in October 1917.[20] By the end of August only 7000 remained. A survey embracing 3559 of these found that only 40 per cent had been party members before the October Revolution and only 20 per cent before February 1917. Some 81.5 per cent were workers—about 5700 in all of Petrograd, as compared to some 28 500 workers—Bolsheviks in October.[21]

But even of these, few were still in the factories. At the Bolshevik Conference of the Northern Region in the spring of 1918 it was noted that

In all organisations without exception party-organisational work has weakened significantly since the October Revolution and in certain cases—true, rare ones—it has almost totally died. Almost all forces of the party have left for government work, the soviets, unions, factory committees, food detachments, red guards—all this has swallowed almost all the forces of the party.[22]

In the course of the first half-year of soviet rule, what remained of Petrograd's factory workers was deprived of its most resolute, dynamic and capable elements. In effect, almost the entire radical leadership stratum, the workers whose initiative had been so crucial in October and who had constituted the real secret of Bolshevik influence among the worker masses, was gone from the factories.

In parallel fashion but on a national scale, the Russian working class lost its natural vanguard developed through three decades of struggle and growth. 'It has already disappeared', wrote the Menshevik Piletskii in May of the Petrograd proletariat,

that vanguard fighter and pathbreaker of the working class of Russia, the genuine pride and glory of the revolution . . . Only slowly and gradually will it be resurrected with Petrograd's industry. The old social democratic guard had disappeared.[23]

Of course, it had not quite 'disappeared'. Many left the factories to play a crucial role in building, running and defending the new soviet state. But in the process they lost their ties with the milieu from which they had come, and the demoralised and emaciated working class still in the factories was in no position to exert any influence or control over them and the new state they had built.

**The 'Obscene Peace'**

In the period following upon the dispersal of the Constituent Assem bly, the main political issue confronting the workers was that of a separate peace with Germany. In a sense, this was the last purely political issue the workers were to face before the outbreak of full-scale war. Henceforth, all questions would be filtered through the economic prism of hunger and mass unemployment. Even so, the choice between an 'obscene', imperialist peace imposed upon Soviet Russia and a revolutionary war confronted the workers of Petrograd at a time of growing disorganisation and demoralisation. Just before the Germans resumed their offensive, an observer of the labour scene noted that

Among the workers, as a result of the unemployment and hunger, interest in political events is diminishing. At the same time, interest in economic questions grows more acute. Political assemblies and meetings are of late poorly attended by workers.[24]

Like most factories, the Phoenix Machine-construction Factory was closed, lacking fuel and orders. According to a report

The mood among the workers is extremely depressed. A general assembly was called three or four times, but only 50–60 people came and it had to be postponed. And only when the committee called the workers to clear snow for pay did almost all show up. The majority of workers are in incredibly bad material straits. They come in groups to the factory and, according to the workers of the factory committee, 'they ask, beg for work and curse their elected representatives', they ask 'to give at least salt water to alleviate their hunger'.[25]

At Rozenkrants

work progresses very poorly. According to the members of the factory committee, the workers scarcely work two hours out of eight. The rest of the time is spent gathering in groups discussing the situation. To any demands for more intense work they reply that their energy is sapped as a result of hunger.[26]

Such was the situation in Petrograd when the German Army began its advance on 18 February, eight days after Trotsky had rejected Germany's peace terms and unilaterally declared that Russia was leaving the war. The peace terms, first presented in early January, called for the separation of Russia from most of her Polish territory, from Lithuania, western Latvia including Riga, the Moon-sund Archipelago and the Ukraine, all to fall under direct or indirect German control.[27]

Before the offensive, opinion among the central Bolshevik leadership had been divided. (The Left SRs, for their part, were vehemently opposed to the peace and left the government over it, though they remained active in the soviets and various governmental agencies, including the Cheka and Red Army.) Lenin, supported by Zinoviev, Kamenev and Stalin, was for accepting the terms after delaying as long as possible. Lenin argued that Russia had nothing with which to fight the German Army. While ultimate victory depended upon revolutions in the West, which indeed were in the making, these were still some way off. In the meanwhile, the Russian Revolution had no right to sacrifice itself in vain. The peace would give the revolution a 'breathing space', allow it to survive and organise itself while the movement in the West matured. A compromise with imperialists that was forced upon the workers was not a betrayal of internationalism.

The Left Communist opponents of the peace, led by Bukharin, claimed that the terms were such that the revolution would in any case be unable to survive. They pointed to the real signs of revolutionary movement in Western Europe—general strikes in Austro-Hungary, Germany, Poland as well as in Bordeaux and Lyons—and to the success of revolutionary agitation against Kornilov's troops in August. To sign the treaty would be a betrayal of the working classes of the West as well as that of Finland, at the time fighting a civil war against its own bourgeoisie, the Baltic countries and the Ukraine.

Trotsky took a middle position, advocating 'neither war nor peace'—a refusal to sign the treaty coupled with a unilateral declaration that Russia was demobilising. This would demonstrate in the strongest possible way to the German workers and soldiers that their government was waging an imperialist war and would give a strong boost to revolutionary anti-war sentiment all over Europe.[28]

At the Bolshevik CC meeting on 12 January Trotsky's position won by nine votes against seven. At the lower party levels in Petrograd sentiment was much more strongly opposed to the treaty. At the PC meeting on 28 December (by which time German intentions had become clear), opinion was overwhelmingly against the peace, for continued internationalist propaganda and, if it came to that, revolutionary war. Samkov, a worker from Vasilevskii ostrov, expressed the common suspicion that something was afoot among the leaders about which they were not being told.[29] Again, as in October, speakers called to put pressure on the *verkhi*. A conference of the party *aktiv* on 7 January voted 32 to 15 against accepting the peace terms.[30] On 18 January the PC formally adhered to the platform of the Left Communists[31] as did the Fifth City Conference, which opened on the eve of the offensive and had to be recessed.[32]

The position was the same in the central and district soviets of Petrograd. On 15 February, the Petrograd Soviet approved Trotsky's action in breaking off the talks and rejecting the peace terms.[33] The

Okhta District Soviet declared that 'it is better to die in the struggle for world revolution than to live enslaved by world capitalism'.[34] And of course, the Red Guards were firmly opposed to the peace.[35]

Attitudes among the worker rank and file are more difficult to gauge because there are few published resolutions in this period—the frequency of meetings declined as the economic crisis deepened. But where opinions were expressed and reached the press, they were consistently opposed to the peace. The Opticheskii workers resolved: 'Speaking with all our hearts against a separate peace with the Germans, we demand energetic steps in the direction of a democratic internationalist peace.'[36] The Opticheskii workers stuck to this even after the Germans had begun to move and the Bolshevik CC reversed itself (5/18 February), qualifying the treaty as a 'betrayal of the Finnish and Baltic working classes'.[37]

Sentiment was the same among the more moderate workers. A joint meeting of the Delegates' Assembly of the Printers Union and representatives of the factory committees pledged full support for soviet power but termed the German conditions unacceptable and called to fight.[38] This was also the case at the Nevskii Shipbuilding Factory, Alexandrovskii, Baltic Shipbuilding and others.[39]

On 21 February, after the Sovnarkom had telegraphed acceptance of the peace terms, the Menshevik *Novyi luch* reported: 'There is strong indignation among the proletariat of Petrograd. A series of factories held huge meetings with resolutions against the action of the Soviet government.' *Novaya zhizn'* also reported that information from Smol'nyi indicated strong opposition to the separate peace among the workers and particularly in the district soviets.[40]

Of course, such sentiment would have been gratuitous unless accompanied by a readiness to take up arms. For the Germans were encountering very little resistance, easily occupying Revel, Rezhitsa, Minsk and Dvinsk. And such willingness did exist, at least among a good part of the workers, who, as in October, acquitted themselves much better than the soldiers. Numerous factories responded to the news of the offensive by deciding on voluntary or universal enlistment in the Red Guards. The workers of New Arsenal declared:

At this time there can be no place for dissension within the working class. Rally behind the soviets, hoping that with a common burst of revolutionary enthusiasm we can hold the Germans back, and the world proletariat will overthrow their oppressor ... Long live the Soviets of Workers', Peasants' and Soldiers' Deputies. Long live the World Revolution.[41]

Summarising the reports from the districts on 9/22 February, the Petrograd Soviet concluded, 'revolutionary enthusiasm, willingness to fight, and the organisation of the Red Guards in progress'.[42] Up to 2 March, the Vyborg District sent out over 3000 armed men, with a similar number awaiting orders.[43] According to Startsev, in the five days of 25 February–1 March, 10 000 people joined the Red Army, bringing its numbers in Petrograd to 15 300. There was a similar number of Red Guards. Other workers formed special partisan units.[44]

Observers from different political currents contrasted the workers' response to that of the soldiers. 'The entire burden of the war falls on the workers', complained *Novaya zhizn*'. 'The soldiers refuse to fight, and there can be no talk of the peasants. Only the workers come forth as defenders.'[45] Zinoviev drew a similarly unfavourable comparison at the Petrograd Soviet between the workers and soldiers, pointing to the workers of the Sestroretsk Arms Factory who had formed an entire regiment and left for the front.[46] The Bolshevik *Workers' and Peasants' Red Army and Navy* reported:

> The working-class districts are agitated; they are full of alarm and enthusiasm. The proletariat is arming itself and leaving in the hundreds and thousands in defence of the revolution for the front. Women and children—even children!—are joining the Red Army. And at the same time—how painful to speak of it!—one observes on the part of the army itself, on the part of the revolutionary garrison, an incomprehensible attitude towards the current events. On the streets one encounters strange scenes. A detachment of civilians, hastily armed and variously dressed, proceeds towards the station singing revolutionary songs. And almost right behind it comes another, also an armed detachment—of soldiers and sailors. They usually have with them a carter pulling a mountain of chests and sacks. They too are on their way to the station. They joke and laugh. They are leaving—but to where?[47]

But enthusiasm was not the only reaction among the workers. On 1 March Shlyapnikov informed the Workers' Section of the Petrograd Soviet that panic was beginning among the workers, who wanted to leave Petrograd. In many places they were demanding six weeks' severance pay as stipulated by law.[48] The workers were beginning to succumb to the mood of the surrounding population. But one must add that this state of mind was fostered by the total failure of the government to clarify the situation. In the very midst of mobilisation for defence, orders were issued to prepare the factories for evacuation or to be rendered inoperative.[49] Such news could hardly have bolstered the spirits of the workers, whose most resolute elements had already left for the front, often with the entire factory committee in the lead.

The panic began in earnest after the 'night of alarm' when the factory whistles announced the fall of Pskov, only 250 kilometres from

Petrograd. At Staryi Lessner, the remaining 300 workers 'alarmed and frightened by the confusion, demanded an immediate settling of accounts. No amount of persuasion by the factory committee or representatives of the Metalworkers' Union had any effect.'[50] Observing what was taking place at neighbouring factories, the Erikson workers demanded guarantees that they would not be left without money if the Germans arrived. Unable to obtain these, they too demanded severance pay.[51] At Nobel, the news of Pskov's capture prompted the general assembly to call for universal enlistment. A flying squadron of 700 was formed. But after a tumultuous week, they decided to shut the factory down completely and take their severance pay.[52]

*Pravda* tended to see in this panic 'dark forces' at work, exploiting the absence of the 'best representatives of the working class gone to fight the German White Guards and speculating on the Germans' arrival to put forth economic demands for those remaining in the rear'.[53] But 'dark forces' aside, the long months of struggle, the uncertain economic and military conditions, the unemployment and hunger, and, indeed, the loss of the most capable and dedicated pro-soviet workers, had all taken their toll on morale. A comparison with the workers' response in the Kornilov and October Days leaves no doubt on this score.

The swift progress of the German forces lent much force to the arguments of Lenin and his supporters and appears to have greatly attenuated opposition to the separate peace. Already on 8/21 February the Petrograd Soviet overwhelmingly approved the Sovnarkom's telegram that accepted the peace terms.[54] Many factories followed suit, including many of those that had earlier insisted on fighting.[55] Although the Petrograd Trade Union Council voted 30 against 22 to reject the treaty, the leadership of the Metalworkers' and Woodworkers' Unions dissented, and on 9 March, a meeting of the Trade Union Council together with 500 representatives of the largest factories voted for ratification of the treaty and for new elections to the Executive Committee of the Council.[56]

Sentiment in the Petrograd Bolshevik organisation also shifted. Although the Fifth City Conference that reconvened after the peace elected an overwhelmingly Left Communist PC, a new conference held a few weeks later decided to end the existence of the Left Communists as a separate faction and to discontinue its organ *Kommunist.*[57] The Vyborg and other districts, with the exception of Narva, supported this decision, as did the Petrograd Regional Party Conference representing Sestroretsk, Kolpino, the Finns and others (a total of 12 582 members).[58]

The usual division between left and right, radical and moderate, seemed to break down over this issue. While groups that had been consistently left in 1917 ended by endorsing the treaty, more moderate elements persisted in their opposition. Among these, aside from the Trade Union Council majority (but significantly not the leaders of the traditionally more radical Metal- and Woodworkers' Unions), were the LSRs, the Mensheviks and SRs, the workers at the Nevskii Shipbuilding Factory,[59] the Baltic Factory,[60] and some shops of the Putilov Works.[61] This perhaps reflected a preoccupation with the isolation of the workers, whom they considered incapable of seeing the revolution through, even with the support of the peasants. At least some of these groups condemned Brest-Litovsk as a retreat from world revolution that would deprive the workers of yet another potential ally, the international proletariat.

### The Opposition—Growth and Failure

During the spring of 1918, the SR and Menshevik advocates of replacing soviet power with the Constituent Assembly continued to gather support among the factory workers. As before, they argued that the civil war and other difficulties the revolution was encountering could not be overcome by the politically isolated soviet régime. The workers and their peasant allies had to transfer power to 'united democracy' through the Constituent Assembly. Also as earlier, the political opposition was nurtured by the workers' economic misery with the occasional boost provided by government repression of worker protests over the food situation.

But the politicisation of discontent so strongly based upon hunger was not without its ambiguities. For if hunger fostered opposition to the régime, it also gave rise to an impatience with politics. In an earlier period this had favoured the anarchists. But by now the latter had lost their appeal for the exhausted workers, who wanted mainly food and calm. 'We are in a zone of declining civic mood among the working class', noted a cultural activist in May.

> At the basis of all this is, of course, fatigue ... Lectures by outstanding speakers on the humanistic sciences draw on the average 15–25 people, and political meetings succeed only when popular names are used as bait. But right alongside this, dance evenings organised by the clubs attract overflow crowds of 1000–1500.[62]

On 9 May, Zinoviev, Chairman of the Petrograd Soviet, spoke at the Putilov Works, where the opposition had been making considerable headway. He explained the serious political and military situation of the republic and warned against the Mensheviks and SRs 'who want only to lure the workers back under the yoke of capitalism'. But presently the meeting grew weary of Zinoviev's political analysis and amidst shouts of 'We've had enough politics, we're tired of it', demanded explanations 'on the food question'. When Volodarskii also began to polemicise with the Mensheviks and SRs, he was interrupted by shouts: 'Closer to the issues! Talk about bread!' In the short run, hunger greatly aided the opposition. But in the longer term, it proved a shaky basis upon which to build a political movement.

Nevertheless, the opposition was really beginning to pick up steam, particularly among the workers whose support for soviet power was only a relatively recent phenomenon. In mid February the Mensheviks reported from Kolpino that 'in connection with a certain shift of mood of late', they had begun to think seriously of rebuilding their organisation which had collapsed after October. The Kolpino workers, employed mainly at the state Izhorskii Shipbuilding Factory, had left the defencists (mostly SRs) only in the late summer, although they had firmly supported the insurrection.[63] Moreover, they failed to demonstrate in favour of the Constituent Assembly in January. But now they seemed to be having second thoughts. A recent meeting organised by the Mensheviks and SRs and attended by prominent figures from all parties did give the Bolsheviks a majority, but it was already a rather slim one.[64]

Another sign of the changing times was the decision of the Petrograd Printers' Union in March to hold new elections intended to oust the Bolshevik executive.[65] These elections, held in April, returned only nine Bolsheviks to the twenty-five-seat executive.[66] Pulled to the left under the impact of the October Revolution, the printers were returning to their traditional moderate leadership.

March also witnessed an expansion in the activity of the Sobranie upolnomochennykh (SU), the Assembly of Delegates of the Factories and Mills of Petrograd, founded by Mensheviks and SRs after the dispersal of the Constituent Assembly to provide an 'independent' alternative to the soviets. Its chief political slogan was 'All power to the Constituent Assembly'.[67]

In its agitation, the SU leaned heavily on economic issues and only very gradually and gingerly moved to more directly political questions. Its appeal to the workers in late March began:

> The war is not over, but our suffering is only beginning. There is little work; a senseless, disorderly evacuation is totally ruining industry. Workers in their tens of thousands are being thrown onto the streets. One cannot leave, and anyway, there is nowhere to go. There is little work anywhere. The last money is being eaten. A hungry summer is on its way.

It did attack the soviets and other Bolshevik-led organisations for doing nothing to help the workers but stopped short of posing overtly political demands, stating merely that 'the Assembly discusses all questions of worker life and seeks means of defending the workers against the oncoming misery'.[68]

This approach was designed to accord with the prevailing mood among the workers, whose acute dissatisfaction with their material situation in most cases had not yet translated itself into opposition to soviet rule. But there were already signs that this might not be long in coming. 'Among the workers', reported a delegate to the Vyborg District Soviet in March, 'there is a panicky fear in face of the terrible misery that approaches.' 'Among the workers a reaction is growing', observed another. 'For they haven't received any of what was promised to them by the soviet régime.'[69]

As time went on, the SU began to act more boldly, calling directly for the transfer of power to the Constituent Assembly, though this was inevitably tied to the issue of hunger. An SU-organised meeting at the Vargunina Paper Mill (Nevskii District) in mid May resolved:

> Having heard a report on the food question, [we] demand the annihilation of the civil war in the country and the convocation of the Constituent Assembly, organs of self-government: city dumas and zemstvos, on the basis of universal, equal, direct and secret ballot, the creation of a unified, firm governmental authority to unite the disintegrated country, to put an end to the multiple centres of power [*mnogovlastie*] in the food sector and to set it in order on an all-state scale.

This was followed by the election of delegates to the SU.[70]

On 12 May at the Obukhovskii Factory a meeting heard reports on the food situation from representatives of the Central Food Authority, who attempted to show their successes in face of harsh objective conditions. But workers responded that these claims did not correspond to the reality, that the fact of hunger disproved them. After this, a delegation that had been sent to attend a session of the Bureau of the SU gave its own report, and the meeting adopted a resolution in support of the SU's position.[71]

A well-attended meeting at the Main Workshops of the Nikolaev Railroad heard the report of its delegation just returned from Moscow, where it had been sent to obtain permission for the workers to buy food collectively. The delegation reported that the government had rejected their request arguing that to permit the free purchase and shipment of food would destroy its efforts to come to grips with hunger by establishing a 'food dictatorship'. The meeting resolved to 'condemn the activity of the soviet government that has destroyed the food apparatus' and demanded the convocation of the Constituent Assembly.[72]

The more penetrating among the sympathisers of the opposition recognised that it was growing largely on the basis of the workers' extreme weariness:

> The ruling party can and will point to the fatigue of the Petrograd workers, to the temporary decline in their faith in a victory close at hand. But is not the proletariat tired all over Russia and is it not being dispersed in a struggle that is beyond its strength? And can one build a victory against the whole world on fatigue?[73]

Fatigue was the very essence of the worker opposition rallying behind the slogans of democratic unity and the Constituent Assembly, slogans that expressed above all a desire to retreat from the latest, extreme phase of the revolution, to end the isolation of the *nizy* and have done with the civil war. 'Not the Constituent Assembly and not a united front, but decisive struggle', exhorted the Bolsheviks.[74] 'Salvation is possible only through the creation of an all-democratic government in the form of the Constituent Assembly', replied the leaders of the opposition.[75]

Support for the Constituent Assembly in the spring on the part of workers who had not raised a finger to defend it back in January can only be understood against the background of their growing exhaustion and desperation over an economic crisis of unimagined proportions. In fact, the workers' preference had always been for a united revolutionary-democratic government that would decisively break with the capitalists and landowners and carry out a truly revolutionary policy. But they finally gave up on this in October–November, concluding that it was unrealisable and pledging their full support for a soviet government that consisted only of left-wing democracy.

Nothing had changed objectively to make democratic unity seem more of a possibility in the spring. But in the meanwhile, the economic situation had gone from bad to disastrous. Defenders of soviet power explained this by the refusal of the educated strata to put their knowledge and skills at the service of a workers' and peasants' government and by the German occupation and the civil war. All these conditions, they argued, had been imposed upon the workers, and the only way out was to fight for the victory of soviet power. They pointed to events in the Ukraine, where a counterrevolutionary régime had replaced the moderate nationalist Rada in April, as proof of the illusory nature of a 'third force' advocated by the SU. 'What the Mensheviks and SRs are proposing', the LSR Proshyan explained to the Putilov workers, 'that is, a common national policy to the detriment of a class policy, can lead the revolution only to Skoropadskii ["Hetman of the Ukraine"]'.[76] They observed further that the Kadets and the Tsarist officers converging on southern Russia were also demanding the Constituent Assembly while secretly dreaming of counterrevolution. That was the real alternative to soviet power. 'Call forth every last ounce of strength', declared Lunacharskii at the Baltic Factory, 'or surrender!'[77]

On its part, the opposition hammered away at the narrow, exclusively worker and peasant base of the régime as the root cause of its inability to govern effectively and to deal with the economic crisis. This was put very bluntly by a Menshevik worker from the Patronnyi Factory at a conference of worker and Red Army delegates at the end of May.

> We warned you that if you signed the obscene peace you would not thus end the war but only intensify the civil war. And this fact is also at hand. All this must be eliminated, but the régime is not capable of it . . . If the evacuation goes ahead without any plan, then one cannot count on the factories' operation. But this too the government is unable to do. Only a people's government, elected by equal and secret ballot, i.e. the Constituent Assembly, can accomplish this . . . Why do we have raw materials, we have fuel [!], but the factories are not open? Because our people are not capable of working there. Now, at our plant a locksmith has been transferred to a turner's job, and tailors [are being appointed] inspector and commissar. Thus, in the Third City [sub] District the honourable comrade Gorbachev is a tailor. Now he is a commissar. He can, of course, sew on a patch well. But can he bring any benefit to the state? Hardly.[78]

This was not an accusation of individual incompetence and corruption, which were widespread enough, as the Bolsheviks themselves constantly complained. They could be corrected. It was rather a claim that the very social basis of the régime rendered it inherently incapable of effective government.

At a meeting on the food situation at the Putilov Works, Glebov, a worker advocate of socialist unity, rebuked Zinoviev, saying that it was inappropriate that

> in such a moment, when Petrograd stands on the eve of real hunger, the commissar who spoke here did nothing but polemicise with the socialist parties, condemning the saboteurs and justifying himself . . . We ask to answer clearly and simply the question: Can the people's commissars feed the hungry and give peace, real peace on the internal and external fronts?

Apparently a significant part of the workers did not think so because a meeting held here on the previous day had resolved: 'Alone, without the aid of national, socialist and democratic forces, they [the People's Commissars] cannot handle the task, and we hurl before their eyes our will, our worker and revolutionary truth: Unite!'[79] The desire for unity, strong among the Putilov workers in October but set aside in face of the defencists' rejection of soviet power, was again coming to the fore under the inpact of the deepening crisis.

Accompanying discontent over the government's failure to reverse the economic decline was a growing feeling among a part of the workers that their elected organisations were no longer responsive to their needs, that they were serving alien interests. In part, this expressed extreme frustration with the difficult circumstances. On 18 March, the general assembly of Metallicheskii discussed the question of back payment for dismissed workers. An agreement had already been reached with the Commissar of Labour, but after the central government moved to Moscow the matter was transferred to the Soviet of the Northern Commune, which amended the decision, forcing renewed negotiations. But in the meanwhile, no money had been paid out, and the workers wanted to know why. The rapporteur from the factory committee explained that despite all the measures taken, including two 48-hour ultimata to the administration with the threat of arrest, payment could begin only in a few days because, apart from everything else, there were difficulties changing big bills. According to a report

The meeting expressed its dissatisfaction with the work of its committee, and five people from among the workers are elected to participate in the task and thereby control [*kontrolirovat'*] the work. The mood of the workers, as one speaker observed, is explained by hunger.

During the discussion, one speaker argued that the government was allegedly hindering the work of the delegates by putting pressure on them. Another, referring to the constant appeals to support the government, wondered how it was possible further to intensify this support—'by holding onto the fenders of the cars when they leave [for Moscow]?'[80]

The atmosphere of conflict between the workers and their organisations—the factory committees, trade unions and soviets —was fostered by the latter's swift transformation from organs of class struggle, whose primary function had been to educate and mobilise the workers, into organs preoccupied more and more with state and economic administration. In a sense, this seemed only natural: a workers' state should be run by the workers' organisations. And nowhere was this transformation more striking than in the Bolshevik Party itself. According to Shelavin, a member of the PC in 1918

A whole series of responsible, highly skilled comrades who had gone through the school of the underground became infected with an exclusively 'soviet' mood, not to speak of the young contingent ... They felt that now the real thing was to organise, for example, the district soviet of the national economy but not by any means to 'ferment' in the district party committee.[81]

Even in ideal economic conditions and under the most representative system, there is still bound to be some degree of conflict between more general needs and those of individuals and groups. But Russia in the spring of 1918 was living through an almost total economic breakdown, general scarcity of all resources, mass unemployment on an unprecedented scale and hunger. The soviet state was unable to meet even the minimum needs of the workers. Under such circumstances it required a high degree of dedication and tolerance on the part of workers to continue to view this state as the incarnation of their interests.

And some workers had a rather primitive view of what a workers' state should be. During the German advance, at a meeting in the Putilov Works, workers who wanted to leave the capital demanded immediate severance pay. One of them declared: 'Give us money and wagons too ... Soviet power—that is our power and must do everything for us ... All that the *nizy* demand it must carry out.'[82]

The sense of estrangement of a growing part of the workers from the various economic and political organisations brought new support to the traditional Menshevik position that workers' organisations should be independent of the various political currents. An appeal of the Bureau of the SU in March describing the workers' suffering declared:

One can expect help from no one. Have the trade unions done much for the unemployed? They are preoccupied not with the unemployed and also not with those who are working. The unions organise the economy and not the workers.

The factory committees have become commissions for the dismissal of workers, state institutions which have no need of our confidence and which lost it long ago. They too will not help us.

It stated further that there was nothing to expect from the soviets either, which only judge, punish, extract taxes, organise the Red Guards and sometimes even shoot. The workers had to begin thinking about their own fate.[83]

In some places workers held election after election of their factory committee in a vain effort to obtain action on their demands. The general assembly of the Printers' Union explained its decision to hold new elections by the Bolshevik executive's failure to support the idea of class struggle, replacing 'the activity of a class organisation with the intervention of the state power ... Carried away by state affairs, it neither wanted nor was able to take action against unemployment.'[84] Similarly, a meeting of the Izhorskii Factory resolved:

> Taking into account that all our workers' organisations—the factory committees, unions and soviets—have ceased to be independent workers' organisations and have turned into state offices, the meeting protests against such a policy of the soviet government and demands the return of the workers' organisations to their class path.[85]

But the alienation and conflict were not only the result of frustration at an objective inability on the part of the organisations to alleviate the workers' hardships. The transformation of these organisations into organs of administration and of the Bolshevik Party into a ruling party, the assumption of new administrative responsibilities by worker militants and their loss of direct continuous contact with the factory milieu inevitably gave rise to a certain 'administrative outlook'. It expressed itself, however imperceptibly at first, in changes of attitude and tone towards the remaining factory masses, in the development of a certain condescension and impatience towards their problems and particularly their protests, and in a growing intolerance of the worker opposition. All of this contributed significantly to the politicisation of discontent.

These changes are most readily evident in the Bolshevik press, in the small space *Pravda* (succeeded by *Petrogradskaya pravda*) now allocated to factory life as well as in its increasingly distorted reporting (though not to be exaggerated in this period) on the worker opposition. This contrasted sharply with the earlier quite broad coverage of the worker milieu and the paper's much more forthright style. In this respect, at least, the Bolsheviks were following in the footsteps of the defencists when they entered the Provisional Government and became quasi-ruling parties.

In an article that was at once a harsh critique of the contemporary party and a grudging eulogy to its recent past, the Menshevik Stroev took note of this transformation:

> The Bolshevik Party, which did not embrace the entire working class with its organised influence, having driven away the intellectual cadres of the socialist parties by its maximalist irreconcilability, is able all the less to service even the purposely simplified governmental apparatus of the Republic of Soviets, which in the opinion of Lenin is accessible even to barely literate workers and peasants.
>
> The best workers have been torn away from their class by government work. The still not consolidated trade union organisations of

the proletariat have been sacrificed to this same Moloch of allegedly socialist statehood.

The political organisation of the working class—the party of social democratic Bolsheviks or Communists—has also, in essence, been smashed. For finding itself in power, it has ceased to live as a party that organises the working class and speaks to it exclusively in the language of omnipotent benevolence or commanding prohibition. The natural healthy growth of the party, the growth of consciousness and organisation in the working class have ceased.[86]

So conclusive a verdict was perhaps still unwarranted in April 1918. And the unequivocal attribution of the left intelligentsia's hostility to Bolshevik 'maximalist irreconcilability' is also more than a little dubious in light of what Stroev's paper itself had written earlier.[87] But he did have his finger on a crucial process: the absorption of the most vital segment of the working class into the new state machinery (including the Red Army) and its transformation into a sort of ruling stratum as it lost its ties with the dying factories.

Government repression against workers' protest, still rare in this period but all the more shocking, was to some degree another manifestation of these changes in attitude. There were two major incidents in and around Petrograd (apart from 5 January) before the end of June that greatly rebounded to the benefit of the opposition.

The first occurred in Kolpino, where already on 7 May there had been a noticeable shortage of food. On the ninth, women queuing for bread were told that supplies had run out. After failing to find the Chairman of the local Food Authority, a large crowd of women moved towards the town square. At this point, Red Guards arrived and, using their rifle butts, prevented a group of women from reaching the fire station in order to sound the alarm. But one youth managed to get through and was shot and wounded by the assistant Red Guard commander. This was followed by a rifle volley into the crowd, causing four casualties, one dead and three wounded. Workers began running out of the shipbuilding factory but were turned back by the Red Guards.

A general assembly at the factory decided to hold new elections to the Kolpino Soviet and to demand the arrest of those responsible for the shooting. It also decided to send delegations to Petrograd to discuss a joint plan of action. But on leaving the factory gates, the workers were met by Red Guards who opened fire, killing one and wounding several others. This was followed by searches and arrests. In the evening, the town was placed under martial law.[88]

The other incident occurred in Sestroretsk and was also initiated by women enraged at the food shortages in early May. A crowd of women went to the arms factory where a meeting was convened. Some speakers called for the overthrow of the soviet régime. From here, a crowd proceeded to the apartments of members of the local soviet and sacked them. Others went to the soviet, dispersing and beating up some of the delegates in the process. A large number of arrests followed, including some factory workers (released after an investigation). The workers responded to this with a strike and the call for new elections.[89] In addition to these two, there was also a number of minor incidents.

This repression of workers was still exceptional in a period of quite broad toleration of the moderate socialists, whose papers as well as the SU continued to exist with little government interference despite their open and extremely hostile agitation against the soviet régime. And these were very desperate times for the régime, with Petrograd on the verge of starvation and the Ukraine, Russia's breadbasket and chief source of coal and iron, being overrun by German and White troops.[90] Just how desperate they were can be judged from Lenin's 11 May telegram to all soviets and food authorities, demanding and pleading for the immediate dispatch of food to save 'the red capital . . . on the verge of perishing'.[91]

The Kolpino events in particular were followed by protest meetings at several factories that demanded the convocation of the Constituent Assembly. Reports from the districts at the 11 May SU session noted that 'the recent shootings at Kolpino have overshadowed the workers' thoughts about hunger'.[92] The meeting at Siemens–Shukkert resolved:

> Having discussed the question of the current moment and hunger, on the basis of which food disturbances arise and the current government employs the force of arms to liquidate them, which is confirmed by the Kolpino events, . . . we demand the unification of all democratic strata of the population and the establishment of a higher state authority by means of universal, direct, secret and equal suffrage, i.e. the convocation of the All-Russian Constituent Assembly, which alone can ease the food situation and all public life.[93]

The Bolsheviks and LSRs were aware of the growing alienation of the factory workers from the organs of power and admitted that the latter's attitudes were often to blame. They were particularly concerned about the district soviets, which had always been closest to the workers and were now often the first targets of their ire. Partly in recognition of this reality and partly in response to Menshevik and SR initiatives in the SU, on the suggestion of the the Inter-District Conference (of District Soviets) the Petrograd Soviet decided in April to convene district workers' conferences to 'clarify the opinion of the worker masses on the current moment'. These conferences were to be

organised by a joint commission of all parties represented in the soviets
and to be elected on the basis of one vote for every fifty employed or
unemployed workers with special representation for the various district organisations (which, of course, favoured the Bolsheviks) and
parties.[94]

The decision to call these conferences was an implicit admission that
the soviets had grown away from the masses. The Narva District
Conference noted that

> The work of the district soviet can be successful only if our deputies
> do not look upon their work as bureaucratic [chinovnichii] and carry
> on a decisive struggle against laziness and slovenliness among those
> who have not yet freed themselves from these vices.[95]

The First City District Conference directed its soviet deputies to
establish closer ties with the workers and to report back to them at least
once a month.[96]

The Bolsheviks themselves saw a major cause of the problem in the
district soviets' detachment not only from the worker masses but from
the party. On 9 April, the PC resolved:

> The weakness and incompleteness of party control over the course
> of soviet work in the districts in the post-October period has led to a
> series of harmful consequences and has had a disastrous effect first
> of all on the activity of the district soviets themselves.[97]

As Stroev had noted, the party's advent to power and the great efflux
of party members into government work had led to its emasculation as
a body that decided policy, educated, organised and led the workers
and to a concomitant freeing of the soviets from its collective influence.

This development was of great concern to the Bolshevik Party
Conference of the Northern Region in April and it especially worried
the Left Communists, who moved:

> The conference, on the basis of reports from the localities, affirms
> that party-organisational work has weakened significantly. The best
> party forces have left for soviet work. A significant part of the
> comrades are torn away from party life, which poses a definite
> danger to the party. Further, the conference affirms that the influ-
> ence of responsible party institutions is little felt in the local organs
> of power. In the soviets above all, questions are decided according to
> the decisions of the soviet fractions, that include not only party
> members but also sympathisers.[98]

In one sense what was being argued was that the administrative point of view was in danger of winning out over the revolutionary-political. At the same time, the headlong rush from party work in the factories and districts was depriving the party of what had traditionally been its most crucial asset—its organic links to the factory masses. Both the Bolsheviks and LSRs felt strongly that the progressive loss of these ties was contributing to the success of the Mensheviks and SRs, who had become very active on the local level since October. In addition, the changes in the composition of the work force, the decline of metalworking and the rise to relative prominence of textiles, paper and print and food processing, provided the opposition parties with an overall much more receptive audience. 'Forces of the right', the worker Khmara wrote to the LSR *Znamya bor'by,* 'utilising the temporary absence of conscious [*ideinye*] revolutionary forces, score temporary successes among the passive workers.'[99]

There was no doubt some truth to this view, although it sometimes distracted attention from the more basic cause of the opposition's growth—the workers' real grievances. In the spring of 1918 there was a good deal of political oscillation among the factory masses, and the presence or absence of an able pro-soviet speaker could sometimes make a difference. Decisions taken at one meeting would be over-turned at the next. Meanwhile, pro-soviet and opposition papers each printed the respective resolutions claiming the workers for their side. This had almost never occurred in 1917.

For example, soon after the Kolpino events, in the absence of the Bolshevik and LSR factory committee members, the Vulkan workers met and decided to hold new elections to the Soviet as well as to call a conference of 'all socialist and honest democratic elements willing to aid the toiling masses and with the aid of socialist and democratic forces to organise the shipment of food'.[100] The Menshevik and SR press made much of this as evidence that even the regime's most loyal supporters were turning away from it. But three days later, this time with the full factory committee present, the workers voted to support the Soviet 'in this difficult moment', rejecting the resolution put forth by the opposition.[101]

Khmara claimed that there were many examples of this. At Nobel the opposition would have persuaded the workers against participating in the May Day celebrations and to demand the convocation of the Constituent Assembly had it not been for 'one comrade maximalist who explained the significance of the resolution to the workers'. 'We cannot leave the masses in the factories without militants [*aktivnye rabotniki*]', he pleaded. 'Comrades in the factories, invite speakers and lecturers, shed light on your factory life in the newspapers, do not yield to the provocations of the conciliationist parties.'[102]

This was also how Shelavin explained the textile workers' vote in the June Soviet elections. In general, the opposition had very limited success among these workers. But in a few mills, particularly in the Nevskii District, on the contrary, they did very well.

> Where nothing is done, or little, there the women are benighted, unorganised, ready to listen to any defencists or 'delegates' and to dance to their tune ... However, the workers of Novaya Bumagopryadil'nya sent Communists to the Soviet and do not want to listen to the defencists. At Novaya Bumagopryadil'nya the party was at work; in the Nevskii District it apparently is only getting ready to work.[103]

This, of course, begs the question of why the Bolsheviks and LSRs were not at work in this most populous of Petrograd's working-class districts in 1918. In the case of Nevskii at least, the specific character of the work force, in particular the moderating influence of the settled, small property-owning workers, was important. The work force of the Urals also contained a significant stratum of workers who owned cottages, garden plots and some cattle; several factories here too were the scene of labour revolts in May 1918 on the background of the food crisis. Here too, the more active, pro-soviet elements were absent, fighting Cossack Ataman Dutov.[104]

What of the militants, the Bolshevik and LSR workers themselves? The contrast here with the fate of the defencist parties in 1917 is striking. While the defencists by the autumn of 1917 had lost almost all of their working-class members, who either joined the Bolsheviks and LSRs or dropped out of politics altogether, in the spring of 1918 the worker members of the latter two parties showed no signs of wavering.

Even the opposition had to admit this. In May the LSR *Znamya bor'by* lamented the fact that 'the masses have lost the ground from under them and are ready to greet anyone who will give them more bread'. It noted an internal struggle within the working class between 'its elected, organised part and the benighted undeveloped [*malosoznatel'naya*] part that does not understand its class interests and has lost its class instinct'. Commenting on this, *Novaya zhizn'* was in general agreement with the analysis but took exception to the part on the 'conscious workers'. The latter had, in fact, long since understood the 'complete hopelessness of soviet irreconcilability, and it is only their inability to deal with the maximalism of the benighted masses and their strong ties to their party that hold them captive of a hopeless, makeshift communism'.[105] But one would have searched in vain in the spring of 1918 for these 'maximalist benighted masses'. In fact, just the opposite was true. The economic crisis, the terrible privations and the civil war (still far from reaching full intensity) were causing a reaction among the factory masses, pushing them away from the radicalism of the October period.

The Petrograd Soviet, still overwhelmingly Bolshevik, firmly supported the government through all the crises. The same was true of the Bolshevik and LSR rank and file in other political forums, where they energetically countered the opposition's attacks.[106] At the Workers' Conference in the Vyborg District, the pro-soviet forces went so far as to call for the exclusion of Mensheviks and SRs from the district soviets as 'counterrevolutionaries and conciliators' and threatened to exclude them from the conference itself.[107]

As one might expect, despite their own grievances, the Petrograd Red Army workers never wavered in their loyalty. In the June Soviet elections they elected fifty-eight delegates—fifty-five Bolsheviks and three LSRs.[108]

Of course, even these worker elements did not spare the government their criticisms. But there was always a bottom line upon which all agreed—soviet power. The government's handling of the food question in particular was cause for much discontent in the party ranks. A Bolshevik conference on this issue revealed great dissatisfaction with the supply authorities, local as well as central. There were two basic positions, one supporting centralisation and the other defending the elective principle and broad district powers. But the latter was far from advocating a broadening of the regime's social base, as the opposition demanded. On the contrary, it insisted on the need to purge the many remaining 'saboteurs' from the food supply organisation. Regarding the Central Food Authority, Kudeshov, a worker from the Vasilevskii ostrov District, stated:

> Its apparatus is good for nothing. It should have been dispersed long ago. Now they want to change it from above. But that is self-delusion. Putting in two or three people won't change a thing. The Central Food Authority consists of thousands—wall-to-wall saboteurs ... We called for a purge of our enemies from the Central Food Authority long ago, but it still is not being done.[109]

There existed among the Bolshevik workers a firm, virtually unshakable faith in the régime. Zikhareva, a Menshevik intellectual, offered the following, perhaps somewhat slanted, portrait of a Bolshevik woman worker. It was in a bread queue, and the women were in good spirits because the ration was up to one-half funt. But one cautioned:

> 'Don't worry. It will be like last time. They will lull us for a couple of days and then again begin to give an eighth of a funt, and then there will be nothing at all.'
> 'Well, no! This time it will hold. And now there will be everything—sugar and butter. During the search [of food stores], it is amazing how much they confiscated.'

This was spoken by Dasha, a tall, pockmarked native of Yaroslavl' Province. I often see her. She never stands at her place in the queue but moves from one group to the next, butts into all conversations and agitates determinedly for the Bolsheviks. There is terrible confusion in her head, but by temperament she is a genuine revolutionary and demagogue. In her desire to defeat the opponent, she does not bother too much about the truth nor is she choosy in her choice of arguments and expressions. Her voice is loud and rather hoarse. Her speech is quick, energetic. They fear her in the queue.

'Yes, well, we all know you are a Bolshevik!'

'Of course, I'm not a Kaledinite. [Cossack general, head of the first White government on the Don.[110]] I am a peasant, from the people, and I follow the people. And I like the Bolsheviks because they care about the simple people and don't give anyone favours. Just give them some time, and they will have all in hand. You'll see what they accomplish then.'[111]

These workers identified very closely with soviet power and they identified soviet power with the *nizy*. At the Workers' Conference of the First City District, the worker V. Ivanov made the following reply to the Menshevik and SR claims of worker estrangement from the régime:

Yes, there is a part of the workers that berates, scolds the soviet régime. But that still does not mean that they don't recognise their own [*rodnaya*] soviet power, just as we see a mother scolding her child, fearing it will get spoiled; and she scolds him precisely because she loves him. But they [Mensheviks and SRs], of course, will never understand this, because they have ceased to be a party of workers, they have left our cause, the cause of the proletarian revolution.[112]

To what degree was this merely wishful thinking, Ivanov's projection of his own sentiments onto the rest of the workers? It is difficult to give a firm answer to this because of the limited and often contradictory nature of the evidence. But there were two major events in the early summer of 1918 which offer more precise insight into the size and nature of the worker opposition and about which there was considerable consensus among the different parties.

On 12 June, the EC of the Soviet of the Northern Commune decided to call the first general city-wide Soviet elections ever. (Until then elections had been held locally on the decision of individual factories.) This decision was taken in part to meet the challenge of the SU and its claim that the workers, disillusioned in the soviets, had chosen it as their genuine spokesperson.

But it is also probable that the pro-soviet parties hoped the result could be used as a mandate to move finally against the SU, whose openly anti-soviet activity had been tolerated until then. For the October Revolution was entering its most critical phase. The food situation was disastrous. After establishing the 'food dictatorship', the Bolsheviks took the fateful decision to organise 'Committees of the Poor' in the countryside in an effort to win the cooperation of the poor peasants in wresting surplus grain from the better-off elements. At the end of May the Czechoslovak troops in Russia rose up against the soviets, seizing Saratov, the central town on the Middle Volga, as well as towns east in Western and Central Siberia along the Trans-Siberian Railroad. In some places, such as Krasnoyarsk and Omsk, the largest city in Western Siberia, the soviets were overthrown by internal uprisings even before the Czechs actually arrived.[113] It was just at this time that the SU was beginning to organise on an inter-city scale with a major conference in Moscow in early June.

The opposition parties maintained that the electoral procedure strongly favoured the Bolsheviks and LSRs since it gave organisations as well as factories a large representation. For example, the Petrograd Trade Union Council sent one delegate for every 5000 organised workers, individual unions with over 2000 members sent two delegates, and smaller unions sent one—in all 144 delegates from the unions. In addition, district soviets each had three representatives and factory committees of closed enterprises that had employed over 1000 workers could also send one each. In all these, of course, the Bolsheviks predominated.

On the other hand, the election results from the factories still in operation were not challenged by the opposition.[114] And while the latter was subject to non-systematic harassment, it remained on the whole free to agitate both in the press and at meetings. Moreover, given the mood in the factories, any limitations on freedom of speech and organisation among the workers would only have played into the hands of the opposition. In any case, it never made an issue of repression in its evaluation of the returns.

Of the two main sources available on the elections, *Severnaya kommuna*, the Petrograd Soviet's paper, is the most complete. Many of the missing returns from the factories can be filled in by *Novaya zhizn'*'s listings. There was no direct information on Vargunina, Pal', Izhorskii, Sestroretsk Arms, Trubochnyi and Skorokhod. But other evidence makes it clear that the first three were oppositional, while Skorokhod was still strongly Bolshevik.[115] The positions of the Trubochnyi and Sestroretsk workers are unclear, though the latter clearly tended towards the opposition during the food crisis of May. The omission of these factories from the tabulation, therefore, somewhat favours the soviet parties. On the other hand, the mode of representation favoured small plants, since although every 500 workers were to be represented by one delegate, enterprises with over 300 could also elect their own delegate, while smaller ones held elections jointly. Small factories, as noted, were traditionally moderate. Finally, a list of closed factories published in *Metallist*, permits the elimination of delegates elected by caretaker factory committees.[116]

On the basis of these sources, factories still in operation elected 262 delegates. This figure appears reasonable since one delegate for 500 workers yields approximately 131 000 employed workers. Official statistics put the number of employed industrial workers on 1 May at 143 000.

Table 8.3 gives the party breakdown. In view of the approximate nature of the data, the Bolshevik–LSR vote could well have been lower, but not conceivably below 50 per cent. Therefore, even if one groups all the non- affiliated delegates with the opposition, it could still not claim to have won over the working class. Moreover, as already noted, the heavily working-class Red Army (the sailors voted separately) returned 55 Bolsheviks and 3 LSRs. And there was a general consensus that the workers had shown a keen interest in the elections. The SU itself, after deciding to participate, conducted an energetic campaign.[117]

TABLE 8.3: *Party Affiliation of Delegates Elected to the Petrograd Soviet from Operating Factories 18–24 June 1918*

| Party[a] | Number of delegates | Percent of all delegates |
|---|---|---|
| Bolshevik | 127 | 48.5 |
| LSR | 32 | 12.2 |
| Mensheviks[b] | 29 | 11.1 |
| SR | 46 | 17.6 |
| Non-affiliated | 28 | 10.7 |
| Total | 262 | 100.1 |

[a] Includes sympathisers.
[b] Includes delegate of United Workers' Party with platform similar to the Mensheviks.
Sources: *Severnaya kommuna* (5 and 6 July 1918); *Novaya zhizn'* (18–26 June 1918).

In evaluating these results, the circumstances in which the voting occurred must be considered. In the very midst of the elections, which took place over seven days, the government announced that the ration would be reduced to one-eighth funt on 24 June and that on 25 and 26 June, instead of bread, one-eighth funt of groats would be distributed.[118] A participant in the election campaign recalled: 'Meetings in the factories and shops were often overflowing with anguish, bitterness and pain. Instead of speeches, the women workers demanded bread. Tears flowed from the eyes of hundreds and hundreds of mothers.'[119] Just before the elections, the soviet authorities began to step up repressions against the opposition outside of Petrograd. Menshevik and SR members of the SU were arrested in Sormovo and Moscow, along with some Petrograd SU delegates in Moscow for the conference.[120] In Tula, Sormovo and Moscow there were incidents involving the use of firearms against workers. [121] On 24 June the TsIK in Moscow voted to exclude Mensheviks and SRs and recommended that local soviets do the same.[122]

If these measures could be expected to intensify hostility to the régime among the workers, the assassination of Volodarskii probably had the opposite effect, as the SR paper *Delo naroda* feared.[123] Volodarskii, the popular Petrograd Bolshevik leader, a tailor by trade who had returned from political emigration in the US after the February Revolution, was shot by an SR, Sergeev, on 20 June while on his way to an election meeting at the Aleksandrovskii Factory in the Nevskii District. Despite the pouring rain, thousands of workers turned out for his funeral.[124] This assassination served to bolster the Bolshevik argument that it was 'either soviet power or Skoropadskii', that there was no retreat but surrender. The active involvement of Right SRs in White anti-soviet movements in Siberia and the Ukraine did not help the opposition either.

These were hard and confusing times that pulled the workers in opposing directions. And the election results reveal a divided working class. The breakdown by factory shows that the opposition did well where the defencists had been strongest in 1917—the Nevskii District, printing establishments, railroad workshops, state metalworking factories, municipal enterprises. The textile workers, however, were an exception that requires special explanation.

The Nevskii District (including Nevskii, Obukhovskii, Aleksandrovskii, Maksvel', Thornton and Porcelain) returned thirteen SRs, one Menshevik, fourteen delegates on the joint Menshevik–SR list, seven Bolsheviks, two LSRs and five non-affiliated. Not included are Vargunina and Pal', which undoubtedly also elected a majority of SRs. But even so, the pro-soviet parties managed to poll a little over one-quarter of the vote, not including any support they may have had among the non-affiliated. The vote at the Nevskii Shipbuilding Factory was 1221 for the SRs, 200 for the Mensheviks and 493 for the Bolshevik–LSR list.

In the two large railroad workshops, the Bolsheviks fared somewhat better, electing three delegates to five for the SRs and one non-affiliated. The situation was similar in the traditionally moderate state factories (Orudiinyi, Arsenal, Patronnyi, Military-Medical Preparations and Baltic). Of twenty-two delegates, there were eight SRs, two Mensheviks, seven Bolsheviks (32 per cent of the delegates) and five non-affiliated. The thirteen printing plants reporting returned fourteen delegates—five SRs, four Mensheviks, four Bolsheviks, one LSR. The somewhat surprising strength of the SRs here relative to the Mensheviks might be explained by the former's more decisive and activist oppositional stance. However, it should be remembered that besides the skilled typesetters, printing employed a considerable proportion of unskilled workers. Finally, in the municipal enterprises (water and power plants), the Mensheviks elected three delegates, the Bolsheviks and LSRs one each.

Despite any previous wavering, the pro-soviet parties retained their following in the traditionally militant (formerly) private metalworking factories such as Nobel, Vulkan, Podkovnyi, Rozenkrants, Cable, Langezipen, as well as the tram depots. These nine enterprises returned twenty delegates—fifteen Bolsheviks, two LSRs, one SR, one Menshevik and one non-affiliated. The soviet parties thus accounted for 85 per cent of the delegates.

They also did well, as noted, in the predominantly unskilled and female textile mills (excluding those in the Nevskii District) as well as at the Treugol'nik Rubber Factory. Here twenty-six of the thirty-one delegates were Bolsheviks, with one LSR, one Menshevik and two non-affiliated. Treugol'nik alone returned seven Bolsheviks and two LSRs. The woman workers, like most unskilled workers, had for the most part turned away from the defencists only after the July Days. Their stalwartness may therefore seem surprising. But unlike most of the unskilled workers, who had already returned to the villages, those who remained had roots in the city and belonged to the urban working-class milieu. Once drawn into political life and radicalised, they apparently tended to remain with soviet power.

On the other hand, the four tobacco factories, also almost exclusively female, gave a majority to the opposition—five Bolsheviks, four SRs, four Mensheviks and three non-affiliated. The Bolsheviks attributed this to party neglect. In any case, it is interesting to note that all four Bolsheviks were elected in one factory—Bogdanova.

Finally, there was the Putilov Works, still Petrograd's largest factory (13 000 workers) and a microcosm of the city's work force. Of the twenty-five delegates elected, there were eleven Bolsheviks, four LSRs, three SRs, two Mensheviks (including one from the related United Workers' Party) and five non-affiliated. As in the industrial work force as a whole, 60 per cent of the delegates belonged to the soviet parties.

In view of the changes in the social composition of the working class, the terrible material conditions and the increasingly repressive policies of the régime towards the opposition, the durability of pro-soviet sentiment is quite remarkable. The election returns indicate that despite all the dissatisfaction, it was mainly the workers with the weakest commitment to soviet power to start with but who had been swept up in the last wave of radicalisation in the autumn of 1917 that turned away from the régime. The predominance of SRs, with their populist as opposed to class appeal, suggests that the workers with the strongest working-class identification tended to stick with the soviets as a 'workers' government' for better or worse.

The limited response to the SU's call for a general strike on 2 July supports these conclusions. The original decision to call a one-day protest strike was taken back in May after the Kolpino events by the Mensheviks and SR PCs and was endorsed in principle by the Bureau of the SU on 12 May.[125] The SU itself, however, agreed to call a strike only if threatened with dispersal.[126]

However, towards the end of May, another reduction in the ration gave rise to a renewed wave of agitation centred in the factories of the Nevskii District. Protest meetings were held, and a strike at the Pal' Textile Mill spread to nearly the entire district as well as to the electrical shop of the Putilov Works.[127] But despite urgings from below to call an immediate general strike, the SU asked the Nevskii workers to return to work for the moment in order to give time to mobilise the rest of the workers.[128]

On 2 June, the SU met again to discuss the strike. While some delegates, especially those from the Nevskii District, reported that all were anxiously awaiting the signal, others were less sanguine.

[The representative from the Nevskii Shipbuilding Factory] expresses doubt about the readiness of the workers of his factory for a political strike, basing himself on the difficult economic situation of the workers in case the factory should stop ...

[Delegates from the printers stated that] although the Delegates' Assembly of Printers passed a resolution protesting against the entire course of the Soviet, there is no certainty of a united attitude among the printers towards a political strike ... In general, it becomes clear that only half of the printers will join the strike ...

Representatives of the tram depots find the declaration of a political strike untimely and call only to prepare for it.

Summing up, the Menshevik Astrov concluded that a strike in the given conditions would not be general, and the meeting again decided to continue preparations.[129]

In the meantime, however, the Moscow SU was arrested along with some of the delegates who had come from Petrograd. But still the SU could not decide. Borisenko, a member of the Bureau, answered the critics on 19 June:

The Petrograd Bureau of Delegates is being accused of lacking decisiveness on the matter of conducting a political strike even after such repressions as the arrest of the Moscow delegates ... The Bureau is not to blame if it does not have at its disposal facts that would permit it to decide on such a measure as the declaration of a political strike.

Borisenko was supported by Smirnov, who pointed out:

A call to the workers to strike, bypassing the firmly expressed will of the delegates themselves, would be an adventure. And such a firm will of the delegates has not once yet been expressed at a meeting—sometimes because they themselves are absent, sometimes because they lack a mandate for this.[130]

On 22 June the Obukhovskii workers and the sailors of the Baltic Fleet's torpedo squadron anchored nearby in the Neva met to discuss the arrest of the SR Ermeev in connection with Volodarskii's assassination. The meeting voted to call a general political strike to protest against government repression of the working class. However, a visit to Uritskii, head of the Petrograd Cheka, obtained Ermeev's release, and the strike was called off. But on 24 June, several hundred armed Red Army troops and sailors arrived and peacefully disarmed the torpedo-boat squadron. Greatly agitated, the workers of the Nevskii District spent the next day in meetings discussing the events. Towards evening, the troops began searching in workers' flats. Four Obukhovskii workers, SRs, were arrested, and the district's two SR clubs shut. (The Obukhovskii Factory had returned five SRs, three non-affiliated and only one Bolshevik in the June Soviet elections.)[131]

When the Obukhovskii workers arrived at the factory gates the next morning, they found a notice informing them that they had been dismissed and that hiring would take place through the labour exchange. (According to *Severnaya kommuna*, thirteen work days had been lost here in May through meetings and seven in the first three weeks of June.[132]) This was followed by a bloodless confrontation with Red Army troops, after which the district was placed under martial law. Searches were also conducted in the Putilov Works, where one SR worker was arrested. Then came the closure of *Delo naroda* 'forever, for expressing approval of the Siberian Government'.[133]

The SU could temporise no longer and on 26 June it called on the workers to prepare for a one-day political strike on 2 July. On 28 June, the Petrograd Soviet resolved to disperse the SU.

The strike did not succeed. Even the workers of Vargunina, who had been insistently pushing for it, made their participation conditional on that of a majority of Petrograd's workers. The strongest turnout was in the Nevskii District. 'In general', observed *Novaya zhizn'*, the strike 'was observed only in isolated factories and even so, not in the largest.' At Putilov, Baltic and others, most workers remained at their benches.[134] *Vechernee slovo*, hostile to the régime, wrote: 'The general opinion is that the strike failed. The worker masses have split into two groups, and the opponents of the strike are significantly more numerous than its supporters.'[135]

The economic situation and the repressions of the previous days certainly played some role in this. But although *Novaya zhizn'* would by no means count all those who did not strike among the régime's supporters, it argued that

It would be superficial [*neser'ezno*] to explain the failure of the opposition parties exclusively by this sort of reason ... The organisers of the strike undoubtedly overestimated the dissatisfaction of the *nizy*, showed insufficient understanding of the psychology of the working class, did not take into account all the threads that, despite everything, still tie the masses to the régime.[136]

Even before the strike had begun, Stroev wrote:

We do not know how broad its dimensions will be—the Communists are too shameless in their use of the police apparatus of state power. Besides that, no matter what one's attitude to the domination of the ruling party or how highly one evaluates the blow dealt to the Bolsheviks by the failure of their candidates, as large factories sent representatives of the opposition (Mensheviks and SRs), all the same, many workers still have not outlived their Bolshevik 'communism' and continue to consider the Soviet régime (whether good or bad—that is another question) as the representative of their interests. To it they tie their fate and that of the labour movement.[137]

The fact that the régime could count on the loyalty of the workers in the state apparatus, whether in the administration or armed forces, obviously rendered less threatening any challenge that might have been mounted from the factories. But the opposition movement in Petrograd failed more from internal than external weakness.

The really activist core of the opposition consisted of workers who had never fully reconciled themselves to the idea of a régime representing only the *nizy*. These activists came mainly from the printers, the Nevskii District and workers of the state factories. These were the same elements that pushed most strongly in October for a homogeneous socialist government, who participated (at least to some degree) in the protest against the dispersal of the Constituent Assembly and who actively supported the July political strike.

But other workers who sent delegates to the SU and passed resolutions in support of the Constituent Assembly did so largely out of desperation over the economic situation. This was fateful for the opposition. These workers were exhausted. When *Novaya zhizn'* asked the Bolsheviks if 'one could build a victory against the entire world on fatigue', it had underestimated the forces behind the soviet régime (although one can certainly question the nature of the victory achieved). But fatigue and hunger were certainly among the main forces behind the worker opposition and these have never provided a satisfactory basis for building a successful working-class movement.

On the other hand, because the discontent was so heavily economic, at least in its origins, 'despite all the dissatisfaction', as an observer sympathetic to the opposition noted, 'significant strata of the workers found the strike too strong a means of struggle against a régime set up by the toilers themselves'. He noted that in discussing the projected strike, the SU delegate from the Putilov works had expressed doubt about the capacity of the Putilov workers to move from a protest on the basis of hunger to the declaration of a political strike'.[138] It is important to emphasise that the SU (and those Mensheviks and SRs in it) were not a 'loyal opposition' demanding merely a change of government or policy within the framework of the existing political régime, soviet power. Their basic slogan—'all power to the Constituent Assembly'—aimed at the complete overthrow of this régime, albeit (at least in most cases) by non-violent means. It was this in particular that doomed the opposition and rendered its influence on the course of affairs much smaller than it might otherwise have been.

Most workers who had greeted the October Revolution as their own were not prepared to support the SU's position in practice. Already in the course of 1917 they had decided that there was no real alternative to soviet power, i.e. a régime based on the workers and (supported by) the peasants. They reached this conclusion on the basis of an essentially defensive and often painful process, the result of the experience of eight months of 'conciliationism' with census society. After the insurrection, they accepted the split in the socialist camp, the exclusively left socialist soviet government. They did so because they had become convinced (for those who still needed convincing) that this split was no caprice of vain leaders but a division between those who stood for soviet power and those who rejected it in favour of some form of continued, if watered down, 'conciliationism'. In similar fashion, in January the great majority of workers showed little concern for the fate of the Constituent Assembly, whose rule promised more of the same, though perhaps with a slightly more left accent.

And now in the summer, the Petrograd workers saw Russian society more irreconcilably polarised than ever and about to plunge in earnest into the civil war. Yet the SU was still offering as its alternative the

Constituent Assembly, a slogan behind which forces that all workers recognised as counterrevolutionary were also rallying (however insincerely).

Since October, the opposition had been hammering away that the civil war was the result of soviet intransigence. In their desperation many workers seemed prepared to listen to this, even though in earlier, less harsh circumstances they had supported the soviets' view of the civil war as a necessary evil imposed upon the revolutionary government. But when it came down to it, to the need to make a choice in action and not only words, the majority of factory workers rejected 'democratic unity' in the form of the Constituent Assembly as an unviable alternative. In the end, though the reality was bitter almost beyond endurance, it was the Bolshevik formulation that carried the day: 'Call forth every last ounce of strength—or surrender!'

# Conclusion

A major underlying concern of this study has been to trace the shifting relations between classes. Fundamental to these was the deepening polarisation between the working class and census society that conditioned the split between the left intelligentsia and the workers and culminated in the civil war. Only viewed against this background can the workers' radicalisation in the course of the revolution be understood as something more than a basically irrational response to 'anarchistic instincts', 'apocalyptic hopes' or the demagogic manipulation of unrealistic demands, all variations on a theme that has long dominated the Western literature.[1]

The workers—and Bolshevik workers were scarcely an exception – started out with an essentially bourgeois–democratic or liberal conception of the revolution and clung to it long after they had begun to surpass it in their practice. As late as the Kornilov affair, even the most militant workers summoned their comrades to the 'defence of freedom', without mentioning socialism as an immediate prospect for Russia (though it remained the ultimate goal, but realisable in Russia only after and through revolution in the West). The workers' massive participation in the Constituent Assembly elections, tactical considerations aside, also represented a belated attempt to reconcile October with February, a working-class-led soviet revolution with an all-national democratic one.

What in retrospect appears as a lag in consciousness in fact expressed the fundamentally defensive nature of the radicalisation process among the workers. Support for soviet power and the broadening struggle for power in the factories were first and foremost responses to the perceived threat to the revolution and to industry posed by census society's increasingly vociferous and active hostility to revolutionary democracy and the workers' organisations in particular, tolerated by a government that was unable or unwilling to move ahead towards the realisation of the revolution's goals. I have tried to show that this radicalisation was not an unconscious working out of elemental drives but a fundamentally reasoned response to a changing situation. (This is not to deny, of course, that the propertied classes were themselves responding to a perceived challenge to their interests. However, census society's aversion to popular revolution and its general hostility to the workers' and peasants' aspirations dated back many years before 1917.)

The workers were not alone in their evaluation of the mood and intentions of census society. In their more candid moments even the moderate socialists, whose entire strategy rested upon an alliance with the liberals, recognised that the latter had turned against the revolution. Where they and the 'labour aristocracy' took issue with the majority of workers was not in their perception of the propertied classes but in their belief that the revolution was doomed to defeat without the latter's at least passive cooperation.

Yet, the workers were not insensitive to the moderates' warnings. They showed themselves acutely aware, particularly after the concrete lesson of the July Days, of the dangers involved in a soviet seizure of power, which threatened them with political isolation and civil war. It is this awareness that largely explains the cautious, indecisive mood that characterised the post-July period despite the almost unanimous demand for soviet power. Such a mood cannot be easily squared with a view of the workers' political evolution as an unconscious, headlong rush towards utopia.

Functionalist sociology and mass society theory portray revolutions as 'value-oriented' movements that aim at putting new ideologies in power.[2] Ideological motivation is contrasted here with the pursuit of more modest, short-term goals, the former being by definition irrational (the choice of values is seen as arbitrary) and the latter, at least potentially, rational. But the evidence tends to point away from such an interpretation and in the direction of stressing as a crucial aspect of the explanation the situation in which the group finds itself and the interests flowing from it. The demands for soviet power, workers' control and later nationalisation were not primarily the result of a desire to realise socialist ideology but means towards resolving concrete problems that the workers faced. The fact that they were in accord with socialist teaching lent them greater force and legitimacy but was far from decisive in itself.

There is no reason to assume that revolutionary politics are less rational than institutionalised politics marked by compromise and a basic acceptance of the existing social and political order. That this view has predominated in the social sciences would seem to be due more to the conservative biases of some social theorists than to the weight of historical evidence.

This is not to deny the role of affective factors and culture. I have placed such heavy emphasis on the rational in the workers' political behaviour because it is a position rarely entertained in the literature and even less frequently supported. But certainly cultural factors—goals, expectations, values derived from the past—such as the ideals of class honour, working-class and socialist unity, 'class separateness' from census society, did serve as a filter accentuating certain features in the objective situation, de-emphasising or perhaps totally screening out others. These acted as intervening variables between the actors and the objective situation. But they were rarely determining in themselves.

Many observers in the years leading up to the revolution, for example, had been struck by the tenacity of the principle of 'class separateness', particularly among the skilled metalworkers of Petrograd, which expressed itself in the rejection of 'fraternisation with the exploiters', of cooperation with management on the plant level and with the liberals and census society on the political level. Yet this norm, if not completely set aside, did not prevent most workers from supporting the 'bourgeois' Provisional Government in the early period of the revolution. Many Bolshevik militants, whose party virtually personified 'class separateness', were genuinely at a loss to explain the moderates' new found support in the working class for the policy of a worker–liberal alliance. What they generally failed to grasp was that the February Revolution, for the moment at least, had created a new situation for the workers, a national reconciliation around the successful democratic revolution.

True, dual power was a guarded form of support for the government, but real nevertheless. There had been no knee-jerk rejection of the traditional class enemy. 'Class separateness' had never been based upon blind hatred for the *burzhui* or envy of the rich and privileged but on the workers' long experience with census hostility to their goals. Similar arguments could be applied to the very potent ideals of working-class and socialist unity, which finally yielded before the objective reality of a split in the socialist camp.

Despite marked differences in political culture among the workers, there were limits to the variations in behaviour that arose from this source. Just as there was extremely broad support in March for dual power, so one finds virtual unanimity in October behind soviet power. The main practical import of political culture in 1917 itself was to accelerate or retard the radicalisation process.

But the consensus around soviet power did hide differences of degree and motivation which later took on real importance as the economic crisis deepened. In particular, the active, militant core of the worker opposition in the spring of 1918 came mainly from the 'labour aristocracy'. Despite widespread discontent among the rest of the workers still engaged in industrial production, they generally stopped short of active opposition to the soviet régime.

Some writers have interpreted the workers' radicalism as political immaturity, a refusal to recognise the objective constraints on the Provisional Government's ability to meet their demands, which were unrealistic in the circumstances.[3] There is some evidence for the existence of such 'maximalist' attitudes, particularly in the autumn and winter of 1917 among the unskilled workers, whose impatience with the new régime's failure to meet their material expectations turned them more and more towards the anarchist opposition.

The fact remains, however, that while the Bolsheviks in the autumn of 1917 had the support of the vast majority of workers for soviet power, the opposition in the spring and summer of 1918 was never able to win substantial support for the actual overthrow—by peaceful or other means—of the soviet régime. The leaders of the opposition themselves recognised that the workers, through all their suffering, distinguished between the failures of the 'bourgeois' coalition government, which they attributed to the pernicious influence of the liberals and the moderate socialists' refusal to break with them, and the failures of the 'workers' and peasants'' soviet government, due partly to incompetence and 'excesses', but mainly to circumstances imposed upon it and beyond its control.

One can debate the validity of this distinction. The point is that most workers were able to and did make it. In the last analysis, they saw soviet power as the only realistic alternative to counterrevolution. In this, and not in the 'irresolute softness and mildness'[4] or other psychological traits of the moderate socialists, lay the basic explanation for the poor showing of the 'democratic' opposition to the soviet régime.

There had always been something puzzling in the moderate socialists' counterposition of 'broad democratic unity' to the 'narrow' social base of the soviet régime. If this 'unity' was to include the Kadets and their supporters, then it was clear that the workers would never accept it. This left the constituency of the moderate socialists, which consisted principally of peasants and the left intelligentsia. The workers indeed desired the peasants as allies, but the soviets already had their passive support, and there was not much more one could expect from them. But if 'democratic unity' meant only the additional support of the socialist intelligentsia, should *they* not adhere to the soviet régime rather than vice versa? This was the reasoning of the majority of workers in October–November and it remained their position, despite the vacillations, into the civil war.

That this view was not entirely unrealistic is attested to by its eventual adoption by the LSRs in November 1917 and a year later by a significant minority of the SR Party. Finding themselves repeatedly confronted with rightist reaction, these moderate SRs offered their active support to the soviets in return for legalisation.[5] (In the spring of 1919 the SR majority itself decided to end the use of force against the soviets and to concentrate all efforts against the Whites.[6]) Many Mensheviks too, despite their party's intermittent persecution at the hands of the régime, fought and acquitted themselves well in the Red Army. One can only speculate whether an earlier and more wholehearted willingness to participate in a soviet régime could have tangibly altered the course of the revolution and the fate of the moderate parties themselves.

In the introduction to the first volume of this study, I argued that the

Russian Revolution was too complex a phenomenon to be reduced to any simple formula. It was, among other things, a soldiers' mutiny, a peasant rebellion, a movement of national minorities. But it was also—and especially—a workers' revolution. Soldiers, peasants, national groups all played their role, but it was in the last analysis a basically negative or passive one in relation to the major antagonists. Their principal contribution to the revolution and the victory in the civil war lay in their failure to support the old régime, the Provisional Government and later the Whites. It remained for the workers to give the revolution direction, organisation and the major part of its active forces. One cannot imagine the victory of the soviet revolution without this active support and participation on the part of the workers. This statement remains valid despite the important changes that occurred in the quality of that participation, particularly in the relations between the rank and file and the leadership after July and especially after October 1917.

However, a revolution cannot be characterised solely in terms of the main popular forces behind it. Certain historians of the English and French Revolutions have persuasively argued that in these too it was the popular urban masses who held the initiative and did a disproportionate amount of the fighting.[7] Yet, the final institutional outcome of these revolutions redounded to the benefit not of these masses but of those holding property in its capitalist or potentially capitalist form. Hence their common designation as 'bourgeois revolutions', despite the apprehension and even aversion with which they were viewed by their eventual beneficiaries.

An analysis of the socio-political system that ultimately issued from the Russian Revolution is obviously beyond the scope of this study. What is immediately clear, however, is that if the revolution did expropriate the propertied classes, it nevertheless failed in the end to give power to the workers. The power that the workers had seized in October 1917 fell completely from their hands in the course of the ensuing civil war. From a dictatorship *of* the proletariat, the soviet state was transformed into a self-proclaimed dictatorship (in the narrow sense) *for* a greatly reduced, physically and morally exhausted proletariat. The state retained, to be sure, certain important links with the working class but it stood above it and beyond its control.

The beginnings of this process could already be discerned soon after the October Revolution. But the final outcome was by no means the result of the working out of logic inherent in the class nature of the soviet revolution or in the ideas of its main protagonists. The victory in the civil war came as a surprise to the Bolsheviks no less than to the moderate socialists. The consensus in 1917 had been that the working class was too small, too weak successfully to make a revolution unless it could find allies. The Mensheviks sought them in the liberal elements of census society. The Bolsheviks looked in part to the peasantry but mainly to victorious socialist revolutions in the developed West.

But the workers remained isolated, and the revolution survived in totally unforeseen circumstances. Census society had been defeated, but the principal active social force on the side the revolution, the working class, had been eliminated as an independent political force by the economic crisis and civil war and the removal of its most vital elements to meet the needs of the new state apparatus. It was this development more than anything else that conditioned the rise of a new absolute state, against which the eventually reconstituted working class of the 1920s was unable effectively to assert itself.

Nevertheless, the developed political consciousness and activism, the initiative and creativity, the deep and genuine preoccupation with democracy and freedom that the Petrograd workers so strikingly displayed in 1917 stand as testimony to the potential of a working-class movement to lead a popular revolution towards a democratic socialist society. Despite the tragic subsequent development of the Russian Revolution, this remains an essential part of its legacy.

# Notes and References

## Chapter 1: Rethinking the Revolution

1. *Rabochaya gazeta* (20 May 1917). See also N. Sukhanov, *Zapiski o revolyutsii* (M.-Berlin-Petersburg, 1921) vol. v, p. 8.
2. *Novaya zhizn'* (19 July 1917).
3. Sukhanov, *Zapiski o revolyutsii*, p. 55; M. P. Price, *Reminiscences of the Russian Revolution* (London: George Allen & Unwin, 1921) pp. 64–5; *Revolyutsionnoe dvizhenie v Rossii v iyule 1917 g.* (henceforth cited as Dok. July) (M., 1959) pp. 294–5, 318–19; *Rabochii put'* (20 Aug 1917).
4. *Ekonomicheskoe polozhenie Rossii nakanune Velikoi oktyabr'skoi sotsialisticheskoi revolyutsii* (henceforth cited as Ek. Pol.), (M.-L., 1957) vol. i, pp. 196, 200–1.
5. Cited in *Novaya zhizn'* (8 Aug 1917).
6. *Proletarii* (10 Aug 1917).
7. Cited in A. K. Tsvetkov-Prosveshchenskii, *Mezhdu dvumya revolyutsiyamy* (M.-L., 1933) p. 133.
8. Sukhanov, *Zapiski o revolyutsii*, p. 110.
9. Ibid., p. 131; *Revolyutsionnoe dvizhenie v Rossii v avguste 1917 g.* (henceforth cited as Dok. Aug.), (M., 1959) p. 360.
10. *Novaya zhizn'* (29 July 1917). On the 'Liberty Loan', see D. Mandel, *The Petrograd Workers and the Fall of the Old Régime* (London: Macmillan, 1981) pp. 72–3. For an account of the repression, see A. Rabinowitch, *The Bolsheviks Come to Power* (New York: Norton, 1976) ch. 3.
11. Price, *Reminiscences*, p. 66.
12. Sukhanov, *Zapiski o revolyutsii*, p. 135.
13. *Novaya zhizn'* (13 Aug 1917).
14. L. Trotsky, *History of the Russian Revolution* (London: Sphere Books, 1967) vol. ii, p. 181.
15. Dok. Aug., p. 370.
16. *Rabochii kontrol' i natsionalizatsiya promyshlennykh predpriyatii Petrograda v 1917–1919 gg.* (henceforth cited as Rab. Kon.), (L., 1949) vol. i, pp. 152–3.
17. *Oktyabr'skaya revolyutsiya i fabzavkomy* (henceforth cited as FZK), (1927) vol. i, pp. 191, 193.
18. Sukhanov, *Zapiski o revolyutsii*, p. 129. See also the assessment of Bazarov, Menshevik–Internationalist economist, in *Novaya zhizn'* (30 Dec 1917).
19. FZK, vol. i, p. 217.
20. See Mandel, *Petrograd Workers*, pp. 133–4.
21. Dok. Aug., pp. 177 and 614.
22. Z.V. Stepanov, *Rabochie Petrograda v period podgotovki i provedeniye Oktyabr'skogo vooruzhennogo vosstaniya* (L., 1965) p. 96.

23. *Izvestiya* (18 Aug 1917).
24. Stepanov, *Rabochie Petrograda*, pp. 140–1; *Revolyutsionnoe dvizhenie v Rossii v sentyabre 1917 g.* (henceforth cited as Dok. Sept.), (M., 1962) p. 197; FZK, vol. II, 1928, pp. 57–8; V. Perazich, *Tekstili Leningrada v 1917 g.* (L., 1927) pp. 75, 90.
25. FZK, vol. II, p. 190.
26. *Znamya truda* (6 Oct 1917).
27. Stepanov, *Rabochie Petrograda*, p. 27.
28. Perazich, *Tekstili Leningrada*, p. 87.
29. The demand for a minimum wage was put forth at the start of the revolution under the strong pressure of the unskilled workers, whose wages—and even the entrepreneurs admitted this—were below subsistence (Mandel, *Petrograd Workers*, p. 90). Although the economic situation of the unskilled workers improved after February, a minimum wage was never enacted and inflation soon ate up what had been won. The low wages of the unskilled and the differentials between the skilled and unskilled wage (which the unions, with only limited success, tried to narrow) remained a constant source of tension between the two categories of workers. Leningradskii gosudarstvennyi arkhiv Oktyabr'skoi revolyutsii i sotsialisticheskogo stroitel'stva (henceforth cited as LGAORSS), fond 1000, opis' 73, delo 16, passim; 4591/1/1 list 40.
30. Stepanov, *Rabochie Petrograda*, p. 81; S. Bruk in A. Anskii, *Professional'noe dvizhenie v Petrograde v 1917 g.* (M., 1927) pp. 127–8; *Rabochaya gazeta* (6 Aug 1917).
31. Perazich, *Tekstili Leningrada*, pp. 64–9.
32. *Novaya zhizn'* (12 and 23 Aug 1917).
33. Stepanov, *Rabochie Petrograda*, pp. 53–4.
34. *Znamya truda* (17 Oct 1917).
35. Stepanov, *Rabochie Petrograda*, pp. 53–4.
36. Sukhanov, *Zapiski o revolyutsii*, p. 173.
37. Stepanov, *Rabochie Petrograda*, p. 67.
38. FZK, vol. I, p. 200.
39. (The correlation between $\dfrac{\text{no. industrial workers employed in district}}{\text{no. eligible voters in district}}$
    and the relative size of the Bolshevik vote in each district was r = 0.6878 at a significance of p(F) < 0.01. Although only a very rough indicator, this high correlation supports the contention that the Bolsheviks' support was heavily working class. Calculations based on data from Stepanov, *Rabochie Petrograda*, p. 30 and *Nasha rech'* (17 Nov 1917).
40. For the social composition of the districts, see Mandel, *Petrograd Workers*, ch. 3.
41. *Delo naroda* (23 Aug 1917).
42. W. Rosenberg, *Liberals in the Russian Revolution* (Princeton University Press, 1974) p. 220.
43. Stepanov, *Rabochie Petrograda*, p. 169; *Raionnye sovety Petrograda v 1917 g.* (henceforth cited as Raisovety), (M.-L., 1968) vol. III, p. 179.
44. See below, p. 222 for the case of the Nevskii District.
45. FZK, vol. I, p. 215.
46. T. Shatilova, 'Professional'nye soyuzy i Oktyabr'', *Krasnaya letopis'*, 2,23 (1927) pp. 179–88.

47. Perazich, *Tekstili Leningrada*, p. 91.
48. See Mandel, *Petrograd Workers*, ch. 2.
49. Perazich, *Tekstili Leningrada*, pp. 79–82, 87.
50. M. Bortik, 'Na Trubochnom zavode', in Anskii, *Professional'noe*, p. 208.
51. K. V. Notman, 'Trubochnyi zavod na Oktyabr'skikh putyah', *Krasnaya letopis'*, 5–6, 50–1 (1932) pp. 249–50.
52. Ek. Pol., vol. I, table 7.
53. 'Piterskie rabochie ob iyul'skikh dnyakh', *Krasnaya letopis'*, 9 (1923) pp. 21–2.
54. Stepanov, *Rabochie Petrograda*, p. 68.
55. Raisovety, vol. II, p. 81.
56. *Proletarii* (17 Aug 1917). See also A. A. Antonov, 'Vospominaniya kommissara Obukhovskogo staleliteinogo zavoda' in *Doneseniya kommissarov Petrogradskogo voenno-revolyutsionnogo komiteta*, vol. I (1957) p. 211.
57. Antonov, 'Vospominaniya kommissara', p. 205.
58. *Proletarii* (13 Aug 1917).
59. O. Znamenskii, *Iyul'skii krizis 1917 g.* (M.-L., 1964) p. 260.
60. *Vtoraya i tret'ya petrogradskie obshchegorodskie konferentsii bol'shevikov v v iyule i sentyabre 1917 g.* (henceforth cited as Vtoraya) (M.-L., 1927) p. 14; *Shestoi vserossiiskii s"ezd RSDRP (b)* (M., 1958) p. 44.
61. *Novaya zhizn'* (8 Aug 1917).
62. Sukhanov, *Zapiski o revolyutsii*, vol. V, p. 190.
63. *Rabochii put'* (28 Aug 1917).
64. Raisovety, vol. I, pp. 80, 89; vol. II, p. 199.
65. Ibid, vol. III, p. 201.
66. Ibid., p. 202.
67. Ibid., pp. 203–4.
68. See for example, M. Mikhailov, 'Rabochiezavoda P. V. Baranovskogo v bor'be za Oktyabr'', *Krasnaya letopis'* nos 50–1 (1932) pp. 205–6.
69. Raisovety, vol. III, p. 204.
70. Sukhanov, *Zapiski o revolyutsii*, vol. V, p. 180.
71. Vtoraya, pp. 62–3.
72. A. Ya. Grunt, *Pobeda Oktyabr'skoi revolyutsii v Moskve* (M., 1961) pp. 200–2; *Materialy po statistike truda severnoi oblasti*, vyp. 1 (1918) p. 10.
73. Trotsky. *History of the Russian Revolution*, vol. II, p. 257.
74. Dok. July, p. 110. See also Dok. Sept., pp. 28, 95.
75. Sukhanov, *Zapiski o revolyustii*, vol. V, p. 154.
76. Ibid.
77. *Izvestiya* (13 Aug 1917).
78. See Mandel, *Petrograd Workers*, pp. 26–8.
79. FZK, vol. II, p. 161.
80. Mandel, *Petrograd Workers*, pp. 24–30.
81. See below, pp. 255–7, 282–3.
82. This is an idea developed by L. H. Haimson. I am indebted to him for pointing out its relevance in this context.
83. Dok. Aug., p. 373.
84. A. Buzinov, *Za nevskoi zastovoi* (M.-L., 1930) p. 92.
85. FZK, vol. I, p. 190.

86. *Rabochii i soldat* (5 Aug 1917).
87. I. Skorinko, 'Vospominaniya rabochego ob Oktyabre', *Krasnaya letopis'*, no. 6 (1923) p. 14.
88. L. V. Golovanova, 'Raionnye komitety RSDRP (b) v 1917 g.', candidate's dissertation (Leningrad State University, 1974) appendix 13, table 17.
89. Stepanov, *Rabochie Petrograda*, pp. 46–7.
90. Golovanova, 'Raionnye komitety', p. 196, table 6.
91. Vtoraya, p. 80.
92. Ibid., p. 75.
93. Ibid., p. 74.
94. Ibid., p. 71.
95. Lenin explained his position in three articles written at this time: 'Tri krizisa', 'K lozungam' and 'O konstitutsionnykh illyuziyakh', *Polnoe sobranie sochinenii* (M., 1962) vol. XXXII, pp. 428–32; vol. XXXIV, pp. 10–17, 33–47. In these articles he argued that there was no choice but for the workers, supported by the poorest peasants (the village, according to Lenin, was undergoing a process of differentiation) to take power even against the will of the soviet majority. The new government would conduct a revolutionary policy and thus win over, or at least isolate, the peasants from 'conciliationist' influence. Lenin rejected the view that the moderate socialist leaders might still embrace a revolutionary policy. Nor did he deny that the new slogan meant civil war under very difficult conditions. He was not, however, writing off the peasantry. He argued rather that the workers could not afford to wait and that it was futile to hope to win over the peasantry without first seizing power and demonstrating through concrete revolutionary measures that it was in the peasants' interest to throw in their lot with the workers.
96. Vtoraya, p. 88.
97. Ibid., p. 80.
98. Perazich, *Tekstili Leningrada*; FZK, vol. I, p. 216.
99. FZK, vol. I, p. 189. Much of the material upon which this section is based is from my article 'The Working Class and the Intelligentsia in 1917' (*Critique*, no. 14 (1982) pp. 67–87), where the issue of worker–intelligentsia relations is discussed at greater length.
100. FZK, vol. I, p. 188.
101. Ibid.
102. Ibid., pp. 206–7.
103. Ibid., p. 208.
104. Ibid., p. 206.
105. Ibid., p. 167.
106. Ibid., p. 191.
107. Lunacharskii was referring to the older generation of worker-intelligentsia formed in close contact with the intelligentsia, particularly before 1905. Most of these workers had either ceased to be active or were defencists. See Mandel, *Petrograd Workers*, p. 42.
108. *Novaya zhizn'* (18 Oct 1917).
109. O. Radkey, *The Sickle Under the Hammer* (Columbia University Press, 1963) p. 159.
110. Vtoraya, p. 28.

424     *The Petrograd Workers and the Soviet Seizure of Power*

111. *Shestoi vserossiiskii s"ezd RSDRP(b)*, p. 45.
112. See *Perepiska sekretariata TseKa RSDRP(b) s mestnymy organizat-siyamy, mart-oktyabr' 1917* (M., 1957) passim.
113. *Rabochaya gazeta* (7 July 1917).
114. Ibid. (30 June 1917).
115. *Revolyutsionnoe dvizhenie v Rossii nakanune Oktyabr'skogo vooruzhen-nogo vosstaniya* (henceforth cited as Dok. Nak.), (M., 1962) p. 152.
116. Mandel, 'Working Class and the Intelligentsia', op. cit.
117. FZK, vol. I, p. 218.
118. Ibid., p. 216.
119. V. Malakhovskii, *Iz istorii Krasnoi gvardii* (L., 1925) pp. 13–14.
120. *Proletarii* (10 Aug 1917). Contrary to what is often claimed, the workers' three demands were not 'peace, bread and land'. The workers' revolution began and remained deeply concerned with political freedom.
121. *Rabochii i soldat* (2 Aug 1917). The choice of words – 'cohabitate' – points to a crucial value in the political culture of this stratum of workers: 'class separateness'. (Mandel, *Petrograd Workers*, pp. 18–19).
122. Sukhanov, *Zapiski o revolyutsii*, vol. V, p. 180. On Bublikov, see p. 214 above.
123. *Znamya truda* (27 Aug 1917).

**Chapter 2: From the Kornilov Rising to the Eve of October**

1. W. H. Chamberlin, *The Russian Revolution* (New York: Universal Library, 1965) vol. I, p. 204.
2. Sukhanov, *Zapiski o revolyutsii*, vol. V, pp. 198–204.
3. Ibid., pp. 207–15.
4. *Novaya zhizn'* (19 Sept 1917).
5. *Znamya truda* (1 Sept 1917).
6. Ibid. (16 Sept 1907).
7. *Rabochii* (31 Aug 1917).
8. *Znamya truda* (3 Sept 1917).
9. K. I. Startsev, *Ocherki po istorii petrogradskogo Krasnoi gvardii i rabochei militsii* (M.-L. 1965) p. 164.
10. *Izvestiya* (5 Sept 1917).
11. Dok. Aug., p. 510.
12. Stepanov, *Rabochie Petrograda*, p. 175.
13. Trotsky, *History of the Russian Revolution*, vol. II, p. 226.
14. M. Mitel'man, B. Glebov and A. Ul'yanskii, *Istoriya Putilovskogo zavoda*, 3rd edn (L., 1961) pp. 645–7.
15. Dok. Aug., pp. 485–6.
16. Ibid., p. 488.
17. Ibid., p. 487.
18. *Rabochii put'* (5 Sept 1917).
19. M. Mikhailov, 'Rabochie zavoda P. V. Baranovskogo', pp. 205–6.
20. Dok. Aug., pp. 485–6.
21. *Znamya truda* (31 Aug 1917).

22. Ibid. (7 Sept 1917).
23. Raisovety, vol. I, p. 356.
24. Dok. Aug., p. 491.
25. Sukhanov, *Zapiski o revolyustii*, vol. V, p. 319.
26. Lenin, *Polnoe sobranie sochinenii*, vol. XXXIV, pp. 133–9.
27. Dok. Aug., p. 227.
28. *Rabochii put'* (3 Sept 1917). See also the Putilov resolution in ibid. (30 Aug 1917).
29. *Rabochaya gazeta* (1 Sept 1917).
30. *Revolyutsiya 17-go goda: Khronika sobytii* (M.-L., 1926) vol. IV, p. 143.
31. Sukhanov, *Zapiski o revolyutsii*, vol. V, p. 337.
32. *Izvestiya* (3 Sept 1917).
33. Trotsky, *History of the Russian Revolution*, vol. II, p. 265; Sukhanov, *Zapiski o revolyutsii*, vol. IV, p. 28.
34. Ibid.
35. Stepanov, *Rabochie Petrograda*, p. 193.
36. *Znamya truda* (6 Sept 1917).
37. Ibid. (2 Sept 1917).
38. Stepanov, *Rabochie Petrograda*, p. 184.
39. *Rabochii put'* (8 Sept 1917). See also ibid. (19 Sept) on Orudiinyi.
40. Ibid. (22 Sept 1917).
41. *Bastiony revolyutsii* (L., 1967) vol. I, p. 168.
42. See *Perepiska sekretariata TseKa RSDRP (b)*, pp. 133–303 passim.
43. Sukhanov, *Zapiski o revolyutsii*, vol. VI, pp. 84–5.
44. FZK, vol. II, p. 21.
45. Ibid., p. 22.
46. Ibid., p. 40.
47. LGAORSS 9391/1/11/31.
48. *Proletarii* (16 Sept 1917).
49. *Pervyi legal'nyi Peterburgskii komitet RSDRP(b) v 1917 g.* (henceforth cited as Peka), (M.-L., 1927) pp. 270–8.
50. *Znamya truda* (16 Sept 1917).
51. Peka, p. 286.
52. *Oktyabr'skoe vooruzhennoe vosstanie v Petrograde* (henceforth cited as Dok. Okt.), (M., 1957) p. 53.
53. Dok. Sept, p. 342.
54. *Izvestiya* (20 Sept 1917).
55. Sukhanov, *Zapiski o revolyutsii*, vol. VI, pp. 135–6.
56. Dok. Sept., pp. 279–80.
57. Sukhanov, *Zapiski o revolyutsii*, vol. VI, pp. 140–62.
58. *Iskra* (17 Oct 1917).
59. Dok. Okt., pp. 98–9.
60. *Znamya truda* (30 Sept 1917).
61. Ibid. (11 Oct 1917); *Novaya zhizn'* (11 Oct 1917).
62. Ibid.
63. Ibid.
64. *Rabochii put'* (11 Oct 1917).
65. Ibid. (2 Oct 1917). See also Dok. Okt., pp. 104–36 passim.

**Chapter 3: Class Struggle in the Factories**

1. FZK, vol. II, p. 7.
2. *Rech'* (13 Sept 1917).
3. See, for example, the report of the Director of the Baltic Shipyards, Stepanov, *Rabochie Petrograda*, p. 126.
4. FZK, vol. I, p. 186; Rab. Kon., pp. 216–17.
5. FZK, vol. I, p. 269.
6. Ibid., pp. 184–6.
7. Ibid., p. 203.
8. Ibid., vol. II, p. 119.
9. Dok. Nak., pp. 275–6.
10. Ek. Pol., vol. I, pp. 414–15.
11. FZK, vol. II, p. 102.
12. *Rabochii put'* (13 Sept 1917).
13. FZK, vol. II, p. 102.
14. Ibid., p. 34. See also ibid., pp. 33–4; Stepanov, *Rabochie Petrograda*, p. 96; *Rabochii put'* (12 Sept 1917).
15. Rab. Kon., p. 175.
16. J. Reed, *Ten Days That Shook the World* (New York: Vintage Books, 1960) p. 8; V. I. Startsev, *Russkie bloknoty Dzhona Rida* (M., 1968) pp. 40–2.
17. Stepanov, *Rabochie Petrograda*, p. 16.
18. *Novaya zhizn'* (4 Aug 1917).
19. Dok. Aug., pp. 207–8.
20. FZK, vol. II, p. 588; Stepanov, *Rabochie Petrograda*, p. 152.
21. Stepanov, ibid., p. 153.
22. *Rabochii put'* (8 Oct 1917); *Znamya truda* (30 Sept 1917).
23. *Rabochii put'* (8 Oct 1917).
24. Dok. Sept., pp. 236–7.
25. *Rabochii put'* (8 Sept 1917).
26. *Znamya truda* (1 Oct 1917). See also FZK, vol. II, p. 68.
27. FZK, vol. I, p. 211.
28. Ibid., p. 269.
29. *Rabochii put'* (20 Sept 1917).
30. Dok. Aug., p. 219.
31. Perazich, *Tekstili Leningrada*, p. 80; A. E. Suknovalov and I. N. Fomenkov, *Fabrika 'Krasnoe znamya'* (L., 1968) p. 105.
32. Dok. Okt., p. 52.
33. Stepanov, *Rabochie Petrograda*, p. 134.
34. *Putilovtsy v trekh revolyutsiyakh* (L., 1933) p. 380.
35. Ibid., p. 390.
36. FZK, vol. II, p. 23.
37. Dok. Okt., p. 52.
38. FZK, vol. II, p. 177.
39. Dok. Okt., pp. 110, 127.
40. Rab. Kon., p. 205; *Putilovtsy v trekh revolyutsiyakh*, pp. 386–91.
41. Dok. Okt., p. 105.

42. Ibid.
43. *Znamya truda* (24 Oct 1917).
44. Dok. Okt., p. 130.
45. *Putilovtsy v trekh revolyutsiyakh*, p. 389.
46. FZK, vol. II, pp. 171–4.
47. Ibid., p. 192.
48. See p. 424, n121 above.
49. FZK, vol. I, p. 92.
50. Ibid., vol. II, p. 192.
51. *Pervaya vserossiiskaya tarifnaya konferentsiya soyuza rabochikh metallistov* (L., 1918) p. 7. See also Schmidt's speech in FZK, vol. I, p. 208.
52. Ibid., vol. II, p. 123.
53. Ibid., p. 122.
54. Ibid., vol. I, p. 216.
55. Ibid., p. 231.
56. Dok. Okt., p. 52.
57. Peka, pp. 313–14.
58. Mandel, *Petrograd Workers*, ch. 3.
59. Dok. Sept., pp. 284–5. See also Rab. Kon., pp. 171–2 and 176.
60. See, for example, J. Keep, *The Russian Revolution—A Study in Mass Mobilization* (New York: Norton, 1976) ch. V, 'Drift Toward Industrial Anarchy'; P. Avrich, 'The Bolshevik Revolution and Workers' Control in Russian Industry', *Slavic Review*, vol. XXII, no. 1 (1973): Moshe Lewin, *Lenin's Last Struggle* (London: Pluto Press, 1975) pp. 7–8, 126.
61. *Pervaya vserossiskaya tarifnaya*, p. 5.
62. Stepanov, *Rabochie Petrograda*, p. 130.
63. FZK, vol. II, pp. 67–8.
64. P. V. Volobuev, *Proletariat i burzhuaziya Rossii v 1917 g.* (M., 1964) p. 239. According to one estimate, 1.1 million workers took part in strikes in September and 1.2 million in October (A. M. Lisetskii, 'Stachechnaya bor'ba proletariata Rossii v period podgotovki i provedeniya Velikoi Oktyabr'skoi sotsialisticheskoi revolyutsii', doctoral dissertation (Kishinev, 1968) p. 42, cited in L. S. Gaponenko, *Rabochii klass Rossii v 1917 g.* (M., 1963) p. 436.) In the January–February 1917 strike wave only 700 000 had participated (G. A. Truken, *Oktyabr'v tsentral' noi Rossii* (M., 1967) p. 217). Gaponenko offers the following aggregate statistics for March–September 1917:

| | March | April | May | June | July | August | September |
|---|---|---|---|---|---|---|---|
| Economic strikes | 27 | 42 | 78 | 76 | 73 | 109 | 117 |

At the same time, there was a growing tendency for strikes to embrace entire industries within a single region (Gaponenko, ibid., p. 386).
65. FZK, vol. II, p. 33.
66. Official strike statistics for 1917 do not exist since the Factory Inspectorate fell into disuse after February and the Ministry of Labour published only aggregate data. This estimate of 10 per cent, which probably exaggerates the proportion of industrial strikers, is based on press reports and published archival material.

67. G. A. Trukan, *Oktyabr' v tsentral'noi Rossii* (M., 1967) pp. 203–17; P. A. Nikolaev, *Rabochie metallisty tsentral'nogo promyshlennogo raiona Rossii v bor'be za pobedu Oktyabr'skoi revolyutsii* (M., 1960) pp. 96–9.
68. Stepanov, *Rabochie Petrograda*, p. 80.
69. Ibid.
70. S. Bruk, 'Organizatsiya soyuza metallistov v 1917 g.' in Anskii, *Professional'noe*, pp. 127–8.
71. Volobuev, *Proletariat i burzhuaziya*, p. 233; Stepanov, *Rabochie Petrograda*, pp. 80–1.
72. Stepanov, *Rabochie Petrograda*, p. 182.
73. *Putilovtsy v trekh revolyutsiyakh*, pp. 384–5.
74. Dok. Okt., p. 116; *Rabochii put'* (18 Oct 1917).

**Chapter 4: On the Eve**

1. Dok. Okt., p. 65. For a somewhat different evaluation of the workers' mood on the eve of October than presented here, see Rabinowitch, *The Bolsheviks*, ch. 12.
2. Peka, p. 313.
3. At the start of October, the Germans occupied the Moon-sund archipelago in the Gulf of Finland, forcing the Russian Baltic Fleet to retreat after offering stiff resistance. Citing this as a threat to the capital, the government announced its intention of moving to Moscow. It soon reconsidered, however, under a barrage of criticism from the left, which saw in this yet another move directed against Petrograd's revolutionary workers. Among the workers, it was widely believed that Kerenskii was planning to leave pacification of the red capital to the German Army. Sukhanov, *Zapiski o revolyutsii*, vol. VI, pp. 218–19, 235–6.
4. FZK, vol. II, pp. 156–9.
5. Even after the TsIK had given in to pressure and set a date for the congress, it urged local soviets not to send delegates. In the autumn, the defencists began generally to play down the significance of the soviets in Russian political life. *Izvestiya*, the organ of the TsIK, went so far as to call for their disbandment, claiming that they had outlived their function. *Izvestiya*, no. 195 (1917).
6. FZK, vol. II, p. 163.
7. Ibid., p. 167.
8. LGAORSS 9391/1/11/43.
9. For a sample of these, see Dok. Okt., pp. 92–135 passim.; Dok. Nak., pp. 277, 295, 325; *Revolyutsiya 1917–go goda* (M.-L., 1926) vols 4 and 5, passim.
10. *Znamya truda* (3 Oct 1917).
11. Dok. Okt., p. 162.
12. *Znamya truda* (17 Oct 1917).
13. S. Mstislavskii, *Sem' dnei* (Berlin–Petersburg-M., 1922) p. 116. See also Martov's statement in *Iskra* (17 Oct 1917).
14. P. F. Kudelli (ed), *Leningradskie rabochie v bor'be za vlast' sovetov v 1917 g.* (L., 1924) p. 116.
15. Trotsky, *History of the Russian Revolution*, vol. III, p. 113.

16. Mstislavskii, *Sem' dnei*, p. 117.
17. Sukhanov, *Zapiski o revolyutsii*, vol. VII, pp. 89–92.
18. *Rabochaya gazeta* (29 Sept 1917).
19. Sukhanov, *Zapiski o revolyutsii*, vol. III, p. 276.
20. *Novaya zhizn'* (15 Oct 1917).
21. Sukhanov, *Zapiski o revolyutsii*, vol. VII, pp. 87–8.
22. Peka, pp. 315–18.
23. *Rabochii put'* (19–21 Oct 1917).
24. *Znamya truda* (21 Oct 1917).
25. *Novaya zhizn'* (13 Oct 1917).
26. Ibid. (15 Oct 1917).
27. Sukhanov, *Zapiski o revolyutsii*, vol. VII, pp. 44–6.
28. Kudelli, *Leningradski rabochie*, p. 113.
29. Sukhanov, *Zapiski o revolyutsii*, pp. 36–7.
30. Peka, p. 313.
31. Dok. Okt., p. 53.
32. See above, pp. 282–3.
33. *Rabochaya gazeta* (29 Sept 1917).
34. FZK, vol. II, p. 192.
35. Peka, p. 171.
36. Dok. Nak., p. 505, note 143.
37. Ibid., p. 296.
38. Ibid., pp. 297–8. See also Sukhanov, *Zapiski o revolyutsii*, vol. VII, p. 69 on Moscow's militancy in October.
39. Peka, p. 313.
40. Stepanov, *Rabochie Petrograda*, pp. 30 and 245. See also Dok. Okt., p. 871, note 30.
41. Peka, p. 313.
42. Ibid., p. 310. There were several thousand Finnish workers in Petrograd in 1917. The Letts were mostly evacuees from Riga's metalworking factories.
43. Raisovety, vol. I, p. 356.
44. *Novaya zhizn'* (13 Oct 1917).
45. Ibid. (3 Oct 1917).
46. *Rabochii put'* (21 Oct 1917).
47. Dok. Okt., pp. 112–13. See also pp. 103–4.
48. See Mandel, *Petrograd Workers*, pp. 69–71, 123–4.
49. Stepanov, *Rabochie Petrograda*, pp. 46–7. See also above, p. 232.
50. Peka, pp. 295–6.
51. Ibid., pp. 299–300.
52. Vtoraya, p. 118.
53. *Petrogradskaya pravda*, no. 5 (1922) cited in Peka, p. 326.
54. Peka, p. 305.
55. Dok. Nak., p. 68.
56. V. Malakhovskii, *Iz istorii krasnoi gvardii*, pp. 23–4.
57. Sukhanov, *Zapiski o revolyutsii*, vol. VII, pp. 234–5.
58. Mstislavskii, *Sem' dnei*, p. 118. See also Trotsky, *History of the Russian Revolution*, vol. III, p. 178.
59. Skorinko, *Vospominaniya rabochego ob Oktyabre*, pp. 137–8.

60. Ibid., pp. 145–7.
61. I. Peskovoi, 'Nakanune Oktyabr'skogo perevorota', *Krasnaya letopis'*, no. 6 (1923) p. 317.
62. V. I. Startsev, 'K voprosu o sostave rabochei krasnoi gvardii Petrograda', *Istoriya SSSR*, no. 1 (1962) p. 137; Stepanov, *Rabochie Petrograda*, pp. 29, 34, 36.
63. Startsev, 'K voprosu', pp. 138, 141.
64. M. Sveshnikov, 'Iz epokhi Oktyabrya', *Krasnaya letopis'*, no. 6 (1923) p. 30; T. Graf, 'Ob Oktyabr'skoi revolyutsii', ibid., pp. 167–9; Skorinko, *Vos pominaniya*, p. 146. See also Peka, p. 330.
65. Startsev, 'K voprosu', p. 139.
66. Kudelli, *Leningradske rabochie*, p. 111.
67. See Mandel, *Petrograd Workers*, pp. 41–2.
68. Startsev, 'K voprosu'.
69. Peskovoi, 'Nakanune Oktyabr'skogo', p. 316.
70. G. Georgievskii, *Ocherki po istorii krasnoi gvardii* (M., 1919) pp. 76–7.
71. Kudelli, *Leningradskie rabochie*, p. 117.
72. S. P. Melgunov, *The Bolshevik Seizure of Power* (Santa Barbara: ABC–CIO, 1972) p. 90.
73. Kudelli, *Leningradski rabochie*, pp. 123–5.
74. E. Pinezhskii, *Krasnaya gvardiya* (M., 1938) p. 62.
75. Trotsky, *History of the Russian Revolution*, vol. III, p. 178.
76. Stepanov, *Rabochie Petrograda*, p. 245.
77. Peka, p. 330.
78. Ibid., p. 314, See also p. 286.
79. Dok. Sept., pp. 375–6.

**Chapter 5: The October Revolution and the Demise of Revolutionary Democracy**

1. Dok. Okt., pp. 351–2.
2. *Novaya zhizn'* (26 Oct 1917).
3. Kudelli, *Leningradskie rabochie*, p. 121.
4. R. V. Daniels, *Red October* (New York: Scribner, 1967) p. 218.
5. Chamberlin, *Russian Revolution*, vol. I, p. 320; *Novaya zhizn'* (20 and 26 Oct 1917); *Znamya truda* (27 Oct 1917); Sukhanov, *Zapiski o revolyutsii*, vol. VII, p. 216.
6. This section deals with attitudes towards the overthrow of the Provisional Government only. The question of the nature of the régime to replace it—specifically, the issue of the all-socialist coalition—which arose only on 27 and 28 October with the formation of the Bolshevik government and the start of the civil war, will be treated separately.
7. This was also noted by A. C. Popov, a Menshevik–Internationalist, in his collection of documents on the October Insurrection, *Oktyabr'skii perevorot* (Petrograd, 1918) p. 361. Most of the material consists of resolutions, which Popov, as a witness to the events, felt accurately reflected the workers' attitudes.
8. *Delo naroda* (28 Oct 1917).

9. Popov, *Oktyabr'skii perevorot*, p. 362.
10. Ibid., pp. 362–3.
11. 'V Oktyabre v raionakh Petrograda' (henceforth cited as V Oktyabre), *Krasnaya letopis'*, no. 2 (23) (1927) p. 178.
12. *Pravda* (4 Nov 1917). See also F. Dingel'shtedt, 'Iz vospominanii agitatora Peterburgskogo komiteta RSDRP(b)', *Krasnaya letopis'*, no. 1(22) (1927) p. 58.
13. Kudelli, *Leningradskie rabochie*, p. 124.
14. Popov, *Oktyabr'skii perevorot*, p. 362.
15. *Novaya zhizn'* (30 Oct 1917). For a different version, see *Rabochaya gazeta* (1 and 2 Nov 1917).
16. Dok. Okt., pp. 855, 890.
17. A. Tanyaev, *Ocherki po istorii zheleznodorozhnikov v revolyutsii 1917–go goda* (M.–L., 1925) p. 141.
18. Ibid., p. 142.
19. Sukhanov, *Zapiski o revolyutsii*, vol. VII, pp. 230–1.
20. Popov, *Oktyabr'skii perevorot*, pp. 363–78 passim.
21. Ibid., p. 372.
22. Dok. Okt., pp. 368, 574, 575; C. Volin, *Deyatel'nost' men'shevikov v profsoyuzakh pri Sovetskoi vlasti* (New York: Inter-University Project on the History of the Menshevik Movement, paper no. 13, 1962).
23. *Novaya zhizn'* (4 Jan 1918).
24. *Pravda* (28 Oct 1917). Similar resolutions from this group were passed by the Sestroretsk Arms Factory (*Znamya truda*, 28 Oct 1917), Schlusselburg Soviet and Powder Factory (Dok. Okt., p. 566), Second Dept of the Putilov Works (*Znamya truda*, 28 Oct 1917), Old Baranovskii Machine-construction Factory (Stepanov, *Rabochie Petrograda*, p. 274), Parviainen Machine-construction (Stepanov, ibid.), Petrograd Metalworkers' Union (Dok. Okt., p. 346), Central and District Strike Committees of the Woodworkers' Union (*Znamya truda*, 28 Oct 1917), Petrograd Council of Trade Unions (*Novaya zhizn'*, 27 Oct 1917), Skorokhod (*Triumfal'noe shestvie sovetov* (M., 1963) vol. I, p. 205 (henceforth cited as Dok. Nov.), and Nevskii Shoe Factories (*Izvestiya*, 3 Nov 1917), the Union of Needleworkers (*Pravda*, 2 Nov 1917) and others.
25. Resolutions of support were passed by Patronnyi (Cartridge) (Dok. Okt., p. 564), Promet (ibid., p. 514), Obukhovskii (*Pravda*, 6 Nov 1917), Aleksandrovskii (*Izvestiya*, 1 Nov 1917)—the latter two in the Nevskii District—and the Soviet of the Kolpino District, where the main factory was Izhorskii (LGAORSS 171/1/1 110p).
26. Ek. Pol., vol. I, 1.7.
27. Dok. Okt., p. 564.
28. Locomotive Workshops of the Nikolaevskii Railroad (Popov, *Oktyabr'skii perevorot*, p. 314) and Main Workshops of the North–West Railroad (ibid.).
29. Union of Textile Workers (Perazich, *Tekstili Leningrada*, p. 97), the Nevka Textile Mill (*Pravda*, 30 Oct 1917), Schlusselburg Cotton-printing (Dok. Okt., p. 560), Novaya bumagopryadil'nya (*Izvestiya*, 2 Nov 1917), Leont'ev Bros (*Pravda*, 3 Nov 1917), Voronin and Co. (ibid., 31 Oct 1917), Kozhevnikovskaya (V Oktyabre, p. 178), Shaposhnikova Tobacco

(Dok. Okt., p. 346), workers of food-processing plants of the Petrograd Food Authority (Popov, *Oktyabr'skii perevorot*, p.309),Treugol'nik Rubber Factory (*Znamya truda*, 28 Oct 1917) and others.

30. *Pravda* (15 Nov 1917).
31. Ibid. (2 Nov 1917).
32. *Iskra* (21 Oct 1917); Popov, *Oktyabr'skii perevorot*, p. 315.
33. Melgunov, *Bolshevik Seizure of Power*, p. 65.
34. This argument is made by Trotsky in his *History*, vol. III, ch. VI.
35. *Pravda* (27 Oct 1917).
36. Ibid.
37. Ibid. (30 Nov 1917); Peka, p. 369.
38. Sukhanov, *Zapiski o revolyutsii*, p. 224.
39. Dok. Okt., pp. 425–6.
40. Skorinko, 'Vaspominaniya rabochego ob Oktyabre', p. 152.
41. Melgunov, *Bolshevik Seizure of Power*, pp. 90–1.
42. Trotsky, *History*, vol. III, p. 250. See also Sukhanov, *Zapiski o revolyutsii*, vol. VII, p. 202.
43. S. A. Piontkovskii, *Sovety v Oktyabre* (M., 1928) p. 53.
44. Malakhovskii, *Iz istorii*, p. 26.
45. *Novaya zhizn'* (29 Oct 1917).
46. Ibid., *Znamya truda* (29 Oct 1917).
47. See, for example, *Iskra* (3 Oct 1917).
48. *Novaya zhizn'* (3 Nov 1917).
49. Ibid. (4 Nov 1917).
50. See Mandel, *Petrograd Workers*, pp. 33–7.
51. *Znamya truda* (6 Nov 1917). Similar resolutions from small factories were passed at Reikhel' (*Novaya zhizn'*, 30 Oct 1917), Odner (ibid., 1 Nov 1917), Ekval' (Popov, *Oktyabr'skii perevorot*, pp. 396–7), the Central Power Station (*Znamya truda*, 3 Nov 1917), and a joint meeting of Brenner, Bruk, Butt, Aleksandrov and Trainin (ibid., 5 Nov 1917).
52. *Znamya truda* (3 Nov 1917).
53. Popov, *Oktyabr'skii perevorot*, p. 296.
54. *Iskra* (5 Nov 1917).
55. *Novaya zhizn'* (3 Nov 1917).
56. Popov, *Oktyabr'skii perevorot*, p. 39.
57. *Znamya truda* (5 Nov 1917).
58. Ibid.
59. Ibid.
60. Dok. Nov., p. 23.
61. *Znamya truda* (2 Nov 1917).
62. *Novaya zhizn'* (4 Nov 1917).
63. *Znamya truda* (7 Nov 1917).
64. Ibid. (2 Nov 1917).
65. Ibid. (3 Nov 1917).
66. Popov, *Oktyabr'skii perevorot*, p. 315.
67. Tanyaev, *Ocherki po istorii*, p. 147. See similar reports on the First and Ninth Districts, ibid., p. 153.
68. Ibid., p. 155.
69. Dok. Okt., p. 758.

70. Popov, *Oktyabr'skii perevorot*, p. 339. Similar resolutions were passed by the white-collar employees of the Putilov Works and Shipyards (*Novaya zhizn'*, 1 Nov 1917), the Central Committee of the Petrograd Port (ibid., 3 Nov 1917), All-Russian Post and Telegraph Union (Popov, *Oktyabr'skii perevorot*, p. 393), white-collar employees of the Treugol'nik Rubber Factory (ibid.), the All-Russian Union of Workers and Employees of the Waterways (*Znamya truda*, 3 Nov 1917). This was also, of course, the position espoused by Vikzhel.

71 Raisovety, vol. I, p. 154. See also the declaration of two days earlier, Dok. Okt., p. 758.

72. Popov, *Oktyabr'skii perevorot*, p. 309. Among the factories and workers' organisations adhering to this position were Admiralty Shipyards (LGA-ORSS 9391/1/11/45), Turret, Locomotive, Boiler and Machine-construction Shops of the Putilov Works (*Znamya truda*, 31 Oct 1917), Main workshops of NW Railroad (Popov, *Oktyabr'skii perevorot*, pp. 315–16), Pulemet Factory (*Znamya truda*, 3 Nov 1917), Nevskii District Soviet of Factory Committees (*Novaya zhizn'*, 4 Nov 1917), Kolpino District Soviet (LGAORSS 171/1/1/17), EC of Petrograd Soviet (*Novaya zhizn'*, 1 Nov 1917), Petrograd Trade Union Council (ibid., 4 Nov 1917), ECs of Textile and Leatherworkers' Unions (*Znamya truda*, 9 Nov 1917), and CS of Factory Committees (*Novaya zhizn'*, 1 Nov 1917).

73. V Oktyabre, p. 174.

74. Ibid.

75. Ibid., p. 173.

76. Peka, p. 330. See also Dok. Nov., p. 155 (Skorokhod).

77. Dok. Nov., p. 161. See also V Oktyabre, p. 178 (Kozhevnikovskaya).

78. It includes Schlusselburg Power Factory (*Pravda*, 4 Nov 1917), Admiralty Shipyards, early November (LGAORSS 9391/1/11/48), Cable (*Pravda*, 4 Nov 1917), Petrograd Tram Depot (ibid., 1 Nov 1917), Petrograd Aircraft Park (ibid., 4 Nov 1917), Treugol'nik Rubber Factory (ibid., 2 Nov 1917), Snaryadnyi (*Znamya truda*, 17 Nov 1917), Sestroretsk Arms Factory (ibid., 3 Nov 1917), Kozhevnikovskaya Textile Mill (V Oktyabre, p. 178), Leont'ev Bros Textile (*Pravda*, 3 Nov 1917), Novaya Bumagopryadil'nya Textile (*Izvestiya*, 2 Nov 1917), Voronin Textile (*Pravda*, 5 Nov 1917), Preparatory Meeting of Women Workers (Popov, *Oktyabr'skii perevorot*, pp. 306–7), EC of Needleworkers' Union (*Pravda*, 2 Nov 1917), meeting of the Conference of 2000 workers and soldiers in Moscow District (ibid., 3 Nov 1917), the food plants of Petrograd Food Authority (Popov, *Oktyabr'skii perevorot*, p. 309), Delegates' Meeting of workers and employees of municipal enterprises (Dok. Okt., p. 573).

79. Perazich, *Tekstili Leningrada*, p. 98.

80. *Znamya truda* (8 Nov 1917).

81. Popov, *Oktyabr'skii perevorot*, pp. 306–7.

82. *Pravda* (9 Nov 1917).

83. Peka, p. 335.

84. Ibid., p. 341.

85. Ibid., p. 342.

86. Ibid., p. 345.
87. Ibid., pp. 345–7 (see also biographies at back of book).
88. Dok. Nov., p. 667.
89. Ibid., pp. 164–5.
90. Ibid., p. 158. See also 'Chetvertaya Petrogradskaya obshchegorodskaya konferentsiya RSDRP (b) v 1917 g.', *Krasnaya letopis'*, no. 3(24) (1927), pp. 58–64.
91. *Novaya zhizn'* (7 Nov 1917); *Znamya truda* (7 Nov 1917).
92. LGAORSS 9301/1/11/45.
93. Ibid.
94. The internationalist wing of the party soon afterwards won a majority in CC, which on 19 November condemned the party's past policies (I. H. Haimson (ed.), *The Mensheviks* (University of Chicago Press 1975) p. 94). Henceforth, with some right-wing exceptions, the party acted as an opposition within the TsIK, rejecting (unlike the SRs) association with attempts to overthrow it by violence.
95. *Znamya truda* (15 Nov 1917).
96. Ibid. (18 Nov 1917).
97. Ibid. (16 Nov 1917).
98. Ibid. (21 Nov 1917).
99. Ibid. (17 Nov 1917).
100. Ibid.
101. Ibid. (17 Dec 1917).

**Chapter 6:  The Constituent Assembly and the Emergence of a Worker Opposition**

1. Peka, p. 375.
2. *Nasha rech'* (17 Nov 1917).
3. See Table 1.1 above, p. 219.
4. *Novaya zhizn'* (14 Nov 1917).
5. *Nasha rech'* (17 Nov 1917).
6. See Mandel, *Petrograd Workers*, ch. 3
7. Ibid., p. 57.
8. O. Radkey, *The Election to the Russian Constituent Assembly of 1917* (Harvard University Press, 1950) p. 80.
9. Ibid., p. 53. See also *Novaya zhizn'* report on Moscow (12 Dec 1917).
10. O. Radkey, *The Sickle Under the Hammer*, p. 291.
11. Radkey, *The Election*, p. 21.
12. Radkey, *The Sickle*, p. 290.
13. Radkey, *The Election*, p. 21.
14. *Pravda* (30 Nov 1917); Peka, p. 369.
15. *Novaya zhizn'* (16 Nov 1917).
16. Mandel, *Petrograd Workers*, pp. 57–8.
17. *Nasha rech'* (17 Nov 1917).
18. *Novaya zhizn'* (12 Dec 1917).
19. *Znamya truda* (30 Dec 1917).
20. *Novaya zhizn'* (11 Nov 1917).
21. Peka, p. 351.

22. *Pravda* (12 Nov 1917). See also *Novaya zhizn'* (17 Nov 1917).
23. *Znamya truda* (30 Nov 1917); *Novaya zhizn'* (3 Dec 1917).
24. *Novaya zhizn'*, ibid.
25. Ibid. (28 Dec 1917).
26. Ibid. (15 Dec 1917).
27. Ibid. (10 Dec 1917).
28. *Znamya truda* (3 Nov 1917).
29. *Novaya zhizn'* (4 Jan 1918).
30. *Znamya truda* (30 Nov 1917).
31. *Novaya zhizn'* (4 Jan 1918).
32. Ibid. (6 Jan 1918).
33. Ibid. (9 Jan 1918).
34. Ibid. (11 Jan 1918).
35. *Znamya truda* (16 Dec 1917). For similar resolutions, see Opticheskii, ibid., and New Shell Dept. of Obukhovskii, Dok. Nov., vol. I, p. 189.
36. *Novaya zhizn'* (6 Jan 1918).
37. Ibid. (12 Jan 1918).
38. Ibid. (11 Jan 1918).
39. Ibid. (17 Jan 1918).
40. Ibid. (11 Jan 1918).
41. Ibid. (9 Jan 1918).
42. Ek. Pol., vol. I, table 7.
43. N. Sveshnikov, *Krasnaya letopis'*, no. 6 (1923) p. 302.
44. *Pravda* (31 Jan 1918).
45. *Novaya zhizn'* (25 Jan and 13/26 Feb 1918).
46. See note 7.
47. *Novaya zhizn'* (21 Jan 1918).
48. *Pravda* (7 Jan 1918).
49. *Novaya zhizn'* (20 Jan 1918).
50. Ibid. (4/17 Feb 1918).
51. Ibid. (22 Dec 1917).
52. *Metallist*, no. 1 (12 Jan 1918).
53. *Novaya zhizn'* (2 Dec 1917).
54. Ibid. (6 Dec 1917).
55. See, for example, the *chernorabochie* at Phoenix, ibid., 20 Dec 1917, and further on Metallicheskii, ibid., 22 Dec 1917. Matters were especially bad in the unskilled chemical industry, ibid., 11 Nov and 21 Dec 1917.
56. *Putilovtsy v trekh revolyutsiyakh*, p. 419.
57. *Novaya zhizn'* (24 Dec 1917).
58. Cited in ibid. (12 Dec 1917).
59. Ibid. (8 Dec 1917).
60. Ibid. (22 Mar 1918).
61. *Metallist*, no. 3 (1918) p. 5.
62. *Novaya zhizn'* (15 Nov 1917).
63. *Pravda* (18 Jan 1918). For similar attitudes, see the resolutions of N. Lessner, *Znamya truda* (20 Jan 1918); Rozenkrants, ibid.; and Skorokhod, *Pravda* (20 Jan 1918).
64. *Novaya zhizn'* (13 Jan 1918).
65. Ibid. (4 Jan 1918).

66. Ibid. (11, 19, 25 Jan 1918); Dok. Nov., vol. II, p. 36.
67. *Novaya zhizn'* (5 Jan 1918).
68. Ibid. (9 Jan 1918).
69. Ibid. (14 Jan 1918).
70. Ibid. (9 Jan 1918).
71. Ibid. (12 Jan 1918).
72. Ibid. (22 Dec 1917). See also Gordienko's account of an encounter between Gorky and three Vyborg workers in 1917, I. Gordienko, *Iz boevogo proshlogo* (M., 1957) pp. 98–101.

**Chapter 7: The October Revolution in the Factories**

1. Lenin, *Polnoe sobranie*, vol. XXXV (M., 1962) pp. 30–1.
2. *Novaya zhizn'* (9 Nov 1917).
3. *Izvestiya* (16 Nov 1917); *Znamya truda* (16 Nov 1917).
4. *Natsionalizatsiya promyshlennosti v SSSR* (henceforth Nats. Prom. SSSR), (M., 1954) p. 78; *Izvestiya* (7 Dec 1917).
5. *Izvestiya* (17 Dec 1917).
6. Rab. Kon., p. 341.
7. *Metallist*, no. 1 (1918) p. 13.
8. *Novaya zhizn'* (23 Dec 1917).
9. Nats. Prom. SSSR, pp. 345–6.
10. Rab. Kon., pp. 325–6.
11. *Novaya zhizn'* (23 Jan 1918).
12. Rab. Kon., p. 285.
13. *Znamya truda* (17 Nov 1917). See also *Izvestiya* (21 Nov 1917).
14. Rab. Kon., p. 285.
15. Ibid., pp. 346–7
16. *Novaya zhizn'* (21 Jan 1918).
17. Rab. Kon., pp. 279, 283.
18. See, for example, *Natsionalizatsiya promyshlennosti i organizatsiya sotsialisticheskogo proizvodstva v Petrograde* (henceforth Nats. Prom. Petrograd), (L., 1958) vol. I, p. 101; *Novaya zhizn'* (15 Nov 1917).
19. Rab. Kon., pp. 346–7
20. Nats. Prom. SSSR, pp. 350–1.
21. Ibid., p. 351.
22. *Novaya zhizn'* (4/17 Feb 1918). For Parviainen, see *Pravda* (31 Jan 1918).
23. Nats. Prom. Petrograd, vol. I, p. 34.
24. Ibid., p. 35.
25. Ibid., pp. 82–6.
26. For a recent example, see J. Keep, *The Russian Revolution*, ch. VI.
27. *Novaya zhizn'* (28 Jan 1918).
28. Nats. Prom. Petrograd, p. 99.
29. *Novaya zhizn'* (4 Jan 1918).
30. Lenin, *Polnoe sobranie*, vol. XXXVI, pp. 521–2.
31. *Novaya zhizn'* (17 Jan 1918).
32. *Metallist*, no. 2 (1918). See also *Novaya zhizn'* (7/20 Feb 1917).

33. *Metallist*, no. 2 (1918).
34. *Novaya zhizn'* (27 Mar 1918).
35. Ibid. (5 Dec 1917).
36. Rab. Kon., pp. 345–7.
37. *Novaya zhizn'* (5 Dec 1917).
38. Rab. Kon., pp. 345–7.
39. *Novaya zhizn'* (26 Jan 1918).
40. Ibid.
41. Ibid.
42. Ibid. (31 Jan 1918).
43. I. Stepanov, *Ot rabochego kontrolya do rabochego upravelniya v promyshlennosti i zemledelii* (M., 1918) pp. 4–14. See also Kosior in *Metallist*, nos 9–10 (1918) pp. 3–5.
44. Rab. Kon., p. 60.
45. *Izvestiya VTsIKa* (5 June 1918).

**Chapter 8: Soviet Power for Better or Worse**

1. S. Strumilin, 'Prozhitochnyi minimum i zarabotki chernorabochikh v Petrograde', *Statistika truda*, nos 2–3 (1918) pp. 4–8.
2. A. L. Mil'shtein, 'Rabochie Petrograda v bor'be za ukreplenie sovetov', in *Rabochie Petrograda v bor'be za pobedu sotsializma* (M.-L., 1963) p. 129.
3. *Novaya zhizn'* (18 Jan 1918).
4. Strumilin 'Prozhitochnyi minimum', p. 5.
5. *Novaya zhizn'* (21 May 1918).
6. Ibid. (30 Apr 1918).
7. Ibid. (5 July 1918).
8. Ibid. (5 Dec 1917); (1/14 Feb and 22 Mar 1918); Nats. Prom. SSSR, pp. 30, 40; Rab. Kon., pp. 273, 289, 412–13, 422, 424–5, 432, 454.
9. Strumilin, 'Prozhitochnyi minimum'.
10. Nats. Prom. Petrograd, vol. II, p. 242.
11. *Bastiony revolyutsii* (L., 1967) vol. I, p. 237.
12. Mandel, *Petrograd Workers*, pp. 9–14.
13. I. Shkaratan, 'Izmeneniya v sotsial'nom sostave fabrichnozavodskikh rabochikh Leningrada 1917–1928', *Istoriya SSSR*, no. 5 (1959) p. 21; *Novaya zhizn'* (23 Mar 1918). Stepanov, *Rabochie Petrograda*, p. 47; K. I. Shelavin, 'Peterburgskii komitet bol'shevikov sed'mogo sozyva v 1918 godu', *Krasnaya letopis'*, no. 2(29) (1929) p. 5; Mil'shtein, 'Rabochie Petrograda', p. 129.
14. P. A. Chugaev, *Rabochii klass Sovetskoi Rossii v pervyi god diktatury proletariata* (M., 1967) pp. 354–5.
15. *Petrogradskaya pravda* (7 Apr 1918).
16. *Novaya zhizn'* (12, 20 Jan and 1/14, 4/17 Feb 1918).
17. Startsev, *Ocherki po istorii petrogradskoi krasnoi gvardii*, p. 280.
18. Ibid., pp. 278, 280.
19. *Petrogradskaya pravda* (27 Mar 1918).
20. Mil'shtein, 'Rabochie Petrograda', p. 129; *Krasnaya gazeta* (18 June 1918).

438 The Petrograd Workers and the Soviet Seizure of Power

21. Chugaev, *Rabochii klass*, p. 92.
22. K. I. Shelavin, 'Iz istorii peterburgskogo komiteta bol'shevikov v 1918 godu', *Krasnaya letopis'*, no. 2 (26) (1928) p. 113.
23. *Novaya zhizn'* (26 May 1918).
24. Ibid. (3/16 Feb 1918).
25. Ibid. (13 Mar 1918).
26. Ibid. (20 Mar. 1918).
27. Chamberlin, *Russian Revolution*, vol. I, p. 396.
28. Ibid, pp. 398–9.
29. Peka, p. 382.
30. *Protokoly Tseka RSDRP (b), avgust 1917 – fevral' 1918* (M., 1958) p. 282.
31. M. N. Potekhin, *Pervyi sovet proletarskoi diktatury* (L., 1966) p. 112.
32. Shelavin, *Krasnaya letopis'*, no. 2 (26) (1928) p. 106.
33. Potekhin, *Pervyi sovet*, pp. 112–13.
34. *Pravda* (14/27 Feb 1918).
35. Ibid. (10/23 Feb 1918).
36. *Znamya truda* (12 Dec 1917).
37. Ibid. (1 Mar 1918).
38. Ibid. (13/26 Feb 1918).
39. *Novyi luch* (8/21 Feb 1918); *Novaya zhizn'* (6 Mar 1918).
40. *Novaya zhizn'* (8/21 Feb 1918).
41. *Znamya truda* (14/27 Feb 1918). See also Main Workshops of the NW Railroad, Russko-Baltiiskii Wagon-construction Factory, Special Conference of the Factory Committees of the Nevskii District, ibid.; Phoenix, Opticheskii, Treugol'nik and others ibid. (1 Mar 1918); Dinamo, *Pravda* (8/21 Feb 1918); Putilov, ibid. (10/23 Feb 1918); Skorokhod, ibid. (14/27 Feb); Nobel, *Novaya zhizn'* (28 Mar 1918).
42. *Pravda* (12/25 Feb 1918).
43. Ibid. (2 Mar 1918); *Znamya truda* (2 Mar 1918).
44. Startsev, *Ocherki po istorii*, pp. 244–5.
45. *Novaya zhizn'* (2 Mar 1918).
46. *Pravda* (2 Mar 1918).
47. Cited in *Novaya zhizn'* (2 Mar 1918).
48. Ibid.
49. Ibid. (20 Mar 1918).
50. Ibid.
51. Ibid. (28 Mar 1918).
52. Ibid.; *Pravda* (2 Mar 1918).
53. Ibid.
54. *Znamya bor'by* (13/26 Feb 1918).
55. See, for example, Treugol'nik, *Pravda* (7 Mar 1918); Okhta meeting, ibid.; Vasilevskii ostrov tram depot, *Petrogradskaya pravda* (14/27 Feb 1918).
56. V. I. Nosach, 'Profsoyuzy Petrograda v pervyi god Sovetskoi vlasti', in *Iz istorii Velikoi Oktyabr'skoi sotsialisticheskoi revolyutsii i sotsialisticheskogo stroitel'stva v SSSR* (L., 1967) p. 142.
57. Shelavin, *Krasnaya letopis*, no. 2 (26) (1928) p. 106.
58. Ibid.; *Pravda* (6 Mar 1918).
59. *Novyi luch* (8/21 Feb 1918).

60. *Novaya zhizn'* (5 Mar 1918).
61. Ibid. (8/21 Feb; 6 Mar 1918).
62. Ibid. (8 May 1918).
63. LGAORSS 171/1/1/10, 11 op.
64. *Novyi luch* (7/20 Feb 1918).
65. *Novaya zhizn'* (26 Mar 1918).
66. Ibid. (30 Apr 1918).
67. G. Ya. Aronson, *Dvizhenie upolnomochennykh ot rabochikh fabrik i zavodov v 1918 godu* (New York: Inter-University Project on the History of the Menshevik Movement, 1960) p. 6; *Novaya zhizn'* (27 Mar 1918).
68. *Novaya zhizn'* (26 Mar 1918).
69. Ibid. (27 Mar 1918).
70. Ibid. (14 May 1918).
71. Ibid.
72. Ibid. (28 May 1918).
73. Ibid. (29 Mar 1918).
74. *Znamya bor'by* (14 May 1918).
75. *Novaya zhizn'* (19 June 1918).
76. Ibid. (28 May 1918).
77. Mil'shtein, 'Rabochie Petrograda', p. 157.
78. Shelavin, *Krasnaya letopis'*, no. 3(27) (1928) p. 167.
79. *Novaya zhizn'* (8 May 1918).
80. Ibid. (22 Mar 1918).
81. Shelavin, *Krasnaya letopis'*, no. 2 (26) (1928) p. 113.
82. *Petrogradskaya pravda* (2 Apr 1918).
83. *Novaya zhizn'* (26 Mar 1918).
84. Ibid.
85. Ibid. (1 June 1918).
86. Ibid. (20 Apr 1918).
87. See pp. 317–18 above.
88. *Novaya zhizn'* (11 May 1918).
89. Ibid. (26 May; 22 June 1918).
90. Chamberlin, *Russian Revolution*, vol. I, pp. 387–8.
91. *Novaya zhizn'* (11 May 1918).
92. Ibid. (12 May 1918).
93. Ibid. (15 May 1918).
94. Ibid. (9 April 1918).
95. *Petrogradskaya pravda* (22 June 1918).
96. Mil'shtein, 'Rabochie Petrograda', p. 137.
97. *Petrogradskaya pravda* (10 April 1918).
98. Shelavin, *Krasnaya letopis'*, no. 2 (26) (1928) p. 115.
99. *Znamya bor'by* (14 May 1918).
100. *Novaya zhizn'* (11 May 1918).
101. *Znamya bor'by* (14 May 1918).
102. Ibid. (24 May 1918). See also the case of the Putilov Works, Shelavin, *Krasnaya letopis'*, no. 3(27) (1928) p. 152.
103. *Krasnaya gazeta* (29 June 1918).
104. Chamberlin, *Russian Revolution*, vol. I, p. 420.
105. *Novaya zhizn'* (1 June 1918).

440    *The Petrograd Workers and the Soviet Seizure of Power*

106. See Shelavin, *Krasnaya letopis'*, no. 3(27) (1928) p. 167.
107. *Novaya zhizn'* (27 June 1918).
108. *Severnaya kommuna* (6 July 1918).
109. Shelavin, *Krasnaya letopis'*, no. 1(28) (1929) p. 74. See also pp. 70–81 passim.
110. Chamberlin, *Russian Revolution*, vol. I, pp. 348, 381.
111. *Novaya zhizn'*, (10 June 1918).
112. Mil'shtein, 'Rabochie Petrograda', p. 135.
113. Chamberlin, *Russian Revolution*, vol. II, pp. 7–8.
114. *Novaya zhizn'* (18 and 21 June 1918).
115. See, for example, ibid. (3 May 1918) and *Krasnaya gazeta* (29 June 1918).
116. *Metallist*, nos 9–10 (1918) pp. 8–9.
117. Mil'shtein, 'Rabochie Petrograda', p. 146.
118. Ibid., p. 154.
119. *Petrogradskaya pravda* (6 Dec 1918).
120. *Novaya zhizn'* (12 June 1918).
121. Chamberlin, *Russian Revolution*, vol. II, p. 48.
122. *Novaya zhizn'* (16 June 1918).
123. Ibid. (22 June 1918).
124. Mil'shtein, 'Rabochie Petrograda', p. 157.
125. *Novaya zhizn'* (14 May 1918).
126. Ibid. (25 May 1918).
127. Ibid. (29, 30 May 1918).
128. Ibid. (31 May 1918).
129. Ibid. (2 June 1918).
130. Ibid. (20 June 1918).
131. Mil'shtein, 'Rabochie Petrograda', p. 154.
132. *Severnaya kommuna* (20 June 1918).
133. *Novaya zhizn'* (26 June 1918). The W. Siberian Commissariat, established on 1 June after the first Czech victories, was headed by the SR Derber and guided by the SR programme: Constituent Assembly and universal suffrage, toleration of the soviets and land committees as non-governmental bodies and gradual denationalition of industry. Within a few weeks, however, it ceded its place to the Siberian Government headed by liberal (Kadet) elements, who had the support of the military force, and proceeded to suppress the soviets on its territory, permitting only "non-political" trade unions. Chamberlin, *Russian Revolution*, pp. 12–14.
134. *Novaya zhizn'* (3 July 1918).
135. Cited in *Krasnaya gazeta* (3 July 1918).
136. *Novaya zhizn'* (3 July 1918).
137. Ibid.
138. Ibid. (2 July 1918).

**Conclusion**

1. Some contemporary examples of this position are J. Keep, *The Russian Revolution*, pp. 68, 77; P. Avrich, *The Russian Anarchists* (Princeton

University Press, 1967) p. 142 and 'Workers' Control in Russian Industry', *Slavic Review*, vol. XXII (1963) p. 63; A. Ulam, *A History of Soviet Russia* (New York: Praeger, 1976) ch. 1; C. Brinton's, *Anatomy of Revolution* (New York: Vintage, 1958) p. 68, is a classic statement of this view in the theoretical literature on revolution.

2. See, for example, C. Johnson, *Revolutionary Change* (Boston: Little, Brown, 1966); N. J. Smelser, *Theory of Collective Behaviour* (New York: Free Press, 1962) especially ch. 10; W. Kornhauser, *The Theory of Mass Society* (Glencoe, Illinois: Free Press, 1959).

3. See, for example, Ulam, *History of Soviet Russia*, ch. 1.

4. Chamberlin, *Russian Revolution,* vol. II, p. 453.

5. Ibid., p. 184.

6. Ibid.

7. See, for example, A. Soboul, *The Sans Culottes* (Garden City, New York: Doubleday, 1972) and B. Manning, *The English People and the English Revolution* (Harmondsworth: Penguin, 1978).

# Selected Bibliography

## I Archives

Leningradskii gosudarstvennyi arkhiv Oktyabr'skoi revolyutsii i sotsialisticheskogo stroitel'stva (LGAORSS)
    fond 171, opis' 1, delo 1 (Kolpino District Soviet protocols)
    1000/73/16 (Petrograd Soviet, Workers' Section protocols, 12 Mar 1917)
    4591/1/1 (general factory assemblies and conferences of the Petrograd Metalworkers' Union, protocols, Mar–Dec 1917)
    9391/1/11 (Admiralty Shipyard general assembly protocols, 12 Apr 1917–9 Dec 1918)

## II Published Documents and Statistics

'Chetvertaya Petrogradskaya Obschegorodskaya konferentsiya RSDRP(b) v 1917 gg', *Krasnaya letopis'*, no. 3(24) (1927) pp. 56–64

Chugaev, D. A., ed., *Rabochii klass Sovetskoi Rossii v pervyi god diktatury proletariata* (M., 1964)

*Ekonomicheskoe polozhenie Rossii nakanune Velikoi Oktyabr'skoi sotsialisticheskoi revolyutsii*, 3 vols (M.-L., 1957) (Ek. Pol.)

*Fabrichno-zavodskie komitety Petrograda: protokoly* (M., 1979)

Lenin, V. I., *Polnoe sobranie sochinenii*, 5th edn, 55 vols (M., 1958–65)

*Materialy po statistike truda severnoi oblasti*, vyp. v (Petrograd,1919)

*Natsionalizatsiya promyshlennosti i organizatsiya sotsialisticheskogo proizvodstva v Petrograde*, vol. I (L., 1958) (Nats. Prom. Petrograd)

*Natsionalizatsiya promyshlennosti v SSSR* (M., 1954) (Nats. Prom. SSSR)

*Oktyabr'skaya revolyutsiya i fabzavkomy*, 2 vols (M., 1927–8) (FZK)

*Perepiska sekretariata TseKa RSDRP(b) s mestnymy organizatsiyami, mart-oktyabr' 1917* (M., 1957)

*Pervaya vserossiiskaya tarifnaya konferentsiya soyuza rabochikh metallistov* (Petrograd, 1918)

*Pervyi legal'nyi Peterburgskii komitet RSDRP(b) v 1917 g* (M.-L., 1927) (Peka)

Piontkovskii, S. A., *Sovety v Oktyabre* (M., 1928)

Popov, A. S., *Oktyabr'skii perevorot* (Petrograd, 1918)

*Protokoly TseKa RSDRP(b): avgust 1917–fevral' 1918* (M., 1958)

*Putilovtsy v trekh revolyutsiyakh* (L., 1933)

*Rabochii kontrol' i natsionalizatsiya promyshlennykh predpriyatii Petrograda v 1917–1919 gg*, vol. I (L., 1949) (Rab. Kon.)

*Raionnye sovety Petrograda v 1917 g*, 3 vols (M.-L., 1966–8) (Raisovety)

*Revolyutsiya 17-go goda: khronika sobytii*, vol. IV (M.-L., 1926)

*Shestoi vserossiiskii s"ezd RSDRP(b)* (M., 1958)

'V Oktyabre v raionakh Petrograda', *Krasnaya letopis'*, no. 2(23) (1927) pp. 173–8 (V Oktyabre)

*Velikaya Oktyabr'skaya sotsialisticheskaya revolyutsiya. Dokumenty i materialy.*

*Revolyutsionnoe dvizhenie v Rossii v iyule 1917 g.* (M. 1959) (Dok. July)

*Revolyutsionnoe dvizhenie v Rossii v avguste 1917 g.* (M., 1959) (Dok. Aug.)

*Revolyutsionnoe dvizhenie v Rossii v sentyabre 1917 g.* (M., 1962) (Dok. Sept.)

*Revolyutsionnoe dvizhenie v Rossii nakanune Oktyabr'skogo vooruzhennogo vosstaniya* (M., 1962) (Dok. Nak.)

*Oktyabr'skoe vooruzhennoe vosstanie v Petrograde* (M., 1957) (Dok. Okt.)

*Triumfal'noe shestvie sovetov*, vol. I (M., 1963) (Dok. Nov.)

*Vtoraya i tret'ya petrogradskie obshchegorodskie konferentsii bol'shevikov v iyule i sentyabre 1917 g.* (M.-L., 1927) (Vtoraya)

## III  Workers' Memoirs

Antonov, A. A., 'Vospominaniya kommissara Obukhovskogo staleliteinogo zavoda', in *Doneseniya kommissarov Petrogradskogo voenno-revolyutsionnogo komiteta*, vol. I (M., 1957) pp. 205–15

Buzinov, A., *Za nevskoi zastavoi* (M.-L., 1930)

Gordienko, I., *Iz boevogo proshlogo* (M., 1957)

Graf, T., 'Ob Oktyabr'skoi revolyutsii', *Krasnaya letopis'*, no. 6 (1923) pp. 164–9

Kudelli, P. F., ed., *Leningradskie rabochie v bor'be za vlast' sovetov v 1917 g.* (L., 1924)

Mikhailov, M., 'Rabochie zavoda P. V. Baranovskogo v bor'be za Oktyabr'', *Krasnaya letopis'*, nos 50–1 (1922) pp. 189–212

Peskovoi, I., 'Nakanune Oktyabr' skogo perevorota', *Krasnaya letopis'*, no. 6 (1923) pp. 315–18
'Piterskie rabochie ob Iyul'skikh dnyakh', *Krasnaya letopis'*, no. 9 (1923) pp. 19–41
Skorinko, I., 'Vospominaniya rabochego ob Oktyabre 1917 goda', *Krasnaya letopis'*, no. 6 (1923) pp. 137–58
Sveshnikov, M., 'Iz epokhi Oktyabrya 1917 goda', *Krasnaya letopis'*, no. 6 (1923) pp. 302–7
*Vogue revolyutsionnykh boev*, 2 vols (M., 1967 and 1971)


**IV  Memoirs of Non-workers**

Dingel'shtedt, F., 'Iz vospominanii agitatora Peterburgskogo komiteta RSDRP(b)', *Krasnaya letopis'*, no. 1(22) (1927) pp. 55–68
Georgieveskii, G., *Ocherki po istorii Krasnoi gvardii* (M., 1919)
Malakhovskii, V., *Iz istorii Krasnoi gvardii* (L., 1925)
Mstislavskii, S., *Sem' dnei* (Berlin–Petersburg–M., 1922)
Price, M. P., *Reminiscences of the Russian Revolution* (London: George Allen & Unwin, 1921)
Shelavin, K. I., 'Iz istorii Peterburgskogo komiteta bol'shevikov v 1918 godu', ocherki I–III, *Krasnaya letopis'*, no. 2(26) (1928) pp. 106–24; no. 3(27) (1928) pp. 146–72; no. 1(28) (1929) pp. 69–88
Shelavin, K. I., 'Peterburgskii komitet bol'shevikov sed'mogo sozyva v 1918 godu', *Krasnaya letopis'*, no. 2(29) (1929) pp. 24–45; no. 3(30) (1929) pp. 12–53
Sukhanov, N., *Zapiski o revolyutsii*, 7 vols (Berlin–Petersburg–M., 1919–23)
Tsvetkov-Prosveshchenskii, A. K., *Mezhdu dvumya revolyutsiyamy* (M.-L., 1933)


**V  Contemporary Press**

*Delo naroda* (SR)
*Iskra* (Menshevik-Internationalist, after closure reopened as *Novyi luch*)
*Izvestiya VTsiKa i Petrogradskogo soveta rabochikh i soldatskikh deputatov* (TsIK and Petrograd Soviet)
*Krasnaya gazeta* (Bolshevik)
*Metallist* (Petrograd Union of Metalworkers)
*Novaya zhizn'* (Menshevik-Internationalist, Gorky's paper)
*Petrogradskaya pravda* (Bolshevik)

*Pravda* (Bolshevik, after closure reopened as *Proletarii, Rabochii, Rabochii i soldat, Rabochii put'*)
*Rabochaya gazeta* (Menshevik-Defencist)
*Rech'* (Kadet, after closure reopened briefly as *Nasha rech'*)
*Severnaya kommuna* (Commune of the Northern Region)
*Znamya bor'by* (Left SR)
*Znamya truda* (Left SR)


## VI Secondary Sources: Histories of Factories, Unions, Industries, etc

*Bastiony revolyutsii*, 2 vols (L., 1967 and 1971)
Bortik, M., 'Na Trubochnom zavode', in Anskii, A., ed., *Professional'noe dvizhenie v Petrograde v 1917 g.* (L., 1928) pp. 268–76
Bruk, S., 'Organizatsiya soyuza metallistov v 1917 g.' in Anskii, pp. 127–8
Notman, K. V., 'Trubochnyi zavod na Oktyabr'skikh putyakh', *Krasnaya letopis'*, nos 5–6 (50–1) (1932) pp. 241–55
Perazich, V., *Tekstili Leningrada v 1917 g.* (L., 1927)
Shatilova, T., 'Professional'nye soyuzy i Oktyabr'', *Krasnaya letopis'*, no. 2 (23) (1927) pp. 179–88.
Suknovalov, A. E. and Fomenkov, I. N., *Fabrika 'Krasnoe znamya'* (L., 1968)
Tanyaev, A., *Ocherki po istorii zheleznodorozhnikov v revolyutsii 1917-go goda* (M.-L., 1925)


## VII Secondary Sources – General

Aronson, G. Ya., *Dvizhenie upolnomochennykh ot rabochikh fabrik i zavodov v 1918 godu* (New York: Inter-University Project on the History of the Menshevik Movement, 1960)
Avrich, P., 'The Bolshevik Revolution and Workers' Control in Russian Industry', *Slavic Review*, vol. XXII, no. 1 (1973) pp. 47–63
Avrich, P., *The Russian Anarchists* (Princeton University Press, 1967)
Brinton, C., *The Anatomy of Revolution* (New York: Vintage, 1958)
Chamberlin, W. H., *The Russian Revolution*, 2 vols (New York: Universal Library, 1965)
Daniels, R. V., *Red October* (New York: Scribner, 1967)
Ferro, M., *La Révolution de 1917* (Paris, 1967)
Ferro, M., *October 1917* (London: Routledge & Kegan Paul, 1980)
Gaponenko, L. S., *Rabochii klass Rossii v 1917 g.* (M., 1963)

Golovanova, L. V., 'Raionnye komitety RSDRP (b) v 1917 g.'
   (Candidates' dissertation, Leningrad State University, 1974)
Grunt, A. Ya., *Pobeda Oktyabr'skoi revolyutsii v Moskve* (M., 1961)
Haimson, L. H., ed., *The Mensheviks* (University of Chicago Press,
   1975)
Johnson, C., *Revolutionary Change* (Boston: Little Brown, 1961)
Keep, J., *The Russian Revolution – A Study in Mass Mobilization*
   (New York: W. W. Norton, 1976)
Koenker, D., *Moscow Workers and the 1917 Revolution* (Princeton
   University Press, 1981)
Kornhauser, W., *The Theory of Mass Society* (Glencoe, Ill.: Free
   Press, 1959)
Lewin, M., *Lenin's Last Struggle* (London: Pluto Press, 1975)
Lisetskii, A. M., 'K voprosu o statistike zabastovok v Rossii v period
   podgotovki Velikoi Oktyabr'skoi sotsialisticheskoi revolutsii',
   *Uchenye zapiski Khar'kovskogo universiteta*, vol. 103 (Kharkov,
   1959)
Mandel, D., *The Petrograd Workers and the Fall of the Old Régime*
   (London: Macmillan, 1983)
Mandel, D., 'The Workers and the Intelligentsia in 1917' *Critique*,
   no. 14 (1982) pp. 67–87
Manning, B., *The English People and the English Revolution* (Har-
   mondsworth: Penguin, 1978)
Mil'shtein, A. L., 'Rabochie Petrograda v bor'be za ukreplenie
   sovetov', in *Rabochie Petrograda v bor'be za pobedu sotsializma*
   (M.-L., 1963) pp. 127–68.
Nikolaev, P. A., *Rabochie metallisty tsentral'nogo promyshlennogo
   raiona v bor'be za pobedu Oktyabr'skoi revolyutsii* (M., 1960)
Nosach, V. I., 'Profsoyuzy Petrograda v pervyi god Sovetskoi vlasti'
   in *Iz istorii Velikoi Oktyabr'skoi sotsialisticheskoi revolyutsii i
   sotsialisticheskogo stroitel'stva v SSSR* (L., 1967)
Potekhin, M. N., *Pervyi sovet proletarskoi diktatury* (L., 1966)
Rabinowitch, A., *The Bolsheviks Come to Power* (New York: Nor-
   ton, 1976)
Radkey, O., *The Election to the Russian Constituent Assembly of
   1917* (Harvard University Press, 1950)
Radkey, O., *The Sickle Under the Hammer* (Columbia University
   Press, 1963)
Reed, J., *Ten Days That Shook the World* (New York: Vintage,
   1960)
Rosenberg, W., *Liberals in the Russian Revolution* (Princeton Uni-
   versity Press, 1974)
Shkaratan, O. I., 'Izmememiya v sotsial'nom sostave fabrichno-
   zavodskikh rabochikh Leningrada, 1917–28', *Istoriya SSSR*,
   no. 5 (1959) pp. 21–38.

Smelser, N. J., *Theory of Collective Behaviour* (New York: Free Press, 1962)

Smith, S. A., *Red Petrograd: Revolution in the Factories 1917–1918* (Cambridge University Press)

Soboul, A., *The Sans Culottes* (Garden City, New York: Doubleday, 1972)

Startsev, V. I., 'K voprosu o sostave Krasnoi gvardii Petrograda', *Istoriya SSSR*, no. 1 (1962) pp. 136–41.

Startsev, V. I., *Ocherki po istorii Petrogradskoi Krasnoi gvardii i rabochei militsii* (M.-L., 1965)

Startsev, V. I., *Russkie bloknoty Dzhona Rida* (M., 1968)

Stepanov, I., *Ot rabochego kontrolya do rabochego upravleniya v promyshlennosti i zemedelii* (M., 1918)

Stepanov, Z. V., *Rabochie Petrograda v period podgotovki i provedeniya Oktyabr'skogo vooruzhennogo vosstaniya* (L., 1965)

Strumilin, S., 'Prozhitochnyi minimum i zarabotki chernorabochikh v Petrograde', *Statistika truda*, nos 2–3 (1918)

Suny, R. J., 'Toward a Social History of the October Revolution', *American Journal of History*, vol. 88, no. 1 (1983) pp. 31–52.

Trotsky, L., *History of the Russian Revolution*, 3 vols (London: Sphere Books, 1967)

Trukan, G. A., *Okyabr' v tsentral'noi Rossii* (M., 1967)

Ulam, A., *A History of Soviet Russia* (New York: Praeger, 1976)

Volin, S., *Deyatel'nost' men'shevikov v profsoyuzakh pri Sovetskoi vlasti* (New York: Inter-University Project on the History of the Menshevik Movement, 1962) paper no. 13

Volobuev, P. V., *Proletariat i burzhuaziya Rossii v 1917 g.* (M., 1964)

Znamenskii, O., *Iyul'skii krizis 1917g.* (M.-L., 1964)

# Index

Printers' Union—*continued*
  condemns restrictions on press, 313
  defencist leadership of: opposed by
    rank and file, 318–19; unseated,
    320, 350
  on separate peace, 387
productivity
  decline in, 265, 270, 359, 380, 385
*Proletarii*, see *Pravda*
Promet Pipe Factory, 318, 431 n25
Proshyan, P. P., 328, 393
Provisional Government
  'directorate of five', 250
  and economic regulation, 265, 289
  fourth coalition, 259
  labour policy of, 215
  in October, 310–12
  plans to leave Petrograd of, 291, 428 n3
  and repression, 213
  worker attitudes to, 218, 242, 260, 261,
    416
Pulemet (machine-gun) Factory, 230,
  433 n72
Purishkevich, V. M., 211
Putilov Shipyard, 332–3
Putilov Works
  anarchists at, 282
  attitudes towards TsIK at, 425 n28
  and Constituent Assembly, 350
  decline in size of work force at, 383
  draughtsmen at, 331
  factory committee, 266–7, 275–9
    *passim*
  in German offensive, 396, 438 n41
  influence of, 348
  June Soviet elections at, 408
  in Kornilov rising, 246
  letter to *Novaya zhizn'* from, 362–3
  Red Guards at, 304–6
  on eve of October, 285–6, 295
  in October, 340, 431 n24, 433 n70
  searches at, 410
  on separate peace, 390
  unskilled wage conflict at, 358
  worker opposition to soviet
    government at, 390–1, 383–5,
    409, 411
  youth at, 230–1, 242, 383

Rabinowitch, A., 420 n10, 428 n1
*Rabochaya gazeta*, 211, 293, 320
Rabochaya pechat' Press, 318–19
*Rabochii*, see *Pravda*
*Rabochii put'*, see *Pravda*
Radkey, O., 237–8

railroad workers, 248, 284, 383
  Conference of, 341
  in June Soviet elections, 401
  in October, 314–15, 318, 330–1
  *see also*, Workshops of NW Railroad
    and of the Nikolaevskii Railroad
*Rech'* (appeared briefly also as *Nasha
  rech'*), 219, 245, 254, 344, 346
Rechkin Wagon-construction Factory,
  355
Red Army, 417
  recruitment to, 383, 388
  SRs in, 386
  vote in June Soviet elections, 403, 406
Red Guards
  in German offensive, 387–8
  moral character of, 304, 307–8
  numbers and composition of, 306–9,
    383
  before October, 241, 245, 257–8
  in October, 297, 304–6, 322–3, 330
  and repression of worker protest, 355,
    361–2, 398
Reed, J., 270
Reikhel' (metalworking) Factory,
  432 n51
Respirator Factory, 283
revolution of 1905, 216, 224, 239
revolutionary defencism, 239
revolutionary democracy
  Bolsheviks accused of splitting, 261
  concern for unity of: after Kornilov,
    245, 247–8, 255, 296–7; in
    October, 327, 329; after October,
    393–5, 399, 417
  split conclusively in October, 341–2,
    412–13
  *see also*, 'homogeneous socialist
    government'
Riga
  fall of, 244
Robert Krug Machine-construction
  Factory, 368
Rodzyanko, M. N., 216, 291
Rosenberg, W., 219, 220, 347
Rovinskii (worker), 254
Rozenkrantz Copper Foundry, 318, 385,
  408, 435 n63
Rozhdestvenskii District
  anarchist influence in, 282–3
  elections in, 218, 220–1, 344, 347
  Soviet, 223–5
  workers' mood in: after July, 243; on
    eve of October, 296, 298; in
    October, 334